POETRY

THE BASICS

Now in its second edition, *Poetry: The Basics* demystifies the traditions and forms of the world of poetry for all those who find it daunting or bewildering. Covering a wide range of poetic voices from Chaucer to children's rhymes, song lyrics and the words of contemporary poets, this book will help readers to appreciate poetry by examining:

- technical aspects such as rhythm and measures
- different tones of voice in poetry
- the relationship between 'everyday' and 'poetic' language
- how different types of poetry are structured
- how the form and 'space' of a poem contribute to its meaning
- some of the ways contemporary poets set to work.

A must-read for all those wishing to get to grips with reading and writing poetry, this book is a lively and inspiring introduction to its many styles and purposes right up to the present-day.

Jeffrey Wainwright is a poet, translator, and critic. He taught for many years at Manchester Metropolitan University where he was Professor in the Department of English.

WITHDRAWN

The Basics

POLITICS (FOURTH EDITION)
STEPHEN D. TANSEY AND NIGEL JACKSON

THE QUR'AN
MASSIMO CAMPANINI

RELIGION (SECOND EDITION)
MALORY NYE

RESEARCH METHODS
NICHOLAS WALLIMAN

ROMAN CATHOLICISM
MICHAEL WALSH

SEMIOTICS (SECOND EDITION)
DANIEL CHANDLER

SHAKESPEARE (SECOND EDITION)
SEAN MCEVOY

SOCIOLOGY
KEN PLUMMER

TELEVISION STUDIES
TOBY MILLER

THEATRE STUDIES
ROBERT LEACH

WORLD HISTORY
PETER N. STEARNS

WORLD MUSIC
RICHARD NIDEL

POETRY
THE BASICS
SECOND EDITION

Jeffrey Wainwright

Routledge
Taylor & Francis Group

LONDON AND NEW YORK

First edition published 2004 by Routledge.

This second edition published 2011,
by Routledge
2 Park Square, Milton Park, Abingdon, Oxon, OX14 4RN

Simultaneously published in the USA and Canada
by Routledge
711 Third Avenue, New York, NY 10017

Routledge is an imprint of the Taylor & Francis Group, an informa business

Typeset in Aldus by
HWA Text and Data Management, London
Printed and bound in Great Britain by
TJ International LTD, Padstow, Cornwall

British Library Cataloguing in Publication Data
A catalogue record for this book is available from the British Library

Library of Congress Cataloging-in-Publication Data
Wainwright, Jeffrey.
Poetry: the basics / Jeffrey Wainwright. – [2nd ed.].
     p. cm.
  Includes bibliographical references.
  1. English poetry–History and criticism. 2. American poetry–History and
  criticism. 3. English language–Versification. 4. Poetics. 5. Poetry. I. Title.
  PR502.W27 2004
  808.1–dc22   2010031308

ISBN: 978-0-415-56615-5 (hbk)
ISBN: 978-0-415-56616-2 (pbk)
ISBN: 978-0-203-80909-9 (ebk)

In Memory of Ken Lowe
1932–2009

CONTENTS

ACKNOWLEDGEMENTS

The following extracts have been reproduced with permission. Whilst every effort has been made to trace copyright holders and obtain permission, this may not have been possible in all cases. Any omissions brought to our attention will be remedied in future editions.

Lyrics from the song *Mamma Mia* by ABBA reprinted by permission of Bocu Music Ltd.

The poem 'That's What You Did and You are My Real Mother' from *Finding the Center: The Art of the Zuni Storyteller,* second edition, translated by Dennis Tedlock, by permission of the University of Nebraska Press. © 1999 Dennis Tedlock. Reprinted with permission of the University of Nebraska Press.

Extracts from 'Safe in Their Alabaster Chambers' and 'Why – Do They Shut Me Out of Heaven?' by Emily Dickinson. Reprinted by permission of the publishers and the Trustees of Amherst College from *The Poems of Emily Dickinson*, Thomas H. Johnson, ed., Cambridge, MA: The Belknap Press of Harvard University Press, Copyright © 1951, 1955, 1979, 1983 by the president and fellows of Harvard College.

Excerpt from Gwyneth Lewis in W.N. Herbert and M. Hollis (eds) *Strong Words: Modern Poets on Modern Poetry* (2000) Tarset:

Bloodaxe Books. © Gwyneth Lewis, reprinted with kind permission from Gwyneth Lewis.

Extract from the poem 'Before the Flowers of Friendship Faded' by Gertrude Stein, from *Before the Flowers of Friendship Faded* (1931) Paris: Plain Edition. © Gertrude Stein, reproduced with permission from David Higham Associates.

Lyrics from 'I'm always true to you my darlin' in my fashion' by Cole Porter. © Cole Porter, reproduced with permission from Warner/Chappell Music Ltd.

Extract from the poem 'Trench Town Shock' from *Touch Mi, Tell Mi* (1983) London: Bogle-L'Overture. © Valerie Bloom 1983, reprinted by permission of Valerie Bloom.

The poem 'How Beastly the Bourgeois Is' by D.H. Lawrence from *The Complete Poems of D.H. Lawrence*. London: Heinemann. © The Estate of Frieda Lawrence Ravagli, reproduced by permission of Pollinger Limited and the Estate of Frida Lawrence Ravagli.

The poems 'An Early Matryr', 'Homage', 'Pastoral' and 'Death the Barber' by William Carlos Williams © 1938 by New Directions Publishing Corp, from *Collected Poems 1909–1939 Volume I* (1988) Carcanet Press/New Directions Publishing Corp, and 'Asphodel that Greeny Flower' by William Carlos Williams © 1944 William Carlos Williams, from *Collected Poems 1939–1962 Volume II* (1991) Carcanet Press/New Directions Publishing Corp. Reproduced by permission of Carcanet Press and New Directions Publishing Corp.

Excerpt from *I Wanted to Write A Poem* by William Carlos Williams, © 1958 William Carlos Williams. Reprinted by permission of Carcanet Press/New Directions Publishing Corp.

Extract from 'Pythagorean Silence' by Susan Howe from *Europe of Trusts* ©1990 by Susan Howe. Reprinted by permission of New Directions Publishing Corp.

Extract from 'Mid-August at Sourdough Mountain Lookout' by Gary Snyder from *Earth House Hold* © 1969 by Gary Snyder. Reprinted by permission of New Directions Publishing Corp.

The poem 'Do Not Go Gentle Into That Good Night' by Dylan Thomas from *The Poems of Dylan Thomas* (1952) New Directions Publishing Corp. © 1952 Dylan Thomas. Reproduced by permission of David Higham Associates and New Directions Publishing Corp.

An extract from the poem 'An American Jay' by Vona Groarke by kind permission of the author and The Gallery Press, Loughcrew, Oldcastle, County Meath, Ireland from *Spindrift* (2009) by Vona Groarke.

An extract from *Speech! Speech!* (2000) by Geoffrey Hill, London: Penguin. © Geoffrey Hill. Reproduced by permission of Penguin Books Ltd and the author.

Extract from the poem 'Crazy Jane Talks with the Bishop' from *The Collected Works of W.B. Yeats, Volume 1: The Poems, Revised* edited by Richard J. Finneran. © 1933 by The Macmillan Company; copyright renewed © 1961 by Bertha Georgie Yeats. Reprinted with the permission of Scribner, a division of Simon & Schuster, Inc. and by kind permission of A.P. Watt Ltd on behalf of Gráinne Yeats. All rights reserved.

Extract from the poem 'Among School Children' from *The Collected Works of W.B. Yeats, Volume 1: The Poems, Revised* edited by Richard J. Finneran. © 1928 by The Macmillan Company; copyright renewed © 1956 by Georgie Yeats. Reprinted with the permission of Scribner, a division of Simon & Schuster, Inc. and by kind permission of A.P. Watt Ltd on behalf of Gráinne Yeats. All rights reserved.

An extract from the poem 'What is the language using us for?' by W.S. Graham *Collected Poems 1942–1977.* (1979) London: Faber. Reprinted by kind permission of the estate of W.S. Graham.

The poem 'The Bedbug' by Tony Harrison from *Selected Poems* (1987) Harmondsworth: Penguin. *Collected Poems* (2007) Harmodndsworth: Penguin. © Tony Harrison. Reprinted by kind permission of the author.

The poem 'I, Being Born a Woman and Distressed' by Edna St. Vincent Millay from *Selected Poems* (1992) Manchester: Carcanet. © 1923, 1951, by Edna St. Vincent Millay and Norma Millay Ellis. Reprinted by permission of Elizabeth Barnett, Literary Executor, The Millay Society.

An extract from the poem 'anyone lived in a pretty how town' is reprinted from *Complete Poems 1904–1962*, by E.E. Cummings, edited by George J. Firmage, by permission of W.W. Norton & Company. © 1991 by the Trustees for the E.E. Cummings Trust and George James Firmage.

Extract from Gjertrud Schnackenberg, *Supernatural Love: Poems 1976–1992* (2000) New York: Farrar, Straus and Giroux. Reprinted by permission of Bloodaxe Books and Farrar, Straus and Giroux.

The lines from 'Aunt Jennifer's Tigers'. © 2002, 1951 by Adrienne Rich. The lines from 'Planetarium'. © 2002 by Adrienne Rich. © 1971 by W.W. Norton & Company, Inc, from *The Fact of a Doorframe: Selected Poems 1950–2001* by Adrienne Rich. Used by permission of the author and W.W. Norton and Company, Inc.

Excerpt from '"When We Dead Awaken": Writing as Re-Vision', from *Arts of the Possible: Essays and Conversations* by Adrienne Rich. © 2001 by Adrienne Rich. Used by permission of the author and W.W. Norton & Company, Inc.

Extract from the poem 'Now the Pink Stripes' by Tom Raworth from *Collected Poems* (2003) Manchester: Carcanet Press. Reprinted by permission of Carcanet Press.

Extract from Edwin Morgan, 'Siesta of a Hungarian Snake', from Edwin Morgan *Collected Poems* (1985) Manchester: Carcanet Press. Reprinted by permission of Carcanet Press.

Extract from Jules Laforgue, *Lettres à un ami*, translated by D. Arkell, *Looking for Laforgue: An Informal Biography* (1979) Manchester: Carcanet Press. Reprinted by permission of Carcanet Press.

Extracts from Matthew Welton, 'She makes her music' and 'We needed coffee but ...' from *New Poetries II An Anthology* (1999) Manchester: Carcanet Press. Reprinted by permission of Carcanet Press.

Extract from Sophie Hannah 'The End of Love' from *The Hero and the Girl Next Door* (1995) Manchester: Carcanet Press. Reprinted by permission of Carcanet Press.

Extract from John Ashbery 'And *Ut Pictura Poesis* Is Her Name', from *Houseboat Days* (1975). ©1975, 1976, 1977, 1999 by John Ashbery. Reprinted by permission of Carcanet Press and Georges Borchardt Inc, on behalf of the author.

Extracts from Eavan Boland 'In Search of a Language' in *Object Lessons: The Life of the Woman and the Poet in Our Time* (1995) Manchester: Carcanet Press, 'The Woman Poet: Her Dilemma' in *Object Lessons: The Life of the Woman and the Poet in Our Time* (1995) Manchester: Carcanet Press © 1995 by Eavan Boland and 'Contingencies' in *Outside History: Selected Poems 1980–1990*, (1990)

Manchester: Carcanet Press. © 1990 by Eavan Boland. Reprinted by permission of Carcanet Press and W. W. Norton & Company Inc.

Extract from Chris McCully, 'Fleur Adcock' in C McCully (ed.), *The Poet's Voice and Craft* (1994) Manchester: Carcanet Press. Reprinted by permission of Carcanet Press.

Extract from Charles Olson, 'Death is a Loving Matter ...', from *Selected Poems* (1993) University of California Press. Reprinted by permission of Carcanet Press and University of California Press.

Excerpts from the poems by Judith Wright: 'Brevity' and 'Dust' from *A Human Pattern: Selected Poems* (2009) Sydney: ETT Imprint. Reprinted by permission of ETT Imprint.

The poem 'What are years?' reprinted with permission of Scribner, a division of Simon & Schuster, Inc., and Faber from *The Collected Poems of Marianne Moore* by Marianne Moore. Copyright © 1941 by Marianne More; Copyright renewed © 1969 by Marianne Moore. All rights reserved.

Final four lines from 'Poetry Corner: Lines on the return to Britain of Billy Graham', *Private Eye*, issue 306, p.15 (7 Sept 1973). Reproduced by kind permission of *Private Eye* magazine, www.private-eye.co.uk.

Extract from José García Villa, 'Sonnet in Polka Dots' from *Volume Two* (1949) New York: New Directions. Permission is granted by the John Edwin Cowen, Literary Trustee for the Jose Garcia Villa Estate.

An extract from Gwen Harwood 'Long After Heine' in *Collected Poems* (1991) Oxford: Oxford University Press. Reproduced by permission of the Estate of Gwen Harwood, copyright © the Estate of Gwen Harwood.

An extract from 'Mr Edwards and The Spider' from *Lord Weary's Castle*, © 1946 and renewed 1974 by Robert Lowell. Reprinted by permission of Houghton Mifflin Company.

The poem 'Ladles and Jellyspoons' from Iona and Peter Opie, *The Lore and Language of School Children* (1959) Oxford University Press. Reprinted by kind permission of Iona Opie.

Extract from Anne Sexton 'The Abortion', *The Selected Poems of Anne Sexton* (1964) Oxford University Press. Reprinted by permission of SLL/Sterling Lord Literistic Inc. Copyright by Anne Sexton.

Extract from *The Arrivants* by Edward Brathwaite, 21 lines from 'Prelude' and 'Ancestors'. By permission of Oxford University Press.

Extracts from R.S Thomas 'Becoming' and 'Welsh' from *Collected Poems* (1995) Phoenix, J.M. Dent. By permission of J.M. Dent an imprint of The Orion Publishing Group, London.

Lines 17–23 of 'Self-Portrait as Hurry and Delay [Penelope at her Loom]' from *The End of Beauty* (1987) by Jorie Graham. Copyright © 1987 by Jorie Graham. Reprinted by permission of HarperCollins Publishers

Extract from 'Gurney, I' in Ivor Gurney *Collected Poems* (1995) P.J. Kavanagh (ed.), Carcanet Press. Reprinted by permission of Carcanet Press.

Extract from Frank O'Hara 'Les Luths', *Selected Poems* (1991) D. Allen (ed.), Manchester: Carcanet. Reprinted by permission of Carcanet Press and Random House Inc., Alfred Knopf in USA.

Two extracts from Thomas Kinsella's 'Downstream', from *Selected Poems* (2007) Manchester: Carcanet Press. Reprinted by permission of Carcanet Press.

Extract from *Strong Words: Modern Poets on Modern Poetry* from Elaine Feinstein in *Collected Poems and Translations* (2002) Manchester: Carcanet Press. Copyright © Elaine Feinstein. Reprinted by permission of Elaine Feinstein and Carcanet Press.

Extract from the poem 'Considering the Snail' in Thom Gunn *My Sad Captains* (1961) London: Faber. Reprinted by permission of Faber and by Farrar, Straus and Giroux in the USA.

Extract from the poem 'Sonnet 23' in J. Berryman *Collected Poems 1937–71* (1990) London: Faber. Reprinted by permission of Faber and by Farrar, Straus and Giroux in the USA.

Extract from 'How to Kill' in Keith Douglas *Complete Poems* (2000) London: Faber. Reprinted by permission of Faber.

The poem 'Shield of Achilles', © 1952 by W.H. Auden from *Collected Poems of W.H. Auden* by W.H. Auden. Used by permission of Random House, Inc and The Wiley Agency /Estate for the UK rights.

AUTHOR'S ACKNOWLEDGEMENTS

For this second edition I should like to thank once more the following students at Manchester Metropolitan University who took time to read portions of my original draft: Claire Milner, Katie Fennell, Katharine Huggett and Katie Watkinson; my colleagues Margaret Beetham, Michael Bradshaw; and Michael Schmidt; Jon Glover and Judith Wainwright.

I should very much like to thank my editor Sophie Thomson and the several anonymous readers whose comments on the first edition and the subsequent proposal and revised manuscript for this volume have been invaluable.

For material in Chapter 9: James Byrne and Anna Smaill of *The Wolf Magazine*; Vona Groarke, Matthew Welton, Antony Rowland, Scott Thurston.

I dedicate the book to the memory to my school English teacher, Ken Lowe who began my love of poetry. All final responsibility is of course my own.

PREFACE TO
THE SECOND EDITION

This book is – and I hope it will seem to be – a work of enthusiasm. My overriding aim is to enhance the pleasure that readers gain from poetry. No special expertise is required to read and enjoy a poem, but, as with most pleasures, it can be greatly enriched by knowledge. This book tries to provide some knowledge and some ideas to all who want to read, study or write poetry.

The majority of you are likely to be students of English Literature at college and degree level and some of you will approach poetry with trepidation. Much more than with fiction or drama, students tend to suspect there be mysteries, if not monsters here. In one cloud is the anxiety that there is only a certain, intuitive cast of mind that will 'get it'. Another fears poetry is fraught with bewildering technicalities. Also, in a quick-paced culture, many find it hard to read slowly, to pause and re-read. Under pressure of assignments and other demands you might be frustrated if a poem is not grasped quickly.

This book – which arose out of my own earliest reading, my writing of poetry and out of my own undergraduate teaching – aims to allay these anxieties. It aims to give clear information about all the major technical aspects of verse and in this respect with its chapter summaries and **Glossary** keyed to the text can be used as a reference book which also presents many examples and readings.

Another feature of poetry that can contribute to its 'difficulty' is the occasional prevalence of allusions. In recent years this problem has become massively reduced: now we can google the Muses and fear no more Madame Sosostris.

But that first cloud of anxiety (Do I have the necessary sensibility for poetry?) is harder for a book like this to disperse. At every turn I have tried to emphasize the *sensuous* dimension of poetry, that its word-use in sound and movement is first of all, in Milton's words, 'simple sensuous and passionate'. If we go slowly, relax and preferably read aloud to ourselves, a good poem will stir us before we have captured its 'meaning'. It is indeed this impression which will make us want to re-read, search out those odd allusions and study how the poem's particular techniques have worked this magic upon us. There is no need to fear or avoid difficulty; indeed, in poetry as in other parts of life, there is much more reason to fear the simplistic. In 'struggling' with a poem we are learning just how complex and demanding language can be. Making sense of it has its own satisfaction but also strengthens our ability to deal with and use language in every aspect of our lives.

Formal studies of literature, in universities and elsewhere, now include composition as well as analysis. The democratization of culture which has encouraged people to be producers of music and visual art has also influenced the language arts, and especially the poem. It is the most practically available literary space. It probably requires paper and certainly some time, but perhaps not as much of either as writing a novel. It needs readers, but not the human and physical resources necessary to realize a play or a film script. Moreover, the development of 'free verse' in the twentieth century has – for good and ill – had the effect of loosening convention, and this, together with the wider availability of knowledge about models in other periods and cultures, has expanded the long-standing practice of verse-making and given the developing poet a great range of possibilities from which to proceed. This is far from confined to formal education and this book is also offered towards creative writing classes and groups as well as individuals, and seeks to encourage all these writers, who *must* therefore be readers, as well as readers who might also practise writing.

To these overlapping readerships I offer knowledge of two kinds. The first is suggested by the topics of the chapters. At the heart of the book are chapters on the most distinctively formal aspects of poetry: the different 'voices' of poetry, the poetic line both measured and 'free', rhyme and stanza. Around these are chapters which attempt to associate poetry with wider language-use whilst establishing the special character of what I shall call the 'deliberate space' that a poem occupies. The eighth chapter explores wider notions about the nature of poetic utterance, 'inspiration', and what it might be to be a poet from an historical point of view. A new final chapter in this edition, 'Writing a Poem Now' aims to describe several different dimensions of contemporary practice.

I hope that the second kind of knowledge gained will be a greater familiarity with a wide reach of poets. The range is drawn from the Middle Ages to the present day, and from poetry across the English-speaking world. Each chapter includes sustained discussion of individual poems as well as briefer examples. I hope that these will develop the way readers might read individual poems closely, and draw them on to explore the work of poets, whether new or familiar, who attract them. (This, as I shall suggest, is now made much easier through the Internet.) Whilst I do not believe we all read a 'different' poem, none of us reads a poem exactly like our neighbour. Reading is a process, and the aim of my readings here is to contribute to the reader's own interior and exterior dialogues about the ideas and the whole experience of individual poems.

One particular idea about the nature of the art recurs in this approach to the 'basics' of poetry. This sees writers and readers working in the midst of a perpetual paradox. At one extreme is the desire to use words to *say* something that is meaningful and memorable: for instance, the kind of substantial statement required by grief or love. At the other is the desire to use words to say *nothing*, that is to free language from meaning and revel in the qualities and associations of words, even inventing new words: ' 'Twas brillig, and the slithy toves / Did gyre and gimble in the wabe.' The creative tension between these poles of interest will be apparent through much of the discussion and I hope that thinking about this will prove part of the pleasure I hope to foster.

INTRODUCTION

BECAUSE THERE IS LANGUAGE
THERE IS POETRY

It's raining, it's pouring
The old man is snoring
He went to bed
With a bucket on his head
And couldn't get up in the morning.

Children as young as two or three can delight in this rhyme and will try to get their own tongues round it. Why is this? Simply it is because they delight in the noise it makes. Just at the time they are sorting words from their whole acoustic world and beginning to use them themselves, here is a piece of language they can understand and whose sounds give them immediate pleasure.

Exploring how this works in more detail, I think we can recognize several particular features in its short span. First it has strong, obvious beats, here shown in bold: 'It's **rain**ing, it's **pour**ing / The **old** man is **snor**ing / He **went** to **bed** / With a **buck**et on his **head** / And **couldn't** get **up** in the **morn**ing.' Moreover there is an intriguing change of pattern within the first four lines. Two strong beats occupy only four syllables in line 3 as against the six or seven of the other lines. Then, in the last line there are three stresses. Line 4 – 'with a **buck**-et on his head' – seems to present a difficulty as the speaker has to scramble over 'with a' to get to the next obviously stressed syllable, '**buck**-et'. Indeed another version of the rhyme gives 'He got into bed / And bumped his head' which is simpler to say because it is more 'regular', and if we combined the two to read: 'He **went** to **bed** / And **bump**ed his **head**' it would be more rigidly patterned still. However the pleasures of verse don't come from rigidity but often from a flexing of a basic scheme, and the 'difficulty' of articulating lines 3 and 4 presents the same kind of enjoyable challenge as a tongue-twister does. If the game is to recite it ever faster the fun increases until the inevitable hilarious breakdown. However arrived at, it is the not-so-simple irregularities of this simple rhyme that account for its rhythmic pleasure.

At the same time this little verse is dominated by clear **rhymes**: raining / pouring / snoring / morning, and bed / head. Standing out from the more normal rhythms and sounds of speech this verse encourages a physical response like clapping or swaying, just as modern pop songs do. The importance of the tune always makes it very difficult to compare poetry and song lyrics but in the words of this Abba song we can broadly see rhythm, rhyme, repetition of word-sound and phrase deployed in just the same way as part of the pleasure:

Mamma mia, here I go again
My my, how can I resist you
Mamma mia, does it show again
My my, just how much I've missed you.

It is just those qualities which make this a children's favourite well before they can make any more sense of the emotional meaning than they can of why a man might go to bed with a bucket on his head.

Rhymes such as these, and even simpler ones like the first lullabies are among the earliest utterances we address to children because we know they will respond to these effects. Through evolution, the human vocal tract has become able to give voice to a variety of particular sounds and their complex combinations. With these we have created languages which can communicate information of very different kinds and to a very high degree of subtlety. As we acquire language we make and respond to sounds, imitating and relishing them, before we learn the particular ones that go to make up words and discover how effectively word sounds denote objects in our world and carry information to others. But however sophisticated our utterances become the sensuous character of language remains.

As the poet **Kenneth Koch** (1925–2002) writes, 'Each word has a little music of its own' which, he goes on to say, 'poetry arranges so it can be heard' (Koch, 1998, p. 28).

> A clock in the eye ticks in the eye a clock
> ticks in the eye.
> A number with that and large as a hat
> which makes rims think quicker than I.
> A clock in the eye ticks in the eye a clock ticks
> ticks in the eye.
>
> (Stein, 1971)

As we have seen with the rhyme and the song chorus, the 'music' of words is further enjoyed in such sequences as a run of the same consonants (*alliteration*), *rhyme*, or the repetition of certain words or rhythmic patterns. The lines above by **Gertude Stein** (1874–1946) show this kind of fascination. Now the intrigue extends to the surprising juxtaposition of word meanings, as does the title of the poem itself, 'Before the Flowers of Friendship Faded Friendship Faded'. Stein called her book *Tender Buttons*. Ponder for a moment what associations come with putting the words 'tender' and 'button' next to each other.

These resources of language, especially *recurrence* – the anticipated pleasure of a sound or shape being repeated – have been used in the pre-literate, oral tradition of all societies for dances, riddles, spells, prayers, games, stories, and histories. The work of the American poet/researcher **Jerome Rothenberg** (1931–) provides a wealth of examples of this from every continent and many cultures. We should not assume though that work of this kind from pre-literate cultures is simple. Often, as Ruth Finnegan shows in her anthology *Oral Poetry*, work such as the Malay form of the *pantun*, which we will meet in its English adaptation in Chapter 7 on **Stanza**, can be very elaborate.

More familiarly, the early enthusiasm for nursery rhymes, chants, schoolyard games, songs, advertising slogans and jingles all feature the same kind of *gestural* characteristics. '*Gesture*' is an important concept here. What I mean by gesture in language are those qualities we employ to signal our meaning strongly by emphasizing particular word sounds, rhythmic sequences or patterns, as we have recognized in the pieces above. Thus the words will catch our attention not only through a grasp of their dictionary meanings, but through their sensuous impression, not unlike indeed, the way we accompany speech by hand gestures and variations of *tone*. The incantatory, 'musical' qualities of beat, drum and dance are close to this and are part of the close relation between poetry and song. Indeed the term which is still key to both – *lyric* – points to this connection. Lyric refers to that kind of *verse* most readily associated with the chanted or sung origins of poetry, traditionally to the harp-like stringed instrument known as the lyre. We still refer to the words of songs of all kinds as lyrics, and poetry closest in style and span to songs, as opposed to poems that tell substantial stories or are the medium for drama, are defined as lyric. I shall have more to say about this *genre* of poetry in Chapter 3, 'Tones of Voice'.

In poetry without music these qualities have become formalized into what are its most prominent distinguishing features: its *rhythms*, that is the way a sequence of words moves in the ear, and its *metres*, that is the regular patterning of such movement into the poetic line. The character of the many different kinds of poetic line will be explored in separate chapters.

So, while the evolution and use of language has obviously been functional, exchanging information with the necessary clarity, its sounds and shapings, both spoken and written, are also inevitably gestural. Of course, those instrumental uses of language will be as simple and direct as possible, like the bald instructions for using a computer: 'Press Enter'; 'Select the file to be moved'; 'Double-click the Mouse icon'. But even the specialized language associated with computers is not literal but *metaphorical*: the mouse, windows, desktop and bin. My computer manual promises 'Right Answers, Right Now', and the simple emphasis of this punchy phrase – repeating 'Right' – is the kind of language I am calling gestural. This snatch of a conversation is invented, but I think it is recognizable:

> So I had to go back to the bank. No sign of it there. Back to the butcher's. No sign of it there. Back to the chemist. No sign of it there.

Back to the deli. No sign. Back to the café. No sign. Where was it?
Slap-bang in the middle of the kitchen table.

The speaker wants to express tedium and exasperation at
mislaying a purse and these repetitive, truncated phrasings with
their slight variations impress this upon the listener. These are the
gestural features of language.

So, the argument of this chapter is that poetry is not really a
peculiar, demarcated zone out of the mainstream of language-
use, but that language is inevitably and intrinsically 'poetic' in
the qualities that I'm calling gestural. However, historically, these
qualities have been highlighted and formalized for particular uses
and occasions. Poetry is a form for special attention and one that
calls unusual attention to the way it is formed.

The ancient ceremonial aspect of gestural language persists in our
desire for special forms of language for particular occasions. We all
know for instance how difficult it is to 'find words' of condolence. In
greetings cards, at weddings, funerals, in sorrow and commemoration
and in love, wherever we feel the need for heightened, deliberate
speech, wherever there is a need for 'something to be said', we turn
to the unusual shapes and sounds of poetry. This is also why we
might be drawn to write poetry in order to form an utterance that
is out of the ordinary and commensurate to the weight or the joy
of the occasion. Always at such times we will encounter the familiar
difficulty of finding what we know to be the 'right words'.

The deployment of impressive sounds and shapes, the deliberate
speech required by that 'something to be said', has been known in
the western tradition as **rhetoric** . In this emphasis, from *Paradise
Lost* to a local newspaper's *In Memoriam* verses, poetry can be seen
to be a part of rhetoric.

However every experience with language teaches us that
communication is frequently less transparent than we would
wish. Disappointment at the failure of language to be clear, and
at its capacity to mislead and sway us into deception has marked
our thinking about language for centuries. Ambiguity, double-
meanings, 'equivocation', intended and not intended, all manner of
'-speaks', result from, or exploit, the potential anarchy of language.
Often it seems 'words run away with themselves' and take us with

them. This may lead into a cheerful gallimaufry of free association and **word-play**, or into saying things we did not mean. Those 'right words' can be very elusive.

As a form of utterance that is especially sensitive to all the various resources of language in both its **semantic** (i.e. meaningful) and sensuous dimensions, poetry has taken upon itself the freedom and opportunity for wordplay, and also its responsibilities. Because language is as it is we might say anything. Because life is how it is we need to watch what we say.

Through language we can convey common information, but also achieve a vast capacity to generalize particulars and to abstract from experience. We can also invent and fantasize and relay any of this to others. Its immeasurable creative flexibility means that 'language enables the promotion of endless associations between any one object/person/event and another', writes the neuroscientist Susan Greenfield (Greenfield, 2000, p. 72). So, since the nature of language itself does not necessarily oblige us to be purpose-like, it also enables associations which may seem purposeless. It is often attractive – even just for the hell of it – to remove its use as far as possible from any externally driven direction.

The philosopher Daniel Dennett observes the essential biological function of language in evolution, but continues, 'once it has arrived on the evolutionary scene, the endowment for language makes room for all manner of biologically trivial or irrelevant or baroque (non-functional) endeavours: gossip, riddles, poetry, philosophy' (Dennett, 1984, p. 48). On this view, *all* poetry, including the most rhetorically purposeful, might be seen as 'baroque', and we shall look at the philosophical problems surrounding rhetoric and **figurative** language in Chapter 8. But when the owl and the pussycat go to sea in a beautiful pea-green boat, then we can see that language can indeed promote Greenfield's 'endless associations' in ways that seem especially 'baroque'. And delightful.

So language can be deployed 'uselessly', and an alternative emphasis to the rhetorical one would see poetry as the space where the glory and freedom of the possibility to say anything is specialized:

an orange the size of a melon rolling slowly across the field
where i sit at the centre in an upright coffin of five panes of glass

Such a relish as this from **Tom Raworth**'s (1934–) poem 'now the pink stripes', may be inspired by a desire to explore the light-spirited freedom afforded by language in a space not subject to instrumental demands. There can be a sheer game-playing element in such poetry, a love of messing with words because we can. Alternatively – or in addition – it may be a response to disillusionment with the use of language in the 'real' world of affairs, transactions and 'information'. This doubt as to whether language really does simply transport common sense from one person to another is deep and long-lived. In **William Shakespeare**'s (1564–1616) *Twelfth Night* the clown Feste complains that language has been so much discredited by being used to lie and deceive that 'words are grown so false I am loath to prove reason with them.' Feste claims here that the character of social discourse has become so unreliable that language itself has become discredited.

Beginning in 1970s the American L=A=N=G=U=A=G=E poets have taken a similar view. This appellation, which comes from the title of one of the principal journals associated with the movement, draws attention to language as itself a material rather than an invisible medium *through* which we make meaning or 'express' ourselves. They question the whole idea of poetry as personal expression of experience, ideas or emotions but focus instead upon the features of words as objects in themselves. Further they challenge the dominance in modern industrialized, business-oriented society of what **Charles Bernstein** (1950–) calls 'authoritative plain style'. Its increasing standardization claims a monopoly over coherence and excludes tones and styles of speaking and writing that do not conform to 'mannered and refined speaking'. How Bernstein and other writers associated with this point of view respond in their own poetic practice will be explored in Chapter 9, 'Writing a Poem Now'.

All of these pleasures and problems are with us because of the character of human language. What we have come to call poetry gives us a constructed, deliberate space in which to enjoy and to tussle with the experience of language. Reading or writing a poem offers a practising awareness of the problems of language and meaning – specifically of what we must say and how we can best say it. *Because there is language there is poetry*: in the rest of this book I shall try to set out some of the principal ways that poetry in the modern English language has been made across the whole spectrum of rhetoric and nonsense.

SUMMARY

In this introductory chapter we have looked at:

- The character of human language, especially with regard to its sounds.
- The pleasure of rhythm and rhyme from children's verses onwards.
- How language operates functionally, uses *gesture*, but can also work 'uselessly' – and enjoyably.
- The problem of finding 'the right words'.
- The basic idea of rhetoric and the challenge of nonsense.
- The continuity between the general use of language and poetry *and* its distinctiveness.

FURTHER READING

Finnegan, Ruth (ed.) (1982) *The Penguin Book of Oral Poetry*, Harmondsworth: Penguin Books.

Hughes, Ted and Heaney, Seamus (eds) (1982) *The Rattle Bag*, London: Faber.

Opie, Iona and Opie, Peter (1959) *The Lore and Language of Schoolchildren*, London: Oxford University Press.

Rothenberg, Jerome (ed.) (1968) *Technicians of the Sacred: A Range of Poetics from Africa, America, Asia and Oceania*, New York: Doubleday.

Trask, R.L. (1988) *Language: the Basics*, second edn, Chapter 3, 'Language and Meaning', London: Routledge.

DELIBERATE SPACE

Jimmy Fryer Esquire,
Walking along a telegraph wire
With his shirt on fire!

I have used the word *gesture* in Chapter 1 to describe those aspects of the nature of language other than those covered by dictionary definition and word-order. These gestures are similar to the physical gestures and tones of voice in conversation. Obviously it is common and important that we use clear, 'cold' instrumental language in everyday life so that we know to meet inside or outside a cinema, or take two per day after, not before meals. But, as we have seen, little or no communication is confined to transmitting information in this way.

All the resources of verse emphasize the gesturing elements of words and their combinations in ways that draw attention and impress. These include sound effects like **alliteration** and **assonance**; repetition; **rhyme**; **rhythm** and **metre**; figures of speech or **tropes**; **limericks**, **sonnets**, **haiku** and all the other verse forms that we shall meet later. (All of these highlighted terms are defined briefly in the **Glossary**.) Even poems that do not manifest such features so obviously – or indeed aim to avoid them altogether – are still *shaping* words in some deliberate form.

This chapter will suggest that poetry can be seen as *a particular space*, created or adapted by the poet out of the flux of language-use with great deliberation. A poem is a part of the functioning and the gesturing of the words we use every day, but it is also set aside. Just as a prayer-mat is made of fabric found everywhere, but, once laid out, marks off a space from the surrounding daily world, so does the shape of the poem organize language into a space for pause and for different attention. It is a space *in time*, just as the prayer is, one marked by the **rhythms** of pace and pause, and the sensations and ideas in every word. This space is shaped in the mind of poet and listener, and when the poem is on the page its impression is also in the formation made by the letters. Some poems, as we shall see, exist primarily, or even entirely in visual space and have virtually no temporal existence.

In later chapters we shall look at the various features which mark out this space and fill it, but first I want to explore what this space might be, and the kind of effects it creates. I shall begin where poetry began in **oral** recitation and performance. I shall look at children's rhymes and oral poetry from Britain and elsewhere, and move from that to look at how strongly visual spaces are created in the familiar space of the printed page.

ORAL TRADITION AND CHILDREN'S RHYMES

As we can see from

> Jimmy Fryer Esquire,
> Walking along a telegraph wire
> With his shirt on fire!

a prime motive for manipulating words in gestural ways is pleasure: the simple sensuous exhilaration that comes of making up such a combination of sense and sound, or of adapting it, or certainly of uttering it. The delight in this verse comes from the **semantic** absurdity – the picture the words show us of someone walking along a telegraph wire perhaps as yet unaware of his predicament is just wonderfully silly, just like the man with the bucket on his head. Besides the relish of others' discomfiture which is so much a part of children's cat-calling, the image's impossibility is also part of its pleasure. Words can be put together in ways that offer a little holiday from reality, a momentary fantasy.

But there is more to it than this. Certain 'manipulations' are more effective than others, and sound, timing and rhythm, for example, are all crucial. Poetry works on the ear. It is a form developed for and in performance, within a long **oral tradition**.

To understand the effects of these oral origins, we can return to the playground and Jimmy Fryer. As we have said, the rhyme offers a certain pleasure through the absurdity of what it describes, but the coincidence of the word sounds is no less striking. The name *'Fryer'* offers the chance of the **rhymes** of *'Esquire'*, *'fire'*, and *'wire'*, although it is just as likely that in earlier versions of the joke the point was to mock the use of the pompous title *Esquire*. It could easily be adapted, for example, to read:

Jeffrey Wainwright Esquire,
Walking along a telegraph wire
With his shirt on fire!

The gender of 'Esquire' would present a momentary problem, but, it's easy to imagine such further adaptations as:

Kylie Fryer Esquire,
Walking along a telegraph wire,
With her skirt on fire.

The schoolyard poet would certainly substitute *skirt*, not *dress*. Any polysyllabic word like *overcoat* or *handbag* would certainly make the line a clumsy mouthful, but not all **monosyllables** are equal. The lighter vowel sound and the soft slipping-away -ss of *dress* would dissolve the mocking bite of harder sounding words like *skirt* and *shirt*. Of such details are successful verses made, and the ear for it is vitally related to the fact that children's verses have an oral existence. Their precision has been honed by repetition and the fact that the playground can be a very critical arena. With one verbal slip the mocker could instantly become the mocked. Imagine for instance the embarrassment of a child eager to pass on this rhyme,

Good King Wenceslas
Knocked a bobby senseless
Right in the middle of Marks & Spencer's

who remembers the content, but not the exact words, and puts in *policeman* or *constable* for *bobby*. The rhythm of the second line would stumble disastrously. It is the predicament of the bad joke-teller. Jokes often turn upon features of language, most obviously puns, which makes them cousin to the **word-play** of poetry. But we all know that it's the way you tell 'em, and so it is. The ability to structure and above all *time* a joke is vital to its success. It is the **cadence**, the arrangement of acceleration and pause, the manipulation of time that matters. The space of these children's rhymes is shaped very precisely to meet these requirements of timing. They choose words with an exact ear for the cadence, the way each sound *falls* in relation to the ones that surround it.

I have emphasized so far the continuity between the gestural features of speech and of poetry, and suggested that in familiar children's rhymes we can see the attractions of verbal gesture in 'poetic' features such as **rhyme** and **rhythm**. Yet just as these verses delight in the peculiarity with which they are constructed, so does their content in the space they occupy in the child's mind. The oddity of King Wenceslas abandoning wherever and whenever it is he comes from, and embarrassing the law in a respectable store like Marks & Spencer's, is a child's cheerful transgression against adult authority as represented by carol-singing and policemen. The happy coincidence that *Wenceslas* rhymes with *senseless* and *Spencer's*, parallels this little disorder because it is in the character of rhyme to be anarchic. By 'anarchic' I mean that because rhyming words have no necessary connection in meaning, following the quest for a rhyme can lead the solemn progress of meaning in quite a different, coincidental direction. (We shall look at this in more detail in Chapter 6 on **Rhyme.**)

We can see the way the forms of children's verses can coincide with their ideas to tweak the nose of the adult world in what Iona and Peter Opie in their classic study *The Lore and Language of Schoolchildren* call 'tangletalk'. This verse travesties the kind of speech-making 'not unknown in their school halls':

Ladles and Jellyspoons,
I stand upon this speech to make a platform,
The train I arrived in has not yet come,
So I took a bus and walked.
I come before you

To stand behind you
And tell you something
I know nothing about.

(Opie and Opie, 1959)

The space of the poem is deliberately separated from the current
of ordinary speech by the way it is shaped. Here the prose norm of
conventional speech is broken into the segments as the child heard
them to form separate lines.

Often too the poem is marked off from the sphere of daily
expectation by the alternative *imaginative* space that it occupies.
As the dignitary rises to speak the children sitting in their obedient
rows hear something different in their heads. It probably makes
little sense to them anyway so they take this to an extreme by
mixing, or 'tangling' it up, substituting words that sound similar
to produce a nonsensical parody. Sometimes it is a more fantastic
space, a realm where pigs take snuff to make them tough and the
elephant, 'a pretty bird',

builds its nest in a rhubarb tree
And whistles like a cow.

All this kind of fancy, and such bold language strokes, might be seen
to have something in common with another delight of children –
cartoon animation. Everything about the words is larger, more
obvious, and the action improbably dramatic.

Drawing again upon children's rhymes, a simple example of a
clapping song can teach a great deal about the fundamental and
powerful poetic techniques used in the oral tradition to impress
stories upon listeners.

When Suzi was a baby, a baby Suzi was
And she went, 'wah, wah, wah, wah.'
When Suzi was an infant, an infant Suzi was
And she went scribble, scribble, scribble, scribble.
When Suzi was a junior, a junior Suzi was
And she went 'Miss, Miss I can't do this
I've got my knickers in an awful twist.'

> When Suzi was a teenager, a teenager she was
> And she went –' Oh ah I've lost my bra
> I've left my knickers in my boyfriend's car.'

The rhyme goes on through Suzi as a mother, granny, skeleton and ghost. The remarkable, simple economy of this life-story is achieved by a number of techniques. Fundamentally we have the signposting structures of repetition: *'When Suzi was...When Suzi was ...'* to introduce each phase of her life. Allied to that is the strong beat on these syllables in the *'When'* lines,

> When **Suzi was** a **ba-by**, a **ba**by **Suzi was**

which coincide with the claps. Interestingly the inversion of the first phrase of this line in its second phrase is in fact a familiar device in ***classical rhetoric*** where it is known as ***anadiplosis***. But reiteration can also be tedious and variation is necessary if the attention of an audience, and of a performer, is to be held. In 'Suzi' the 'wah wah' and 'scribble scribble' pattern soon looks likely to be boring, hence the shift of phrase and of rhythm with

> And she went – 'Miss Miss, I can't do this
> I've got my knickers in an awful twist.'

These lines alter the rhythmic pattern and introduce rhyme at the same time as they take the girl out of infancy.

All of these reiterative techniques also work as a stalling device which helps the clappers to be sure they remember the next line. Indeed this whole clapping song is a small-scale instance of the memorizing, or ***mnemonic*** qualities of oral recitation. Poetry is far more ancient than print or even written cultures, and it is devices such as ***rhyme***, ***beat***, and ***recurrent*** structure that enable singers, clappers and story-tellers to organize and remember their material for the audience.

Orality is the major reason for the primacy of the *verse line*. (We shall look at this in detail Chapters 4 and 5.) A recurrent pattern, defined by repeated sequences of ***beats***, together with related aural effects such as rhyme and other formulaic constructions, enabled the pre-literate makers of poetry not only to 'remember their lines', but to hold their audience. We still use *mnemonics* as an aid to memory as in this old History lesson revision aid:

In fourteen hundred and ninety-two
Columbus sailed the ocean blue.

and we know that verse in set forms is easier to memorize than prose. So the clappers of 'Suzi', with some twenty-plus lines to remember, have beat, rhyme, reiteration of both phrase and structure to help them through the narrative which is in any case structured by its progress through the span of a life.

ORAL TRADITION IN EPIC AND NARRATIVE

If we turn to the great stories of ancient Greece and other communities told for generations before they were ever written down, we can understand more about how the space of poetry was organized for large and lengthy purposes. We shall see that 'remembering' is hardly an accurate term for the way in which these oral poems of the past existed within their tradition.

Perhaps the poems best-known to us of the ancient oral tradition are the Greek heroic epics attributed to Homer: *The Iliad* which tells the story of the Greeks' long war against Troy, and *The Odyssey* which recounts the protracted voyage home from Troy of its hero Odysseus. These are poems which in present-day conventional English editions will occupy some 450 pages each, but they existed, long before they were written down in the 6th century BC, only in the mind and voice of their poets and narrators. In 1934 the researcher Milman Parry heard a Serbian bard, whose tradition is thought to be related to the ancient Greek manner of Homer, recite a poem as long as *The Odyssey*, and take two weeks to do so in twice daily sessions each lasting two hours. This would not be done by remembering the poem line by line but by a process of continuous re-composition. The bard was working with a knowledge of the narrative outline and an ingrained sense of the movement of the verse line. This given structure acts as a channel through which he could convey the story's larger and more detailed incidents. These in turn would include an array of formulae which allow set repetitions of such things as the arrival of a messenger, how he is received, and how he delivers his missive. Description of natural objects and persons would also be made in appropriate given forms.

So this huge poem is being re-made as its recitation goes along, but in accordance with strongly established conventions. In his *The World of Odysseus* the historian M.I. Finley reckons that about one third of the *Iliad* and the *Odyssey* is composed of lines or blocks of lines that appear elsewhere in the poem. All of this shows us the importance of creativity in the recitation of oral poetry, and that performance is vital to it. Much nearer to our own time and experience, the process is somewhat similar to the way we might improvise the verses of a pop song whilst returning to the chorus, or the way football crowds adapt songs to hymn their club or particular players. Incidentally the *collective* character of the composition of such songs and chants shows us another continuing feature of the **oral tradition**.

The experience of the anthropologist John Tedlock is interesting here as it highlights a further aspect of the relationship between oral performance, the full meaning of a work and the nature of poetry's deliberate spaces as against conventional prose. In the 1960s Tedlock set himself to record the narrative poetry of the Native American Zuni people in the south-western United States. Transcribing his many hours of tapes Tedlock found himself dissatisfied by pages of written prose which seemed to capture so little of the experience he had heard. Most specifically he writes, 'there is no silence in it', and the varying pauses of the Zuni narrators, together with their varieties of level, are part of the body of the story. Consequently, influenced also by poetry readings in his own culture, Tedlock devised a written version of the Zuni stories set out in *'free verse'* lines to point the pauses and with capitals and different letter sizes indicating voice levels:

"THAT'S WHAT YOU DID AND YOU ARE MY
REAL
   MOTHER," That's what he told his mother. At that
moment
   his mother
embraced him
     embraced him.
His uncle got angry
     his uncle got angry.
He beat
his kinswoman
     he beat his kinswoman.
That's how it happened.
The boy's deer elders were on the floor.
     His grandfather then
spread some covers
     on the floor, laid them there, and put strands of turquoise
       beads on them.

                                        (Tedlock, 1972)

Tedlock's translations make use of the gestural features of poetry, including the deployment of white space on the page, to render what might otherwise have been thought of – especially had they been transcribed by pen rather than by tape-recorder – as prose narratives. He found that prose doesn't capture performance, where varying emphases and plays of sound and silence are part of story and its meaning. Verse lines and the deployment of deliberate poetic spaces do. His experience he writes, 'convinced me that prose has no real existence outside the written page'. Introducing Tedlock's collection of Zuni work, Jerome Rothenberg asserts:

> We have forgotten too that *all* speech is a succession of sounds and silences, and the narrator's art (like that of any poet) is locked into the ways the sound and silence play against each other.

It is exactly this interactive play of varyingly stressed sound and silence that constitutes the deliberate space of poetry.

OUT OF THE ORAL TRADITION – TOWARDS THE PAGE

As these instances suggest, the relationship between oral and written forms of poetries that certainly have their origins in the oral tradition is complex. As the editor and translator Michael Alexander writes of the Old English epic *Beowulf,* 'it is likely that the poem had more than one oral stage and more than one written stage.' This has implications too for our conception of the *authorship* of poetry which I shall discuss in Chapter 8. For the moment however I want to continue to explore the influence of the oral origins of poetry upon its shapes.

In English the '*ballad* tradition' carries all these complexities of origin and transmission. As a consciously defined 'tradition' this usually refers now to the gathering of poems by F. J. Child as *The English and Scottish Popular Ballads* published between 1882 and 1898. However the form had attracted a lot of literary interest and imitation much earlier, especially in the eighteenth century and most prominently by **William Wordsworth** (1770–1850) and **Samuel Taylor Coleridge** (1772–1834) whose joint volume *Lyrical Ballads* appeared in 1798. Formally the *ballad* is usually a poem that tells a story and is written in short stanzas. The stories tend to have simple plots, straightforward characterization and are frequently dramatic and violent. They often feature encounters with the supernatural, love tragedies, sons lost at sea, and adultery. Here are some lines from the mediaeval ballad *Little Musgrave and Lady Barnard,* a tale in which the lady, having fallen in love with a young man at church, and he with her, takes him off to her 'bower at Buckelsfordbery where 'Thou's lig in mine armes all night'. Told of this by 'a little tinny page', the Lord Barnard discovers them:

> With that my Lord Barnard came to the door,
>   And lit a stone upon;
> He plucked out three silver keys,
>   And he open'd the doors each one.
>
> He lifted up the coverlet.
>   He lifted up the sheet:

"How now, thou Little Musgrave,
    Doest thou find my lady sweet?"

"I find her sweet," quoth Little Musgrave,
    "The more 'tis to my pain;
I would gladly give three hundred pounds
    That I were on yonder plain."

"Arise, arise, thou Little Musgrave,
    And put thy clothes on;
It shall nere be said in my country
    I have killed a naked man.

"I have two swords in one scabbard,
    Full dear they cost my purse;
And thou shalt have the best of them.
    And I will have the worse."

(From The English and Scottish Popular
Ballads, Francis James Child (ed.) (1965))

Many of these ballads are very lengthy and so it is necessary to quote at some length to give an idea of how any incident unfolds. In these lines we can see how the **narrative** is built piece by piece in each self-enclosed stanza: Lord Barnard arrives at the door; lifts the sheet – and here the repetition acts both as part the reciter/singer's **mnemonic** and as suspense; Musgrave's reaction; Barnard's chivalric challenge to a duel in two parts – the command to Musgrave to dress, and the donation of the better sword.

Each of these stanzas has the same two features to its structure. First each rhymes the second and fourth lines: *'upon'/'one'; 'sheet'/'sweet'; 'pain'/'plain'*. Rhyme schemes are conventionally notated, in this example: **ABCB**. (See Chapter 5 for a fuller discussion of **rhyme**.) Secondly each has the same **metrical** pattern, that is the **beat** or **stress** – like the claps in the clapping song – falls upon syllables in each line in a way that corresponds to related lines. Again we shall study **metre** more fully later (Chapter 4), but broadly this means that the first and third lines contain *four beats* and the second and fourth lines *three beats*:

'He **lifted up** the **coverlet**,
  He **lifted up** the **sheet**;
How **now**, how **now,** thou **Little** Mus**grave,**
  Does thou **find** my lady **sweet.**'

This then is the marked-out working space of the ballad. To the singer/reciter this pattern would be grooved as a channel in which to carry the narrative, a basic framework in which to fit details and devise variations. Especially since it often includes 'pause' reiterations, it helps the performer recall the content, or if necessary improvise. In this stanza we can see how it serves the purpose of the story. The key action is of course the lifting of the bedclothes so **lift** and **up** are bound to carry stress and their reiteration lends suspense. The last line of the ballad stanza is often the punchline of that part of the narrative and in this stanza the key content is contained in the three words **find, la**dy and **sweet**. The rhyme **sheet/sweet** – less expected than ballad rhymes often are – is brilliantly impressive as it reveals the Lord Barnard's sensual, sardonic psychology, the way his mock interest in Musgrave's experience of his wife is sinisterly controlled. Ballads are often represented as painting action and character with a very broad brush, but this detail, resting as it does in that one word 'sweet' is wonderfully resonant.

What we see in John Tedlock's work transcribing Zuni stories and Child's record of the ballads is the influence of the written word. Tedlock's experience is interesting in that he distinguishes between *written* prose and *written* poetry. As with the ballads, the original performances have nothing to do with such categories. But the 500 years of the printed word since the flourishing of the ballads have made their demands and largely decided the way they are now experienced as fixed texts. Print has been a centralizing and standardizing force, which is why so many social and political struggles have always centred round access to the press. In this context it is not surprising that oral cultures have remained most important to groups with least access to standard publication. The African-American Blues tradition is one prominent instance, and, more strictly in verse than in song, so is the oral poetry of the

African-Caribbean, especially Jamaica, both on its home ground and in African-Caribbean communities in Britain and elsewhere.

This poetry is composed in dialect and is usually *narrative*, often using the manner of conversation to cover material ranging from outraged denunciation to neighbourly gossip. One example is the work of **Louise Bennett** (1919–2006) who emerged in Jamaica in the 1940s. The poetry persists in both authored instances such as Bennett's, and in traditional transmission, often of memorized verses hundreds of lines long. The verse scheme is usually similar to the ballad in that it uses a four-line stanza rhyming *abab*, and either a four *beat* line or an alternation of four and three beats. But, in context, most important is the dialect, for in the shaped sound-space of the poem the ordinary language of the people proclaims its seriousness and demands respect. It returns pleasure and recognition to its own speakers and reminds 'standard' speakers of the capacities of varieties of English other than their own. The space of the poem is thus doubly deliberate: first in its formal shaping and then, through this, as an act of cultural assertion.

Valerie Bloom (1956–), a successor to Louise Bennett, performs her work in character and often in costume, mobilizes the apparently lightsome qualities of her tradition to serious purposes. Here she adopts the manner of a street gossip telling a relative the story of a boy shot dead by police in a dispute at a picture house. Skilfully she uses the repeated phrase 'a soh dem sey' ('or so they say') to make an ironic comment on different versions of the incident. These are the last three verses of 'Trench Town Shock (A Soh Dem Sey)' in which the teller describes how the official version is that the boy pulled a knife and was thus shot through the head in self-defence, something that happens often:

> 'Still, nutten woulda come from i',
> But wha yuh tink, Miss May?
> Di bwoy no pull out lang knife mah!
> At leas' a soh dem sey.
>
> Dem try fi aim afta im foot
> But im head get een di way,
> Di bullit go 'traight through im brain,
> At leas' a soh dem sey.

Dry yuh yeye, mah, mi know i hat,
But i happen ebery day,
Knife-man always attack armed police
At leas' a soh dem sey.'

(Bloom, 1983)

SPACE ON THE PAGE

The 'deliberate space' of the poems we have looked at so far is created primarily by patterns of sound and we follow the poems by ear. Sound is nearly always important to poetry, but with the wider dispersal of literate culture, especially following the advent of printing by movable type from the fifteenth century onwards, the poem's effect is complemented by the shape of the space it occupies on the page. Now I want to look at a series of poems in which the visual becomes of increasing importance.

As I wrote in Chapter 1 we often turn to poetry in the midst of strong feeling, especially grief. Several of the poems we shall look at in the next few pages are linked by featuring tears. Although we are primarily concerned with the shapes of these poems, in theme and **imagery** the globe of the tear might be said to occupy its own small space within the poetic tradition.

'Luveli ter of luveli eyghe,   [lovely ...eye]
   Why dostu me so wo?   [give me such woe]
Sorful ter of sorful eyghe,   sorrowful]
   Thu brekst myn herte a-to.'   [you break my heart in two]

This beautiful little refrain from the mid-1300s, possibly a love lyric but certainly part of a devotional poem to Christ, conveys its tender feeling with the most minimal deployment of four simple lines. It alternates four and three **beat** lines, though in the first and third lines ensuring that the beats *start* the lines (these stressed **beats** are shown in bold):

'Luveli ter of luveli eyghe ...
Sorful ter of sorful eyghe'

This ensures a heavier emphasis, an effect that pushes forward the sense of the expostulation of grief and mimes a tolling measure befitting the mournful subject. *Measure* is a term often applied to poetry and these lines with their simple solid balance of these key stresses on key words, convey the powerful sense of being measured, in the sense of calibration *and* of restraint, whilst also holding the sense of bursting forth that is weeping. These common Old English words *luveli* and *sorful* (sorrowful) are just allowed to impose their accumulated weight both in the strong sound of consonant and vowel, and of their roots and associations of meaning in *love* and *soreness*. The second and third lines, are differently, but no less strongly stressed,

> 'Why **dos**tu **me** so **wo** ...
> Thu **brekst** myn **herte** a-**to'**

but that slight difference opens a break in the beat through that unstressed *why* which is almost like a tiny catch in the voice. Short, with obvious beats and reiterated vocabulary, these four lines appear to make little inventive use of their space, and yet these minimal means achieve remarkable emotional power.

Not weeping, but still lamenting, **Geoffrey Chaucer** (1340–1400) in this poem with the interestingly paradoxical title 'Merciles Beaute', has a refrain of similar affecting economy:

> 'Your yen two wol slee me sodenly;   [eyes will slay me suddenly]
> I may the beautee of hem not sustene.'   [survive]

In these longer, ten syllable lines – counting *yen* as two – Chaucer gets the pain into his rhythm by obliging a tiny pause after *yen* and then accelerating the line through the sibilance of *slee* and *sodenly*. The second line has three beats much stronger than the others, on **beaut**ee, **not** and *sus***tene** which intensifies the emotion after that apparently equable **may**. *Sostene* – which is made to rhyme in the whole with *kene*, *grene* and *queen* – seems to me a particularly effective choice because it picks up the *s* sounds of *slee* and *sodenly*. The word in this sense of *withstand, endure,* is unusual, and thus gives the sense of the poet casting urgently about to find the proper word to convey the pressure. Again, a small space carrying a potent effect.

But the pleasures of the poetic space can be less doleful:

> There once was a poet called Donne,
> Who said "Piss off!" to the sunne:
>> The sunne said "Jack,
>> Get out of the sack,
> The girl that you're with is a nun."

Not all **limericks** are so indelicate, although this one easily could be more so, and, as it has transmuted into a popular joke form, many are. The origins of the form are obscure and it has always, it seems, migrated back and forth between written and oral traditions. The pattern however is broadly the same: five lines, with numbers three and four shorter, usually two beats, and a rhyme scheme of *aa bb a*. Especially because the form, like all joke formulae, has become so well-worn, the first two lines can often use their length to produce a knowingly laborious, even pedantic quality. This must however then be recovered by the acceleration of the short lines, and, vitally, by surprise in the final rhyme, even if – as in 'Hickery dickory dock' – it repeats the first rhyme word and gains its effect by second-guessing what the listener expects. In this case the deliberate anti-climax might only serve to highlight the real inventiveness that is in the third and fourth lines. This, by **Edward Lear** (1812–1888), is an example:

> There was an old man of Thermopylae,
>> Who couldn't do anything properly;
>> But they said "If you choose
> To boil eggs in your shoes,
> You shall never remain in Thermopylae."

But in all cases it is shape that satisfies, a fixed form within which wit can devise surprises. As always the *cadence*, or fall, is a matter of timing.

Another short form that shows the appeal of distinct shape is the **haiku**. Originally a Japanese poetic form developed in the thirteenth and fourteenth centuries, it attracted western imitation around 1900. Although there are variations both in the Japanese tradition and in western practice, the commonest definition of the haiku is that it has seventeen *syllables* distributed over three lines in the pattern of 5-7-5. Its interest for English language poets, especially for **Ezra Pound** (1885–1972) and the *Imagist* poets of the early twentieth century, is that its extreme compression purges verse of dilation and decoration in order to concentrate on a single noticed thing. Pound himself did not in fact write any true haiku though the influence of the form can be seen in such poems as 'Alba', 'In a Station of the Metro' and the satiric squib 'The New Cake of Soap'. Later, the associations of the haiku with Zen Buddhism attracted the attention of poets exploring eastern religion and philosophy, and the influential translations of R.H. Blythe of the Japanese poets **Bashō**, **Buson** and others, represent the form in both shape and tone, but cannot always translate it exactly in terms of that syllable structure:

> The coolness:
> The voice of the bell
> As it leaves the bell!

> (Buson in Blythe, 1978)

The precision and pregnancy of the form makes it continually appealing, not least to *parodists*. The Internet might be seen as a contemporary site for the oral tradition and familiar frustrations with its technology are a frequent feature of its exchanges. The haiku seems an appropriate form to express such infuriation, as it suggests the brevity of computer commands and the technology's nearly mystical inscrutability. Here, composed in English and thus able to follow the template exactly, are two of many in circulation:

> Windows NT crashed.
> I am the Blue Screen of Death.
> None will hear your screams.
>
>   * *
>
> With searching comes loss
> And the presence of absence:

"My Novel" not found.
Press Exit in tears.

We shall look in more detail at the set spaces poets use in Chapter 7 on the *stanza*. However, returning to the theme of tears, and to Jack the Poet, the opening of **John Donne**'s (1572–1631) farewell to his lover as he departs overseas, 'A Valediction: of Weeping', is a striking contrast to the simplicity of the haiku. Here we see a poet figuring a more elaborate space in which to work:

Let me pour forth
My tears before thy face, whilst I stay here,
For thy face coins them, and thy stamp they bear,
And by this mintage they are something worth,
    For thus they be
    Pregnant of thee;
Fruits of much grief they are, emblems of more,
When a tear falls, that thou falls which it bore,
So thou and I are nothing then, when on a divers shore.

The *idea* of an enclosed space – the globe of his tear containing the reflection of his lover – governs this *stanza*. It is then expanded in the poem's two succeeding stanzas as the tear becomes first an image of the world and then of the seas in which he might drown. The anguish of parting lies in the sense of fragility: the imminence of their last moment together, and the possibility that the break might never be repaired whether because of disaster or change of heart. The falling tear is an exact image for this fragility, and its enclosure is paralleled by the stanza that holds it. It opens with the outbreak of weeping carried by the bursting forth of that short first line, and ends with the dissolution of the tear as it hits the ground – 'thou and I are nothing then'. The space between contains the speaker's urgent thoughts as they tumble forward, stopping and starting as he grasps at connecting words, *whilst, for, when, that, so*, to sort out his logic. Like the first line, the other two short lines are moments when the emotion is most forceful. Their heavy and irregular stresses, and crude *be/thee* rhyme, punctuate the effort in the longer lines to hold back the fall of the tear, and so the parting, by inventing so much to see in it. All the anxiety about the relationship – brevity, fragility – is represented in the instant of the falling tear, held up, as though in slow motion, by the space between line 1 and line 9.

It is interesting to ponder the degree to which such distinct shapes as the limerick and haiku are held in the poet, reader or listener's mind as sound or as a visual shape. My own sense is that since the printed page is so much part of our mental landscape, even the shapes of poem that arise out of the oral tradition like the ballad stanza and the limerick occupy a visualized space in our imagination. Some early sixteenth- and seventeenth-century printings of *lyrics* and sonnets drew a series of arcs down the right-hand margin linking together the rhyme words in order to illustrate that there is a visual, normally an elegantly symmetrical pattern to the poem which complements its harmonies of sounds. Drawing these arcs and then turning the page through ninety degrees, the rhyming of some elaborate stanza forms, such as **John Dryden**'s (1631–1700) 'Song for Saint Cecilia's Day', can be seen to have a nearly architectural structure. Again, we shall look at this in more detail in Chapter 7 on the *stanza*.

Visual shape then, is the other dimension of the poem's deliberate space. Such shapes as the *quatrain* and the *sonnet* have a presence on the page and in the ear. But prior to their realization they can occupy a distinct working area within the poet's mind during composition. For a variety of reasons the poet's first motivation may be to write a *sonnet*, or a *villanelle* or some other set form. Less specifically he or she may see the poem in the mind's eye at an early stage of its gestation as composed of *quatrains*, or six-line stanzas or some other configuration. In the same way that the twentieth-century Russian poet Osip Mandelstam said that a poem first of all existed for him as 'a musical phrase ringing insistently in the ears' even before the words came to him (Nadezhda Mandelstam, *Hope Against Hope: A Memoir*, 1975, p.82), so poets might glimpse the beginning of a poem as a shape. All the poetic forms have this visual, even sculptural, dimension.

EMBLEMS AND 'CONCRETE' POEMS

Some poems, like the *emblem poems* of the seventeenth century, foreground the visual dimension by patterning the words on the page so as to present a visual image of the poem's subject. This is **George Herbert**'s (1593–1633) 'Easter Wings':

Lord, who createdst man in wealth and store,
Though foolishly he lost the same,
Decaying more and more,
Till he became
Most poore:
With thee
O let me rise
As larks, harmoniously,
And sing this day thy victories:
Then shall the fall further the flight in me.

This is one of a pair of poems that can be read this way, and turned through ninety degrees to present the image of two angels standing with wings outspread. *Emblem* poems were often, although not exclusively, religious, and aim to convey their point briefly and vividly. In 'Easter Wings' the outside, longer lines treat of the expansiveness of God while the inside lines waste to the near vanishing point of human frailty. The poem's meaning therefore is carried both in word and image.

In the twentieth century several poets have been drawn to this tradition, among them **Dylan Thomas** (1914–53) with a number of poems both imitating Herbert's wings and inverting it to produce a diamond shapes on the page. **Geoffrey Hill**'s (1932–) 'Prayer to the Sun' is composed of three short poems, each in the shape of a cross, stepped diagonally down the page, and **John Hollander**'s (1929–) 'Swan and Shadow' is figured as a swan on the water together with its exactly inverted reflection.

These poems all make use of visual effect to endorse the meaning. *Concrete poetry* of the twentieth century may also do so, but many of its practitioners are most interested in the nature and variety of *text*. This is **Edwin Morgan**'s (1920–2010) 'Siesta of a Hungarian Snake':

S SZ SZ **SZ** SZ **SZ** SZ **ZS** ZS **ZS** ZS ZS Z

The poet and editor Richard Kostelanetz defines text broadly as 'anything reproducible in a book', and since concrete poems have often appeared as posters or other forms of art-work, even his definition may be too narrow. In the twentieth century 'concrete' poets have used the expanding resources of typography and modern printing techniques to emphasize the material nature of the poem and of words themselves. The page consists of (usually) white space and letter and /or number forms. While there is only one kind of empty space there are myriad forms, including – now that photographic means of mechanical reproduction are the norm – handwriting. The emphasis of concrete poetry, or text in Kostelanetz' sense, is to weaken or remove the *semantic* properties of words, letters and figures, that is to reduce their attachment to meaning.

Morgan's poem above might not qualify as a 'pure' concrete poem since its effect depends on at least three things: a rudimentary knowledge of the character of the Hungarian language with its clusters of consonants and apparent plethora of Zs; our understanding of the words *siesta* and *snake*; and upon the *onomatopoeic* convention by which cartoons and comic-strips denote snoozing. All these go together to create a verbal and visual joke.

But **Jose Garcia Villa**'s (1908–97) 'Sonnet in Polka Dots' is more inscrutable. The first quatrain reads:

```
O  O  O  O  O  O  O  O  O
  O  O  O  O  O  O  O   O  O  O
  O  O  O  O  O  O  O   O  O  O
O  O  O  O  O  O  O  O  O
```

(J.G.Villa in Kostelanetz 1980)

and continues through the whole fourteen lines in the classic 8 and 6 division of the *sonnet* form. Villa's text seems to be playing a game with the abstraction of poetic form: it is in the shape of a sonnet but its content is zero. **Matthew Welton** (1969–) elaborates a variation on Villa in his sequence 'Six Poems by themselves' in which the twelve lines of each poem reads: '_____', but with each poem comprised of a different stanzaic pattern.

Morgan's 'Hungarian Snake' might also be considered a *sound poem*, that is a work that takes the physiological qualities of voice-sounds, whether they are words, or are part of words, or onomatopoeic sounds like 'sz', or sounds with no semantic features at all, as its key feature. Tongue-twisters such as

> Betty bought a bit of butter
> But she found the butter bitter
> So she bought a bit of better butter
> To make the bitter butter better,

are close to sound poems since the consonants or vowels are so prominent. But they still use words. More radically, and towards the nonsense end of this spectrum is Morgan's own hilarious performance poem in which Nessie the Loch Ness Monster slowly surfaces and returns to the depths. The poem consists simply of a series of bubblings, exhalations and snorts from Morgan's virtuoso sinuses. Most recently, PC Multimedia offers resources whereby a poet might compose a text by making simultaneous use not only of the semantic properties of the words, but their typography, their utterance, together with layerings of other sound and music as well as images.

PERFORMANCE POETRY

The prominence of the printed page and the book since the sixteenth century has perhaps served to obscure the continuing importance the physical voice for poetry. Certainly reciting aloud was a very important part of the life of poetry in the nineteenth century, and in contemporary poetic culture 'performance' has assumed a significant enough place for many towns and cities to have poetry 'nights' of different kinds as part of their cultural scene.

Many elements play into this phenomenon, two of the most important from outside the metropolitan culture of the English-speaking world. The influence of the oral tradition of Jamaica and other parts of the Caribbean already described, and its updating in a British urban context in the work of **Linton Kwesi Johnson** (1952–) and other *dub* poets, is one of these along with the *rap* poetry that has emerged from African-American culture. Both show the power of the fundamental characteristics of verse of *beat* and *rhyme*. Moreover the association of these styles with popular music, formally and culturally, is another component in its success which has meant that they have become imitated, adapted and disseminated well beyond their original sources.

The influence of popular music on poetry can be seen in one very simple borrowing: the microphone. Only at the rare, big traditional poetry readings might the reciting poet encounter (usually uncomfortably) a microphone, but for contemporary poets who see their natural context as the kind of club or performance space shared with bands, the microphone is a necessary tool and one that enhances and stretches the capacity of the reciting, or as it becomes, the *performing* voice.

So, drawing on these influences, and the poetry events of the *Beat* poets of the 1950s and 1960s, *performance poetry* has grown to be a popular and highly visible part of the contemporary poetry landscape. The *slam* in which poets compete against each other to win by audience acclaim has encouraged not only skill in the verse itself but greater actorly skills in voice, gesture, costume and persona. But equally the phenomenon of the 'open mic' at performance poetry events embodies the ethos of performance poetry: the entertainment of a live audience and an unmediated, do-it-yourself openness towards expression and technical skill. Here poetry lives alongside and sometimes fuses with other parts of the entertainment world, popular music and stand-up comedy. In many ways it is the present-day space of the oral tradition in which poetry began.

CONCLUSION

Always the poet is working between the poles of the minimal and the full, between economy and plenitude. The one side draws towards compression – how briefly can I put this? – the other towards expansion, dilation – how richly, how extravagantly can I put this? Both extremes will eventually disappear into nothingness: silence, the blank page, or an endless, shapeless spume of words.

Between these poles poetry uses conventions to demarcate and organize a space in time and/or space – perhaps 'space-time'– for the words to dwell. These bounds draw and intensify attention. Just as the structuring of a joke will have us listening for and expecting the punchline, so the techniques of eloquence will have us straining for the key points of the argument or the point of inspiration. All are verbal spaces, marked out deliberately, *with* deliberation, and *for* deliberation. The poet feels for a space that seems at once demanding and accommodating, whether given by tradition or 'made anew'. It is a space marked for special attention. Indeed poets accept outlines in order to achieve the powers of concentration and effect that come from limitation. **John Crowe Ransom** (1888–1974) argued, for instance, that formal measures obliged him to think harder, made him reject his first words because they would not fit, and therefore to discover other more interesting things that he would never have written had he not made himself meet the restrictions he had imposed upon himself. **Thom Gunn** (1929–2004) puts it like this: 'As you get more desperate, you actually start to think more deeply about the subject in hand, so that rhyme turns out to be a method of thematic exploration.' (*Shelf Life*, 1993, p.221). **Walt Whitman** (1819–92), on the other hand, in a spirit we might recognize in contemporary performance poets, sought to write 'as though there were never such thing as a poem'.

In practice the very decision to write poems presupposes *some* conception of what a poem is, and this will relate to the *space* and *sound* that it is. This does not mean however – as Whitman demonstrated – that the expectations that compose any genre cannot be expanded and renewed in the work of new poets. Whether these shapes, short or long, are accepted from the existing tradition or invented anew, the poet will discover workable outlines to contain the work: the deliberate space of the poem.

SUMMARY

In this chapter we have considered:

*   More of what is meant by gestural language.
*   The nature of the oral tradition in poetry and the importance of its devices for recitation and memorability.
*   Children's rhymes, including the relation of clapping and poetic rhythm.
*   The oral tradition in epic and narrative poetry both ancient and modern, including the ballad, and its continuation in contemporary performance poetry.
*   The development of sound and shape as poetry moves from the oral to the page.
*   Poems as visual artefacts.

FURTHER READING

Bloom, Valerie (2002) *Hot Like Fire*: *Poems*, London: Bloomsbury.

Donne, John (1998) *Selected Poetry*, Carey, John, (ed.) London: Oxford University Press.

Frost, Robert 'The Figure a Poem Makes' and Glyn Maxwell, 'Strictures' in Herbert, W.N. and Hollis, M. (eds) (2000) *Strong Words: Modern Poets on Modern Poetry*, Tarset: Bloodaxe.

Furniss, Tom and Bath, Michael (1966) *Reading Poetry: An Introduction*, Prentice Hall, see Part I, 1, 'What is Poetry? How Do We Read It?'

Grigson, G. (ed.) (1975) *The Penguin Book of Ballads*, Harmondsworth: Penguin.

Holub, M. (1990) *The Dimensions of the Present Moment*, Young, D. trans, London: Faber.

Koch, K. (1998) *Making Your Own Days: The Pleasures of Reading and Writing Poetry*, New York: Simon & Schuster.

Ong, W.J. (1982) *Orality and Literacy: The Technologizing of the Word*, London: Methuen.

Opie, Iona and Opie, Peter (1959) *The Lore and Language of Schoolchildren*, Oxford: Oxford University Press.

Pinsky, R. (1988) *Poetry and the World*, New York: Ecco Press, see 'Poetry and Pleasure'.

Wade, Stephen (2002) *Writing Performance Poetry*, Brighton: Straightforward Publishing.

TONES OF VOICE

My view is
Far too complicated
To explain in a
Poem.

> (E.J. Thribb, 'Lines on the Return to Britain of Billy Graham')

Master Thribb, the English satirical magazine *Private Eye*'s spoof schoolboy poet, clearly thinks that poetry is not the appropriate vehicle to do justice to the intricacies of his views on religion. Whether or not some subject matter is beyond the capacities of verse, we can readily see that the tone struck by a poem needs to be appropriate to its content. Our merriment in reading E.J. Thribb comes from enjoying the disparity either between the dignity of his chosen topics and the banal inertia of his verse, or between the ambition to write high-flown verse and the trivial character of his concerns. It is exactly the disjunction that all ***parody*** uses to gain its effect, and by recognizing the incongruity we are also reminded of the importance of an appropriate fit between subject and tone of voice.

I use the term 'tone of voice' in this chapter for two reasons. First, in reading poetry, we often have the impression that the poet is 'speaking' to us. This is partly because of the long association of poetry with the spoken word, but more specifically because the predominant poetic mode has become one in which one person is telling – or *singing* to us – often about emotional experience. This ***lyric*** mode fosters a sense of intimacy, and is the model we also see in words set to music from Schubert to the popular songs of our own day. As I shall show later, this notion of how a poem 'speaks' needs serious qualification. The second reason however is that there are respects in which the system of tones adopted by poems can be equated with those we employ in daily speech, and it is this variety that I want to explore in this chapter.

WAYS OF SPEAKING

In conversation we adopt different ways of speaking according to circumstance and to whom we are speaking. To people we know well we will speak more allusively, drawing upon shared knowledge and assumptions, whereas with strangers, or in more formal situations, we might strive to be more explicit and precise in vocabulary and sentence structure. We always work with a loose system of formalities, adjusting how we say things according to the situation. For instance, we may only use that kind of intonation of our voice which aims to tell the listener that we mean the opposite of what we are saying – for example remarking 'Lovely day' when it is cold and raining – if we are confident that they will understand what we really mean. In many languages the same part of speech can mean entirely different things depending on how the spoken sound is pitched. English does not work like that, although contouring the sound ironically, as in '*Lovely* day', is part of the way we pitch the *tone* of our speech. Indeed intonation can generate meaning all by itself: think how many ways there are of saying 'Yes' and 'No'. These have their counterparts in many kinds of writing. As we shall see later, the *stress* patterns of the verse line are a special resource for deploying *pitch* of this kind.

Linguists often use the term *register* when picking out the formalities appropriate to speaking to various audiences, and in this chapter I want to argue that we can see the different *sub-genres* of poetry as registers of this kind. The lament for the dead in an *elegy*, the inwardness and song-like qualities of the *lyric*, the wryness or vituperation of the *satire*, the considered mixture of public and private concern in the *ode*, all these are examples of how the traditional modes of poetry have evolved to fit a tone of voice composed of word-choice, rhythm and shape to the appropriate occasion. Employing the resources of such modes is akin to finding the appropriate way to speak in public, or to a friend, whether in celebration, condolence, gossip or any other situation.

'NATURAL' AND 'UNNATURAL'

Now it can be objected that emphasizing the place of traditional modes denies the spontaneity or naturalness of poetry. This takes us back to that valued association between the verse and the poet as speaker. The American poet **Kenneth Rexroth** (1905–82) stated that 'I have spent my life trying to write the way I talk'. Rexroth evidently thought that his verse should approximate in tone to the way he talked. Presumably he valued the idea of consonance between these different speech acts, indeed different parts of his personality. Since we tend to think of our ordinary speech as 'natural', it seems obvious that he wanted to cleanse his verse of 'artificial' expression. Interestingly however, since Rexroth says that he has spent his life on this quest, it seems the pursuit of the 'natural' is not easy. Settling to work upon a poem, he encounters an expectation for a certain, specialized language and manner, acting strongly upon him. Although he speaks every day of his life, it is a lifetime's work to write in just the way he speaks.

If this suggests that 'natural' is not in fact so natural, it does not eclipse the longstanding demand for poetry to achieve a tone close to 'everyday speech', what **William Wordsworth** (1770–1850) called 'the speech of ordinary men'. Wordsworth was reacting against a poetic manner that he thought had become stultifying, and the changes of poetic styles have often been driven simply by an intuitive sense that poetry can't work that way anymore, a sense that is often related to how close or how distant poetry and common speech should be. But we should recognize that in speech too audience and occasion will usually influence, even determine, the *tenor* of how we talk, and that within these conventions we will choose our words. There is then no simple distinction here between the 'natural' and the 'artificial'. Artifice – by which I mean considered making – is not only unavoidable, it is 'natural'. None of this is to say that the time will not come when impatience with set forms, transgression, innovation and irreverence will be as appropriate and necessary in poems as they are in life.

But we can ask whether an 'ordinary' tone is what we want in poetry. Might we not want extraordinary speech, choice of words, a *diction*, that we do not encounter everyday? At present, after half a century in which the informal, the conversational, the 'unpoetic' manner has dominated poetry in English, we might think so. The following discussion of the different registers that have been used over the preceding centuries might help us decide.

AUTHORITY AND AUTHENTICITY

In considering the different classifications of poetry as 'tones of voice' I shall be making a broad division between 'public' and 'personal' registers. But in both spheres – and of course they are not wholly distinct – one aspect of the 'voice' is bound to concern us. As we encounter a poem we will pick up a **tone** and want to ask, as we do mentally or explicitly with an unexpected phone-call, 'Who is speaking here?' We ask this not in the literal biographical sense, but in search of assurance as to the *authority* of the voice, that is whether we want to give it our trust. This might mean trusting the poem to tell us a story with a secure grasp of its plot and with compelling embellishment of description and character. It might mean being confident that the ideas the poem contains are intelligible and substantial rather than arrantly prejudiced. It might mean being convinced that the emotional world of the poem is plausibly and affectingly conveyed. None of these things necessarily depends upon our knowing the poet's credentials in the sense that she or he was an eye-witness to events, or a profound philosopher, or actually experienced the pain or joy described. Authenticity in a poem is a matter of rhetoric: of how the poet draws us into trust, makes us inhabit the events, ideas or emotions of the poem as we read. Finally this is done only by the words themselves on the page and in the ear. Of course, as with all trusting, we might come to feel we were misled.

PUBLIC VOICES

Although we now often see poetry as the most intimate of the literary genres, through most of its history it has worked as a public medium. Yet again this has to do with its oral origins, the transmission of the poem by voice to an audience.

Narrative, as we have seen with the ballad, is the most obvious of poetry's traditional functions and storytelling has been the principal purpose of poetry, or significant component of it, for centuries. In his massive collection *The Canterbury Tales* **Geoffrey Chaucer** (?1340–1400) makes the pleasure and purpose of storytelling the very method and substance of his work. The Host of Southwark's Tabard Inn, from which Chaucer's varied company of characters will leave on their pilgrimage to the shrine of St Thomas à Becket, exhorts each of them to tell a tale or two along the way as the ride will be cheerless if they ride 'the weye doumb as stoon' [dumb as stone]. He himself will give a free dinner as the prize for the best story,

> That is to seyn, that telleth in this caas   [say; case]
> Tales of best sentence and moost solaas   [solace]
>
> ('Prologue' l. 797–8)

'*Sentence*' here encompasses theme and significance, and '*solaas*', solace, amusement and pleasure. But there is another dimension to this double purpose that Chaucer takes pains to set out, and that is his aim to represent the tale of each of his companions exactly as spoken. Of course this is a fiction, but it is a significant one and his bold apology for it is significant:

> For this ye knowen al so wel as I,
> Whoso shal telle a tale after a man,
> He moot reherce as ny as evere he kan   [rehearse; near]
> Everich a word, if it be in his charge,   [every]
> Al speke he never so rudeliche and large,   [rudely]
> Or ellis he moot telle his tale untrewe,
> Or feyne thyng, or fynde wordes newe.   [pretend]
> He may nat spare, although he were his brother;   [flinch]
> He moot as wel seye o word as another.
> Crist spak hymself ful brode in hooly writ,
> And wel ye woot no vileynye is it.   [you know]
>
> ('Prologue' l. 730–40)

[Gloss: You know as well as I that anyone who repeats another's tale must keep as close as he can to each and every word, no matter how crude they might be, or else he is being untruthful, pretending and putting in new words. He must not flinch from that even to save his brother's blushes but say one word as straight as another. After all, in the Bible Christ spoke broadly and as you know there's nothing unfit in that.]

The poet claims that being true to what is actually said, and *how* it is said, even if the words are 'rudeliche and large', is his first duty even if this 'vileynye' offends against decorum. His licence to do this he takes from the Gospels in which Christ himself speaks 'ful brode'.

The **register** of *The Canterbury Tales* then is presented as natural speech. Implicitly the work is setting itself apart from literary decorum. In the 1300s too it was important that the work is in the English tongue rather than the more prestigious Latin or French. The poem is declaring itself for a 'middle' style of verse, one that will include voices of various social degrees in the context of convivial, improvised storytelling.

Yet Chaucer is assigning himself a greater task because this naturalistic effect needs to vary according to the different manners of his narrators. It is striking how often in the brilliant character sketches of the Prologue the poet remarks upon the vocal character and sometimes precise sound of voice of the pilgrims. Thus the Knight's Squire is 'Syngynge ... or floytynge, al the day' [singing .. fluting]; the Prioress sings the divine service 'Entuned in hir nose ful semely' [properly refined]; the sweet-talking Friar's speech is unparalleled for 'daliaunce and fair langage' [stylish show]; of the fashionable Wife of Bath he writes 'In felaweshipe wel koulde she laughe and carpe', part of the social skills that have brought that 'worthy womann' five husbands; in his cups the Summoner falls into Latin, though only the form of a few clichéd tag-terms; the venal, arrogant Pardoner, come straight 'fro the court of Rome', is reduced by the observation 'A voys he hadde as small as hath a goot' [goat]. Two contrasting examples might show how Chaucer fits his verse to create the impressions of different registers.

Here the Miller, who can barely stay on his horse, brushes aside the Reeve to insist on being next after the Knight's tale, a challenge to precedent and status which effects a striking cultural shift in the sequence of the *Tales* in itself, and for which Chaucer affects to apologize.

```
    This dronke Millere spak ful soone ageyn
    And seyde, "Leve brother Osewold,
    Who hath no wyf, he is no cokewold.        [cuckold]
    But I sey nat therefore that thou art oon;
    Ther been ful goode wyves many oon,        [many a one]
    And evere a thousand goode ayeyns oon bade.
    Thou knowestow wel thyself, but if thou madde."
```
('The Miller's Prologue' l. 3150–6)

[Gloss: This drunken Miller was soon off again: 'By your leave, brother Oswald, if a man isn't married he can't be a deceived husband. Not that I'm saying you're one – there are a thousand good wives for every bad one. You know that yourself, unless you're mad.]

The ribald quip that if you don't have a wife then you can't be cuckolded is followed by some clumsy verse reeking of inebriation. Trying to speak it ourselves we find the metre stumble towards the same rhyme word 'oon' [one], a word that also comes up in the next line. Putting 'Thou knowestow wel thyself, but if thou madde' into a separate sentence makes it one of those 'And another thing ...' of the button-holing drunk, a lurching afterthought banged home with the big stress on 'madde'.

The corrupt Pardoner whose handsome living depends upon his seductive eloquence selling fake pardons and relics to the faithful, begins the preface to his own tale like this:

```
    "Lordynges," quod he, "in chirches whan I preche,
    I peyne me to han an hauteyn speche,        [take pains; highflown]
    And rynge it out as round as gooth a belle,
    For I kan by rote that I telle.        [know by heart]
    My theme is alwey oon, and evere was –
    Radix malorum est cupiditas."        [love of money is the root of all evil]
```
('The Pardoner's Prologue' l. 329–34)

[Gloss: 'My lords,' he said, 'when I preach in church I take pains to use a highflown kind of speech and to ring it out clear as a bell for I've it all by heart. My theme is always and ever has been the same: *the love of money is the root of all evil*.]

The haughtiness of his manner is immediately evident as is his own high opinion of his delivery, which contrasts so clearly with what we have already been told about his goat-like tone. After that first sentence he rounds off his paragraph with a sophisticated turn by contriving a couplet mixing English and Latin. His choice of Latin text shows an effrontery which anticipates irony. As with so many such characters, the 'solaas' in the Pardoner's self-portrayal comes of his outrageousness, and the 'sentence' in the poet's depiction of ecclesiastical greed.

So in the different ways Chaucer has these characters speak we can see their character. The Miller's 'rudelich', knockabout verse reveals his heedless heartiness, whilst in the Pardoner's affected smoothness we see a condescending superiority, convinced as he is that his audience is too stupid to see through his hypocrisy. In these instances we see a deployment of tone that is akin to characterization in dramatic speech.

Another simple feature of *The Canterbury Tales* is the way virtually every tale begins with a geographical placement. The scene may be Oxford, Syria, Holderness, Tartary or Trumpington, but the audience is always immediately told. Alternatively the provenance of the tale, for instance Arthurian legend or the Roman authors, is announced at the outset, but both procedures serve to situate the audience at once. Thus we know where and when we are, and so are able to take our bearings, to '*naturalize*' the situation as the sequence of the tale unfolds. These are two aspects – characterization through speech, and physical placement – of the 'voice' of the *Tales* which compose the overall register in which Chaucer endeavours to create a narrative mode suited to actual storytelling before a varied audience.

EPIC AND THE MUSES

Traditionally the grandest type of narrative poem is the *epic*. The model of epic is a large poem whose story is of great historical significance for the group or nation from which it comes. In the western tradition Homer's tale of the ten year war against Troy in *The Iliad* (see Chapter2) and its sequel *The Odyssey* telling of the return home of the hero Odysseus, also known as Ulysses, form the defining myths of the Greek culture from which they sprang. Similarly Virgil's Latin epic *The Aeneid*, which begins with the escape of Aeneas from the ruins of Troy and tells of its hero's wanderings and the eventual fulfilment of his destiny to found the city of Rome, was deliberately composed to recount and sustain the founding myth of the city and its burgeoning empire.

For poets setting themselves a narrative task of this magnitude which calls so much more for 'sentence' than for 'solaas', the issue of authority weighs to an extraordinary degree. How can a single mind embrace the historical span and spiritual significance of a people's identity and also have the technical skill to engage and excite an audience? Traditionally the answer is ***inspiration*** (see also Chapter 8). Our common notion of inspiration is of an idea or sense of possibility that comes to us individually and unbidden without conscious mental process, as though from 'elsewhere'. The classical poets looked to the gods and to the ***Muses*** for aid, and in the Middle Ages the Italian poet **Dante** (1265–1321), lost in the dark wood of doubt and depression, recounts how he is sent divine assistance to enable him to start his imaginary journey and thus his poem. Occasionally the muses' assistance is sought in drama, as when the Prologue in **William Shakespeare**'s (1564–1616) *King Henry V* yearns for reality to replace the stage's shadow-play:

> O, for a muse of fire, that would ascend
> The brightest heaven of invention;
> A kingdom for a stage, princes to act
> And monarchs to behold the swelling scene!
>
> (Act I, Sc I, l.1–4)

This is 'a muse of fire' because fire, the lightest of the elements, is associated with poets whose work aspires upwards towards the spiritual realm.

For us the important thing about poetry that presents itself in this manner is that the poets are acknowledging that the process of composition is not a simply individual matter but an effort that requires support, and is in some sense collective. Whether or not the particular poet literally believes in the touch of a Muse, Aphrodite, or the Virgin Mary, he or she is seeking a confidence and authority that transcends their own individual voice. The poet is saying that behind these verses is a weight of precedence and knowledge greater than my own, that I am a channel through which this gathered force of knowledge flows. The epic tone therefore aspires to be impersonal. The unnamed figure clad in a long black cloak who traditionally spoke Shakespeare's choruses is therefore an appropriate figure for this register.

What lies behind this kind of writing is well shown in the work of perhaps the last writer in English to attempt it with full seriousness, **John Milton** (1608–74). In *Paradise Lost* Milton sets out to write an epic in the classical manner, but, even more adventurously, in English rather than either of the anciently prestigious languages of Latin or Greek. The poem will retell the foundation story of the Judeo-Christian religion: the loss of innocence of the human race through Adam and Eve in the Garden of Eden. For Europeans of Milton's time there could be no greater story, and since it is told in the sacred text of the Book of Genesis, Milton's attempt could well be seen as presumptuous in the extreme. Milton is aware of this, referring to his poem as

> ... my adventurous song,
> That with no middle flight intends to soar
> Above the Aonian mount, while it pursues
> Things unattempted yet in prose or rhyme.

> (*Paradise Lost* I, l. 13–16)

In these early lines Milton is doing two things. He is invoking the assistance of the Muses and of the Christian Holy Spirit as metaphysical aid. He is also girding himself with his palpable awareness and knowledge of the poetic and religious tradition – 'the Aonian mount' and other references. But it is also important to Milton as a Christian that he surpasses this classical and pagan literary tradition. The 'Aonian mount' is Mount Helicon, in Greek mythology the sacred home of the ***Muses***, and his own poetic flight is going to take him above that. By these devices he asserts his vision of the transcendence of his religion. He also makes it seem that it is not merely John Milton, born in Bread Street, Cheapside, who sings, but the 'heavenly muse', who is, by implication, no less

than God himself. Midway through the poem he calls for renewed
strength to continue:

> Descend from heaven Urania, by that name
> If rightly thou art called, whose voice divine
> Following, above the Olympian hill I soar,
> Above the flight of Pegasean wing.
> The meaning, not the name I call: for thou
> Nor of the Muses nine, nor on the top
> Of old Olympus dwell'st, but heavenly born,
> Before the hills appeared, or fountain flowed,
> Thou with eternal Wisdom didst converse,
> Wisdom thy sister, and with her didst play
> In presence of the almighty Father, pleased
> With thy celestial song. Up led by thee
> Into the heaven of heavens I have presumed
> An earthly guest, and drawn empyreal air,
> Thy tempering;

> (*Paradise Lost* VII, l.1–15)

These lines are dense with classical and Christian allusion. Once
more he claims to be flying above 'the Olympian hill', or the height
reached by Pegasus, the winged horse of legend. Urania is the Greek
Muse of Astronomy, thus the most heavenly. She was the Muse
Christian writers 'adopted' for inspiration and the one Milton
calls upon and associates with his own God. All of this is meant to
display his knowledge, his humility, and his determination to reach
and survive in the most rarefied altitudes of poetry and spirituality.
Milton's epic poetic voice is not a singular thing but a composite of
what he saw as proper influences. To adopt Coleridge's metaphor, he
has giants' shoulders to mount on and will thus see further. This is
how this author seeks to establish his authority.

For all the apparent command of its manner, *Paradise Lost* is a
poem of embattlement and struggle. It is after all a story of loss,
of how Adam and Eve's disobedience of God's ban on eating the
forbidden fruit 'Brought Death into the World, and all our woe'. The
theme of such momentous loss is common in the grand narratives of
the world. It figures for instance in a modern poem that can properly
be called epic, *The Arrivants* by **Edward Kamau Brathwaite**

(1930–). Subtitled *A New World Trilogy*, its matter is the history and the culture of the Caribbean, a subject which, from the self-styled metropolises of western culture might appear marginal, but embodies the massive and enduring themes of a spoiled 'new world': migration, transportation and the effort to find a homecoming.

But unlike Milton, who has those few verses of the book of Genesis to expand upon, Brathwaite has no set preceding narrative. Instead he makes his own creation myth for the islands of the Caribbean in the *image* of a stone thrown across water that 'skidded arc'd and bloomed into islands ... curved stone hissed into reef ... flashed into spray / Bathsheba Montego Bay'. The scattering implicit in this image can also describe his sources which are fragments of a lost history, indeed a lost language: the stories and words of the native American people and of the slaves brought there from Africa. Thus,

> Memories are smoke
> lips we can't kiss
> hands we can't hold
> will never be
> enough for us;

('Prelude', *The Arrivants* 1973: 28)

Brathwaite sees about him a shattered history, a contemporary culture split into folk fragments and marked by the experience of further emigration. Alongside highly formal western education for a few is mass illiteracy. All this means that a single voice is surpassingly difficult to establish. Within the different sections and sub-sections of his trilogy therefore, Brathwaite cuts between a great variety of voices, often, as in the lines above, employing a pared, staccato style of stops and starts, as far as possible from the grand progress of Milton's heroic style. Indeed the first lines of the whole sequence seem to invoke a source in unvoiced sound and image:

> Drum skin whip
> lash, master sun's
> cutting edge of
> heat,

and it is out of this that the poet says 'I sing / I shout / I groan / I dream'. To see how different the registers can be in sections barely a page apart, we can compare these passages from the third book of the trilogy, *Islands* in a section called 'Ancestors'. The first is a simple, apparently autobiographical, recollection:

> Every Friday morning my grandfather
> left his farm of canefields, chickens, cows,
> and rattled in his trap down to the harbour town
> to sell his meat. He was a butcher.

This matter-of-fact voice shifts into a dreamier remembrance of his grandmother 'telling us stories / round her fat white lamp …

> And in the night, I listened to her singing
> in a Vicks and Vapour Rub-like voice what you would call the blues

> 3
> Come-a look
> come-a look
> see wha' happen

> come-a look
> see wha' happen

> Sookey dead
> Sookey dead
> Sookey dead-o

(lines 239–40)

The subject of *The Arrivants* is too large and various to be covered in one register alone. Milton strove for an encompassing English voice believing that he could render the true interpretation of Scripture to his people. For Brathwaite there is no 'scripture' for his subject. Instead there are fragmentary histories, songs, murmurings, intuitions, memories like smoke. Thus the poem is comprised of many styles and tones, some jagged and furious, others ruminative, some descriptive, others in song. Often, as in passages quoted, the poem moves quite suddenly between the different kinds of English included in what Brathwaite himself has called the 'prism of languages'.

PUBLIC ANGER AND SATIRE

In view of its subject-matter it's not surprising that an angry note is often struck in *The Arrivants*. But this is no modern novelty: historically poetry has frequently been scorched by anger, and whilst we might readily assume that this might be an eruptive, unbridled phenomenon, it can be related once more to the association poetry has with those deliberate styles of public speaking known as *rhetoric*. In *classical* rhetoric there were *ways* of getting mad. In Latin, *vituperatio* – vituperation – was a special, calculated mode of speech to express fury. In this poem **D.H. Lawrence** (1885–1930) may simply seem to be stamping his foot, but in fact he does so in time. It takes its title from the first line:

> How beastly the bourgeois is
> especially the male of the species –
>
> Presentable, eminently presentable –
> shall I make you a present of him?
> ...
> Oh, but wait!
> Let him meet a new emotion, let him be faced with another man's need,
> Let him come home with a bit of moral difficulty, let life face him with a
>   new demand on his understanding
> then watch him go soggy, like a wet meringue.
> Watch him turn into a mess, either a fool or a bully.
> Just watch the display of him, confronted with a new demand on his
>   intelligence,
> a new life-demand.
>
> (Lawrence, 1957)

Lawrence is clearly angry but the rage is not inchoate. Structurally the poet marshals it into a series of *anaphoric* clauses, 'Let him ... Let him ... Watch him... Watch him' together with those *alliterated* 'b' sounds and the refrain 'How beastly the bourgeois is / especially the male of the species'. These are stock rhetorical devices often heard in speeches by which the orator seizes the ear. Of course the vituperative mode might often speak direct to the object of disgust rather than, as here, to a supposed third person. Perhaps however Lawrence is being disingenuous. Perhaps he suspects that a good part of his contemporary readers will start to wonder, 'Might he mean me?' Such wiliness is not the most full-on manner of vituperation, though it is outspoken, enraged, and brooks no qualification.

A subtler and more extensive version of the critical register is *satire*. The traditional targets of satire are pride and presumption, and the satirist's stance is that of the undeceived observer who relentlessly spies the gap between pretension and reality. The serious satirist has a philosophical view of the limitations of humankind and is enraged by the spectacle of fellow-creatures who persist in vanity and self-deception of every kind. In this poem the anonymous **Miss W–** is provoked by the calumny on women she has seen in **Jonathan Swift**'s (1667–1745) scatological poem 'The Lady's Dressing-Room'. Swift had chronicled, in stomach-churning detail, the realization of a particularly soppy lover that his lady, far from being an ethereal creature, has bodily functions. Miss W– retaliates with an equally scabrous denunciation of the habits of the male sex, 'The Gentleman's Study'. She concludes:

> Ladies, you'll think 'tis admirable
> That this to all men's applicable;
> And though they dress in silk and gold,
> Could you their insides but behold,
> There you fraud, lies deceit would see,
> And pride and base impiety.
> So let them dress the best they can,
> They still are fulsome, wretched Man.

Although here Miss W– means the male sex by 'Man', her insistence is upon the chasm between appearance and reality. Dress hides nothing from the satirist's X-ray eye.

It is because of this disparity that the ironic tone features so prominently in satire of all kinds. *Irony* is the mode in which what is said is the opposite of what is meant. For example, when the songwriter **Randy Newman** (1943–) croons 'Short people got no reason to live', we are taken aback until we recognize that he is making a proposition he knows to be ludicrous in order to mock prejudice. Ironic effect often involves such a time-lag between our first hearing the idea and realizing its true meaning – rather as in any 'wind-up' joke. In verse the *couplet* (see also Chapter 7 'Stanza') is a device particularly suited to such delayed revelation of the underlying truth. A couplet is a pair of successive rhyming lines, and our wait to see what the second rhyming word will be is an interval that can be exploited. **Mary Barber**'s (1690–1757) 'An Unanswerable Apology for the Rich' takes this ironic tone in sympathizing with the wealthy 'Castalio':

> No man alive would do more good,
> Or give more freely, if he could.
> He grieves, when'er the wretched sue,
> But what can poor Castalio *do*?
>
> Would Heaven but send ten thousand more,
> He'd give – just as he did before.

The 'apology' is of course a caustic condemnation of Castalio's lack of charity. We are led to wonder if he would be more generous if he had yet *more* money, but when told he would do as he did *before*, we realize that means he would do nothing. In these next lines, in which **Alexander Pope** (1688–1744) sardonically skewers the casual habits of judges and jurors, we see the couplet deployed to full effect:

> Meanwhile, declining from the noon of day,
> The sun obliquely shoots his burning ray;
> The hungry judges soon the sentence sign,
> And wretches hang that jurymen may dine.

Although the comfortable progress of the first two lines is becoming disrupted by the signing of the sentence and especially the image of hanging, it is not until the last syllable that the full import of his complaint is clear: the wretches are off to the scaffold because the court wants its lunch. The passage comes to a point, and what is distinctive about the satiric register is its acuteness. The wit to produce surprise in which things become instantly clear is the successful verse satirist's weapon. But the stance is not without its dangers, for seeming to be so perspicacious, so certain, and so ready to mock and correct, opens such writers to charges of presumption and simple peevishness. Deciding what in the poet's tone is properly critical, and what is merely spiteful, is one of the difficulties and fascinations of reading satire.

PASTORAL AND SIMPLE SPEAKING

Concerned as it is with foibles and manners, often as symptoms of a greater malaise, satire is the most social of poetic modes. *Pastoral* by contrast is a form which criticizes worldly sophistication not by pillorying it but by staying apart from it. The notion of pastoral goes back to classical Greece and the poet **Theocritus**, reckoned to have been at work around 270 BC. It claims its source and inspiration from the simple songs of shepherds which is why the reed pipe, Milton's 'oaten flute' in his 'pastoral elegy' 'Lycidas', is its familiar emblem. But this attribution should not be taken literally, for pastoral is largely a feigned form, a style employed by poets as a means to criticize their own sophisticated society by contrasting it with the unaffected virtues of the 'humble' shepherd's life.

It is also a mode through which poets can seek another kind of idealized return: to a simpler, less elaborate manner of writing. For Milton the pastoral was the style for the poetic beginner, but for **Wordsworth**, certainly at the outset of his career, it is an ideal in itself. For him it respects the unnoticed lives of the rural poor and provides a purified diction for poetry based in ordinary language. Here in 'We Are Seven' the voice can sound determinedly straightforward:

> I met a little cottage Girl:
> She was eight years old she said;
> Her hair was thick with many a curl
> That clustered round her head.

The short lines, alternating between four and three beats, the predominant use of *monosyllables*, of familiar words and the unremarkable nature of what is described, all go to comprise a register that is defiantly plain. It is indeed a kind of anti-poetry. Elsewhere, and increasingly as his career goes on, Wordsworth does develop a more elaborated style using the longer, unrhymed, *blank-verse* line of Milton whom he revered. But in his pastoral manner he had first worked to strip and simplify his style to create a voice that sounds closer to that of the subjects and characters in his poems. Thus he does not seem to be speaking from the mountain of poetic tradition, and his 'authority' might appear less forbidding. Indeed, in 'We Are Seven' we hear the encounter of two voices, the poet and the 'cottage girl'. As she insists, against adult rationality, that there are seven in her family, including the ones living away and the two who 'in the churchyard lie', her view of the world confounds her senior. It is a poem in which Wordsworth seeks to dismantle his own – and others' – educated authority.

A similar turn towards the simple voice can be seen in twentieth-century *modernist* poetry. **William Carlos Williams** (1883–1963) was an American poet writing in urban New Jersey, about as far from the life of humble shepherds as you can get. But he sought to write about the daily life in the streets about him in a deliberately simple way, and he titled several of his poems 'Pastoral'. This poem, 'An Early Martyr', published in 1935, is in this style:

> Rather than permit him
> to testify in court
> Giving reasons
> why he stole from
> Exclusive stores
> then sent post-cards
> To the police
> to come and arrest him
> – if they could –
> They railroaded him
> to an asylum for
> The criminally insane
> without trial

(Williams, 1988)

For Williams the development of this manner was involved with how he felt he related – or did not relate – to the accepted poetic tradition. 'From the beginning I felt I was *not* English', he wrote. 'If poetry had to be written I had to do it in my own way' (*I Wanted to Write a Poem*, 1958, p. 14). In 1913 he had begun a poem 'Homage' like this:

> Elvira, by love's grace
> There goeth before you
> A clear radiance
> Which maketh all vain souls
> Candles when noon is.

(Williams, 1988)

Here, clearly, he is using a voice that he thinks is the one appropriate to verse but one foreign to his sensibility. His shedding of that manner is a search for authenticity, a simple 'natural' style not governed by precedent. But, as with Wordsworth, the style serves immediate, unsung subjects. These lines are from one those he called 'Pastoral' in which he is walking through a poor district:

> the fences and outhouses
> built of barrel-staves
> and parts of boxes. All,
> if I am fortunate,
> smeared a bluish green
> that properly weathered
> pleases me best
> of all colors.

(Williams, 1988)

In *I Wanted to Write a Poem*, Williams later described what he was doing like this:

> The rhythmic unit was not measured by capitals at the beginning of a line or periods within the lines ... The rhythmic unit usually came to me in a lyrical outburst. I wanted it to look that way on the page. I didn't go in for long lines because of my nervous nature. I couldn't.

> The rhythmic pace was the pace of speech, an excited pace because I
> was excited when I wrote. I was discovering pressed by some violent
> mood. The lines were short, *not* studied.
>
> (*I Wanted to Write a Poem*, 1958, p. 15)

PERSONAL VOICES

It is clear in this discussion of the pastoral register how we have
come back to the notion of the distinctively individual voice and
Rexroth's ideal of writing in the way one speaks. Williams uses the
phrase 'lyrical outburst'. As we saw in Chapter 1, lyrical poetry
has its origins in song – an important sense which survives in the
term 'song lyrics'. But as this kind of poetry has evolved, it has also
come to refer to poems which carry an immediately felt emotion
compulsively expressed. The **lyric** has become predominantly the
medium for the personal voice.

This is an anonymous lyric known, with its music, from the
early sixteenth century, though it may be older:

> Westron wind, when wilt thou blow,   [western]
>   The small rain down can rain?
> Christ, if my love were in my arms
>   And I in my bed again!

We know nothing of the circumstances surrounding this poem but
the melancholy atmosphere created by the images of wind and rain
takes us into the author's sadness. Then the rhythmic surge of the
exclamation 'Christ', followed by the **stresses** on the two key words
'love' and 'arms', carries us into the sense of loss and longing. It
is an exact simple example of that 'immediately felt emotion
compulsively expressed' and to convey that immediacy is its whole
burden. If we as readers or listeners feel this, it comes entirely from
these particular words, not from anything we know outside of them.

But we could not claim that these lines are 'ordinary speech'.
There is obvious artifice in the use of the **image** of rain and wind, in
the **metrical beat** and in the use of **rhymes**. These are what comprises
the lyric's 'musical' qualities. The poem may be felt, and we may

feel its emotion, but it is *composed*. This, I believe, is the essential quality of the lyric of emotion: that it can convey its sincerity through artifice.

We might see this working in an idiom much closer to our own in this contemporary lyric by the songwriter **Nick Cave** (1957–). It is a love-song called 'Into My Arms', and the phrase, 'Into my arms, O Lord' is its refrain. It is hard to think of a few words that can more directly convey a lover's simple longing. But the song also has a more elaborate scheme. It begins:

> I don't believe in an interventionist God,
> But I know darlin' that you do.
> But if I did I would kneel down and ask Him,
> Not to intervene when it comes to you:
> Not to touch a hair of your head,
> To leave you as you are,
> If He felt He had to direct you
> Then direct you into my arms,
> Into my arms, O Lord,
> Into my arms, O Lord
> Into my arms, O Lord
> Into my arms, O Lord.

The lyrical longing is powerfully there, but built around it is this pondering about belief in a God who steps into our lives. It becomes a prayer, though one perhaps uttered with tongue-in-cheek since it is phrased conditionally: 'If I did [believe] … If He felt He had to direct you …' The song is intriguing because of its mixture of love-longing and a weighty religious idea, and the possibility that the singer is playing with both these elements ironically.

When we recognize this complexity two questions might occur. First, is he sincere? We might answer that by trying to research the song's background in Nick Cave's life or some other aspect of its sources. But if – as it is – the song is performed by someone else, how can we know if the singer is sincere? Of course we don't expect performers to have felt and experienced everything they sing, but to rely on tracking back from the singer to what we might discover about the composer's life or sources, is surely a convoluted approach to evaluating our response to hearing the lyric. First and foremost we must enter the little world the song creates for us and be convinced and entertained by that alone. If we are to connect it to a real life let it be our own.

Second, is its felt emotion undermined by the song's construction around the religious idea – is it too blatantly artificial? If we think 'sincerity' depends upon conveying a direct, unambiguous feeling as simply as possible, then perhaps so. If however, we think it might include shades of feeling, and its complication by ideas about that feeling, as I believe Cave's song does, then no. All verbal expression involves artifice. The 'personal voice' of Cave's lyric is the more interesting and enjoyable because of its complexity of structure and feeling.

But here is a spanner for these works. Long after I had formulated my own reading and ideas about Cave's song as set out here, I heard him tell an interviewer that the subject of the song was not in fact 'a lover' but his own father. How does that information affect your reading?

PERSON AND PERSONA

It was largely because of the too-ready association of the 'I' in the poem and the 'I' who is the author that some poets have cast their poems in the voice of distinct, named characters. This strategy of the *dramatic monologue* is used most notably by **Robert Browning** (1812–89) in such poems as 'My Last Duchess', 'Andrea del Sarto' and 'The Bishop Orders his Tomb'. All these have Italian Renaissance settings and so while the poems feature an 'I' speaking to us, the reader recognizes the distance from Browning when his Fra Lippo Lippi, painter and monk, says, 'You understand me: I'm a beast I know.'

Modernist poets of the early twentieth century, especially keen to break the identification of the individual poet with what is spoken in the poem, adapted Browning's example. **Ezra Pound** (1885–1972) used free translation, playing variations upon the literally translated meaning, as another way of achieving this in such poems as 'The River-Merchant's Wife: A Letter' which is taken from the Chinese, and 'Homage to Sextus Propertius' which adapts the Latin poet Propertius. The 'voice' becomes a *persona*, or mask which enables the poet to explore a personality which might include some indistinguishable part of him or herself but can range more freely, much as a dramatist can in creating a character. Such figures are **T.S. Eliot**'s (1888–1965) anxious, fastidious 'J. Alfred Prufrock', Pound's struggling poet 'Hugh Selwyn Mauberley' and **W.B. Yeats**' (1865–1939) 'Michael Robartes' and 'Crazy Jane'.

Later in the century some poets – or perhaps more accurately some critics – came to see the casting-off of any mask as a virtue in itself. For enthusiasts of what came to be called the 'confessional' school of poetry the manner of speaking should be open, easy, even slangy, and the openness should reveal personal intensity and pain. This is the ending of 'The Abortion' by the American poet **Anne Sexton** (1928–74):

> *Somebody who should have been born is gone.*
> Yes, woman, such logic will lead
> to loss without death. Or say what you meant,
> you coward ... this baby that I bleed.

(Sexton, 1964)

Major poems have been written by poets often lumped simplistically together as the 'confessional' school of the 1950s and 1960s, usually taken to include John Berryman, Robert Lowell and Sylvia Plath as well as Sexton. However the critical fashion has tended to insist that the success of the poetry depends upon the guarantee that the experiences in the poem are biographically true. The extremes of painful experience, abortion, madness, suicidal impulse become seen to be the stuff of poetry. This is a perilous model and, in view of the distorted prominence given to the suffering and the suicides of Plath and Sexton, perhaps an especially dangerous one for women poets. The distinction between the self who writes and the self who 'appears' in the poem is put well, I think, by **John Berryman** (1914–72):

> ... poetry is composed by actual human beings, and tracts of it are very closely about them. When Shakespeare wrote [in Sonnet 144] "Two

loves I have of comfort and despair", reader, he was *not kidding* ... but of course the speaker can never be the actual writer who is a person with an address, a Social Security number, debts, tastes, memories, expectations.

(*The Freedom of the Poet*, 1976, pp. 316 and 321)

'WHAT IS THE LANGUAGE USING US FOR?'

The broad assumption so far in this chapter has been that the poet chooses his or her 'tone of voice' for a poem just as, hopefully, we choose when we speak and write in everyday life. But is this simply true? We have all had the experience of letting our tongue run away with us so that once started on a way of speaking – sarcasm for example – we say more than we mean because the force of that tone becomes irresistible. Similarly we sometimes strike the wrong note, perhaps make a joke at the wrong time. In these instances the tone we begin with seems to have a power all its own.

This is surely part of the character of language. As we learn to speak and then to write, we learn language's component parts and how to put them together individually and creatively. But at the same time we are absorbing many ways in which it has already been put together in set phrases, sayings and associations. We also speak and write as others have done before us and around us. As we have seen above, *epic* poets turned this to their advantage, but for poets like Wordsworth in the '*romantic*' period and his successors, who set so much more store by originality, the idea that our 'expression' is not all ours has been more discomfiting.

The twentieth-century philosopher R.G. Collingwood in his *The Principles of Art* (1938) wrote this about emotion and expression:

> 'Expressing' emotions is certainly not the same thing as arousing them. There *is* emotion there before we express it. But as we express it, we confer upon it a different kind of emotional colouring; in one way, therefore, expression *creates* what it expresses, for exactly this emotion, colouring and all, only exists *so far as it is expressed*.

So, in a poem, the materials of language like vocabulary and syntax, the 'background noise' we hear of preceding and contemporary language-use, and especially how it has and is used in poetic convention, might drive the poem as much as the emotion or idea which is 'there before we express it'.

It is this sense that language speaks us rather than the other way round that provoked **W.S. Graham** (1918–86) to write

> What is the language using us for?
> Said Malcolm Mooney moving away
> Slowly over the white language.
> Where am I going said Malcolm Mooney.
>
> Certain experiences seem to not
> Want to go in to language maybe
> Because of shame or the reader's shame.
> Let us observe Malcolm Mooney.

(Graham, 1979)

Notice the little transgressions against the norms in these lines: the *image* of 'moving away' over language and its being called white; the absence of a question mark at the end of the first stanza; the awkwardness of the split infinitive over lines five and six 'seem to not / Want to go in to ...', and the splitting of 'in to' to mime the reluctance. These, following the slightly paranoid opening line, testify to Graham's sense of tussling with this force called language. Another of his poems, 'Language Ah Now You Have Me', suggests the same unease: 'Here I am hiding in / The jungle of mistakes of communication.'

This jungle is treacherous. Language, especially 'everyday language', is subject to the wear of custom, and words and phrases which once seemed pithy and exact lose their currency and become cliché. The attention to language that goes into the poetic space will always want to reject cliché in favour of new ways to speak. Moreover that attention will also be aware of the *echoing* of history, social usage, and **connotation** in language. All these things affect the '**tone**' we try to adopt. The poet both uses and is used by the conventions of the craft. The voice of the poem is both the poet's own and the voice of other poets. 'Beauty', writes Pound, 'is a brief gasp between one cliché and another.' It makes writing poetry difficult, but is not a reason to despair. The American poet **Susan Howe** (1937–), from 'Pythagorean Silence':

age of earth and us all chattering

a sentence or character
suddenly

steps out to seek for truth fails
falls

into a stream of ink Sequence
trails off

must go on

waving fables and faces

SUMMARY

In this chapter we have looked at:
- What is meant by 'tone of voice' in poetry and how different registers in speech can be said to correspond to different poetic styles.
- The relationship of speech to poetry and what we might mean by 'natural' and 'unnatural' style.
- The concept of the author's authority, and authenticity in the poem.
- Public styles for poetry: narrative poetry and characterization.
- The Epic and the idea of the Muses in composition.
- Poems of anger, and satire.
- The simple voice in poetry and the pastoral style.
- Poetry as personal expression and the idea of the persona.
- The pressures of language on 'free' expression.

FURTHER READING

Brathwaite, E.K. (1973) *The Arrivants: A New World Trilogy*, Oxford: Oxford University Press.

—— (1995) *History of the Voice: The Development of Nation Language in Anglophone Caribbean Literature*, New York: New Beacon Books.

Leech, G.N. (1969) *A Linguistic Guide to English Poetry*, Harlow: Longman, Introduction and Chapter 1.

Mayes, Frances (1987) *The Discovery of Poetry*, Orlando, FL: Harcourt, Brace, Jovanovich, see Chapter 4 'The Speaker: the Eye of the Poem'.

Preminger, A. and Brogan, T.V.F. (eds) (1993) *The New Princeton Encyclopedia of Poetry and Poetics*, Princeton, NJ: Princeton University Press, see entry on 'Tone'.

Tomlinson, C. (1972) *William Carlos Williams: Penguin Critical Anthology*, Harmondsworth: Penguin, see articles in Part One.

MEASURES

THE VERSE LINE

True ease in writing comes from art, not chance,
As those move easiest who have learned to dance.

(Alexander Pope)

Transcribing her husband's most famous poem, Mary Hutchinson Wordsworth picked up her pen one day and wrote *'I wandered like a lonely…'* At this point she stopped and realized her mistake. If we read aloud these two lines:

I wandered like a lonely cloud

and

I wandered lonely as a cloud

we will realize why she paused. Does not the first sound clumsy, awkward in the mouth and ear? In this small difference we hear the essential importance of ***rhythm*** to poetry. In these two versions the sentiment expressed is the same, the image used to convey it is the same, the number of ***syllables*** and even the placing of the ***beats*** is the same. Nonetheless, and not only because of familiarity, *'I wandered like a lonely …' sounds* wrong. Analytically, the reason must be that *like*, though a vital part of speech, is too weak a word to bear a stress at this point in the impetus of the line. Putting it there delays the important idea of loneliness, especially as associated with the *I*, whereas the stresses placed in *'I **wand**ered **lonely**…'* enables the line to gather its meaning into the long and important syllable ***lone-*** so that the line pivots upon it in both rhythm and meaning. But *'I wandered like a lonely cloud'* simply sags.

THE POETIC LINE

What is often called 'poetic' language is usually marked by a high incidence of *imagery*, *metaphor* and the 'rich' sounding of words. But these features might just as often be encountered in prose (which, for all its apparent spaciousness, would in itself have to be described as a 'form'). What most marks off poetry is the *line*. In Chapter 2 we saw how the claps in the schoolyard rhyme 'When Suzi was …' defined the verse. Each clap is a *beat*, and the beats are put together in lines. The *rhythm* created in the line is a sound in the head and the ear, and in written form becomes a defined space on a page. These lines of rhythm have been fundamental to the practice and concept of poetry, both as a *mnemonic* and a device working on the senses.

Once more we must recall poetry's *oral* roots. During its speaking, the way that the poem manipulates the time by deployment of pace, length of *syllable*, and emphasis, or *beat*, is decisive. These qualities comprise the *cadence* of the words (see Chapter 2 above). 'Cadence' comes from Latin and Italian words meaning to fall, and this description, as when the wistful Orsino in Shakespeare's *Twelfth Night* says of a song 'It had a dying fall' (Act I Sc i, 4), is as often used of verse as of music. Under 'cadence', the *Oxford English Dictionary* quotes George Puttenham writing in 1589 of

> the fal of a verse in euery last word with a certaine tunable sound which being matched with another like sound, do make a concord.

Poetry highlights the element of time, and timing in how the particular sounds of words fall against each other and so compose 'a concord', or pleasing harmony of sound. It is in this respect of course that poetry is closest to music and both share such terms as 'rhythm' and 'beat'. It is here too that the question of whether poetry is 'sound' or 'meaning' is most acute. **Ezra Pound** (1885–1972), a poet who was also a composer, saw the different roles of words as musical 'concord', and words as items which carry meaning in a poem like this: 'The perception of the intellect is given in the word, that of the emotions in the cadence.' This division may be simplistic, but it does address the experience of poetry in which we apprehend an idea and feel the same kind of sensuous surge that we derive from music at one and the same time.

The principal means that poetry employs to create its particular cadences is the *measure* of the poetic line. The line gains its effect by *recurrence*, the reappearance of notable features in the language time and again. It is the same principle that makes the chorus of a song its most important and memorable feature – the point where we can all join in.

One way of creating recurrence in early English verse was to use *alliteration*, that is to repeat the same consonant throughout a line and, as the line *recurs* to the left-hand side of the page, or announces itself in the voice, it repeats the trick with another consonant:

Swart swarthy smiths besmattered with smoke
Drive me to death with din of their dints.

The alliteration defines the line.

Until twentieth century explorations of '*free verse*', lines usually recurred in the sense that their lengths and patterns had the same *measure*, or that the same measures recurred within reach of one another. 'Free verse' will be considered in a later chapter (Chapter 5), but here I am concerned with the working of the poetic line as it uses set measures, or *metres* – what is often described as 'formal verse'.

RHYTHM AND METRE

At this point I should distinguish the terms *rhythm* and *metre* since they are often confused and used interchangeably. *Rhythm* refers to the way the sound of a poem moves in a general sense either in part or through its whole length. *Metre* is more specific and refers to a set pattern which recurs line by line:

Hickory dickory dock,
The mouse ran up the clock.

A 'free verse' poem will not have a fixed measure like this since measure is one of the things it seeks to be free of. But, unless it is to be quite inert, it *will* have rhythm as in these other varied lines from Lowell's 'Fishnet':

The line must terminate.
Yet my heart rises, I know I've gladdened a lifetime
knotting, undoing a fishnet of tarred rope;

If we read these two examples aloud one after the other we will hear the regularity in the first and the irregular flow of the second. But the difference is not between a fixed tick-tock and a more liberated 'flow'. A poem written in set measures will have a rhythmical movement of its own which includes the effects of the measure unless it is to sound tediously mechanical. The aim of this chapter is to describe the characteristics of set measures and then point to the ways in which their regularity varies to produces particular rhythmic effects.

DIFFERENT METRES

Traditionally these measures are made by one of four different systems depending on what they count. They might count:
  a *syllables*, that is the segments of sounds that make up individual words (*syllabics*),
  b *quantity*, that is the length of varying syllables (*quantitative*),
  c *beats*, that is where the *stress* or *accent* falls on different syllables in normal speaking patterns, (*accentual* or *strong stress*).
  d the number of *stressed and unstressed* syllables, often in an alternating pattern

When a poem measures its lines by one or other of these systems it is said to have *metre*, and the procedure for identifying and describing their working is *scansion*. In poetry in English by far the most used of these metres is (d) – *accentual* or *stress-syllabic*. However, because it is important to understand **syllables** and **stress** separately, I have placed **accentual-syllabic** last in this series so that we can work towards it. Here is a fuller description of each of the four systems.

SYLLABICS

The recognition of **syllables** is crucial to the composition and the study of formal measures. If we are to be absolutely precise the syllable is difficult to define and is in part a concept as well as a concrete item. That we speak of putting something 'in words of one syllable' suggests that that concept has to do with simplicity, of breaking things down to basics. But, in the sounds of a language, the **phoneme**, not the syllable is the most basic item. Phonemes are the sounds actually used by a particular language that will make a difference to the meaning of a word. Thus if the phoneme that is the **k** sound in *cat* is replaced by the **m** phoneme we have the entirely different meaning of *mat*. The number of different phonemes will vary according to the language, as will the permitted sounds. English has some forty-plus phonemes (there is a margin of variation in practice) some of which will not feature at all in other languages: for instance the *th* sound as in *thin* is not a French phoneme just as the Welsh *ll* as in *Llanelli* is not an English one. Our respective difficulties in pronouncing such sounds occur because they fall outside the phonological range we learn as children.

A **syllable** however might be made up of a number of phonemes: *k/a/t* go to make up the single expressed voicing of *cat*. We do not articulate all its component sounds separately (*'k/a/t* spells *cat'*) but when we say *catarrh* we must voice two separate sounds, *cat-arrh*, for *catapult* three: *cat-a-pult*, for *catamaran* four: *cat-a-mar-an*. The difficulty in precise definition comes from occasional doubt as to how many syllables a word has. For instance an especially resonant actor might declaim 'O for a muse of fire, that would ascend / The brightest heaven of invention' in such a way as to give *fire* the two syllables many speakers would recognize anyway even though Shakespeare only counts it as one. Similarly many English north-country speakers might shorten *poetry* in a way that makes it sound like *po'try*. Within **polysyllables** too we might not always be sure where the divisions fall: is it *pol-y* or *po-ly*? These are factors which make linguists pause before providing a suitably scientific definition of the syllable. What is especially important for poetry however is to recognize that different syllables have very different sounds and therefore contribute very different *rhythmic* qualities to speech. For instance the briefly voiced syllable *a* sounds very different from the long-vowelled *fire*; *tarred* is quite different from *rope*. We might go further than Kenneth Koch and say that not only does every word have 'a little music of its own', but that every syllable has too.

Nevertheless the sound feature we call the syllable with the different sounds it can contain is generally recognizable and the number and the disposition of them is essential to all kinds of verse line. Since this is so, it might seem that the most obvious measure of a line is to count syllables. In fact, however, this method, *syllabics*, has not been much attempted in English poetry because, as we shall see below, stress is so prominent a feature of spoken English that it is bound to become a dominant feature in any sequence.

Where *syllabics* have been attempted, notably in the twentieth century, they have often been employed specifically to disrupt the accentual expectations of the traditional line by letting the stresses fall where they may. But then how do we distinguish a syllable-counted line as poetry from say / the last ten syllables of this sentence? We have seen already (Chapter 1) that the *haiku*, adapted from the Japanese form, is constructed in lines counting syllables in the pattern of 5-7-5. This shaping is one way by which the distinction from consecutive prose is made.

But a prose-like manner is likely to be an aim of syllabic verse and may often emphasize this by eschewing the use of capital letters at the opening of new lines in the way that poems conceived of as verses normally do. This is the first stanza of 'Considering the Snail' by **Thom Gunn** (1929–2004):

The snail pushes through a green
night, for the grass is heavy
with water and meets over
the bright path he makes, where rain
has darkened the earth's dark. He
moves in a wood of desire,

(Gunn, 1961)

Careful counting will reveal that each of this poem's lines has seven syllables. It seems as though Gunn is simply being contrary in imposing his chosen count in ways that break up the syntax, for example separating 'green / night', and isolating the first word of a new sentence 'He / moves'. In some other poems he accompanies syllabics with **rhyme** – in 'Considering a Snail' there is the lightest of **half-rhymes**: green/rain, heavy/he, over/desire – which increases its difference from prose. But, as he has said in an interview subsequently, he was drawn to use syllabics as a way of changing the way he was writing:

> ... because after you've been writing metrically for some years, you have that tune going in your head and you can't get rid of it or when you try you write chopped up prose. My way of teaching myself to write free verse was to work with syllabics. They aren't very interesting in themselves. They're really there for the sake of the writer rather than the reader.
>
> (*Shelf Life*, 1993, p. 219)

Exactly what Gunn was trying to get rid of we shall look at when we study stress-syllable metres, and, in Chapter 7, examining stanza-form in a poem by Marianne Moore, we shall see just how much can be made of syllabics. Apparently the most crudely mechanistic of the ways to measure a line, it can be tooled to produce the most singular effects.

QUANTITATIVE – THE CLASSICAL TRADITION

Quantitative measures were the principal way of making verses in Greek and Latin poetry. The measure depends upon the sound lengths, or **quantity**, of different syllables, although the degree to which this followed in actual pronunciation is debated, and it may simply have become a convention. A line is defined by the number of syllables being divided into distinctive arrangements of long and short syllables: *heart* like *tarred* would be a long syllable and *hit*, like *rope*, a short one. Educated in Latin and Greek, many European **Renaissance** poets of the fifteenth, sixteenth and seventeenth centuries composed poems in those 'classical' languages and looked to those forms as ideal both for reasons of prestige and an aesthetic liking for their complexity. Some tried to reproduce the *quantitative* method in verses in their own native languages. However these have been only rarely successful, for certainly in English measuring quantities takes poets too far from the rhythms of the spoken language.

The main reason now for readers of poetry in English to know anything of quantitative metre is because this long-standing devotion to the *classical* tradition has influenced the vocabulary used to describe verse measures. As we shall see later, scansion of lines that are in no way quantitative employs technical terms drawn from this classical tradition. It is useful to know the fundamentals of that terminology so that we can describe metrical features when we encounter them.

There are five principal types of metrical *foot* and their names derive from Greek. Originally a foot is a distinctive arrangement of short and long syllables:

	Types of quantitative poetic feet	
i.	**iamb**: one short and one long syllable, notated	˘ ‒
ii.	**spondee**: two long syllables, notated	‒ ‒
iii.	**trochee**: one long and one short syllable, notated	‒ ˘
iv.	**dactyl**: one long and two short syllables, notated	‒ ˘ ˘
v.	**anapestic**: two short and one long syllable, notated	˘ ˘ ‒

A classical quantitative line is therefore made up of a set number of feet, the type depending upon the requirements of the poem. The conventional terms for these lengths of line are drawn from Latin:

These terms, both for groupings of syllables and lengths of line, have been taken over in order to describe lines based upon *stress* – the main metrical feature of verse in English that we shall approach later. Instead of long and short syllables English scansion has come to recognize *stressed* and *unstressed* syllables, with stress often marked and unstressed **v**. *In subsequent quotations here I have marked stressed syllables in* **bold type**.

Lengths of quantitative line
Dimeter: two feet
Trimeter: three feet
Tetrameter: four feet
Pentameter: five feet
Hexameter: six feet

STRESS OR ACCENT

Stress or ***accent*** refers simply to the prominence some syllables have over others in speech. In some languages, Italian for instance, where the stress falls is sometimes indicated by marked ***accents***: *possibilit*à, caff**é**. English rarely uses such marks except for words borrowed from other languages, but any English word of two or more syllables will be accented. Thus we say, **heav**-en it-**self**. Sometimes the same word in different forms will be stressed differently, for example the noun is **con**-flict but the verb con-**flict**. The modulations here are not always exact. For instance do we say 'syllable' by stressing only **syll** and leaving -ab and -le unstressed, or do we put a lesser accent on the last to give **syll**-ab-**le**? I think I would go for the former but there are variations. Do we say 'dis-**trib-**ute' or '**dis-**trib-ute', '**con-**trib-ute' or 'con-**trib-**ute'? Some of these are much more marked with different language groups providing quite different accents. English football fans will speak of United's de-**fence**, whereas American sports crowds chant '**de-**fense, **de-**fense'. In the English Midlands the city is **Birm-**ing-ham, but in Alabama it can be Birm-ing-**ham**.

Notwithstanding these differences ***accent*** or ***stress*** is a prominent feature of English speech and therefore of verse. In a sequence of ***monosyllabic*** words some will be stressed more prominently than others as in '*we* **will** be **glad** to **send** you **cash**'. Usually the stress will be on the items most important for carrying the meaning with the grammatical items such as a, the, from, at, some, and suffixes like -ed and -ing being unaccented. When listening for stress in verse lines it is helpful to think of that clapping song in Chapter 1: 'When **Su**zi **was** a **ba-by**, a **ba**by **Su**zi **was**'. We clap on the stressed syllable.

In some measured verse stress is the main recurring feature:

Why why why De-li-lah?

These are known as *pure stress* or **strong stress** metres. Besides their alliteration those blacksmiths lean heavily on stress to create their recurrent effect:

Swart swarthy smiths besmatt**ered** with **smoke**
Drive me to **death** with **din** of their **dints**.

Here we have a preponderance of stressed syllables, in this case clearly aiming to mime the blows on the anvil. In other instances the line will be defined by having a set number of stresses (two, making it a *dimeter*) but ones that are strong enough to vault across two unstressed syllables.

There **was** an old **wo**man
    And **what** do you **think?**
She **lived** upon **noth**ing
    But **vict**uals and **drink**
Victuals and **drink**.

In another set pattern these lines each have four stresses, making it a *tetrameter*, with a regular alternation of stressed and unstressed syllables.

Half a **pound** of **tupp**enny **rice**
    Half a **pound** of **trea-cle**
Mix it **up** and **make** it **nice**
    Pop goes the **wea-sel**

But in reciting the rhyming words 'treacle' and 'weasel' are stretched to give two stresses as against their conventional values of '**trea**cle' and '**weas**el' thus emphasizing both the beat and the rhyme.

Strong-stress elements can be used for urgent purposes as in **Percy Bysshe Shelley**'s (1792–1822) indignant sonnet 'England in 1819' which begins:

An **old**, **mad**, **blind**, des**pised**, and **dy**ing **king** –
Princes, the **dregs** of their **dull race**, who **flow**
Through **pub**lic **scorn** – **mud** from a **mud**dy **spring**;

These are ten syllable lines but what dominates them is the heavy hitting of certain clustered syllables as in 'An **old**, **mad**, **blind** ...' However, the most used formal line in English poetry is one that employs a set pattern of stressed *and* unstressed syllables.

PATTERNED STRESS

Patterned-stress, or, as they are sometimes known **accentual-syllabic**, or **stress-syllable** metres, may vary in the length of lines but have *a set number of syllables and a set number of stresses*. Most often they will alternate like this opening of Shakespeare's Sonnet 12:

When **I** do **count** the **clock** that **tells** the **time**

Or, from Sonnet 9:

Is **it** for **fear** to **wet** a **wid**ow's **eye**
That **thou** con**sum'st** thy**self** in **sing**le **life?**

Each of these lines has ten syllables, and each stresses them alternately in the pattern of

ti-**tum**, ti-**tum**, ti-**tum**, ti-**tum**, ti-**tum**.

If we devise a slightly different version of that first line, still using just ten syllables, '*When I count the clock's strokes to tell the time*' we don't have the same pattern. Scanned, it might sound like this,

When I **count** the **clock's strokes** to **tell** the **time**

which sounds simply clumsy and certainly has none of the regular measure of the clock's ticking with its implications of relentlessness.

This alternating, 'duple' pattern is predominant in verse in English. Why this might be so is a complex and fraught matter which has long divided scholars. In essence the argument is how far, if at all, the *artifice* of **patterned stress** metres is derived from the cadences of 'natural speech'. Certainly, as the *The New Encyclopedia of Poetry and Poetics* points out, it is easy to fall into this binary, on-off pattern in such sentences as 'I'll have a Whopper and a can of Coke'. In another example does the common expression *free and easy* rather than *easy and free* result from a deeply-imbued preference to keep stressed syllables close to each other (i.e. **free** and **eas**y not *eas*y and **free**; **bright** and **shin**ing / *shin*ing and **bright**)? This is a fascinating area for further study but requires too much complex linguistic discussion for our present purpose.

The *patterned-stress* lines given above are called *iambic pentameter*, a term composed from the classical vocabulary referred to earlier. This means that they consist of five *'feet'* (hence **pentameter**), each of which is a pairing of unstressed and stressed syllables (*ti*-**tum**) which are known as *iambs*. This line pattern is the fundamental basis for all of Shakespeare's sonnets, and the staple too of stage-speech in his and his contemporaries' plays in Elizabethan theatre. Indeed it is the most common formal measure in English verse. But as soon as I assert this I must qualify it by saying that iambic patterns are in practice subject to a lot of variation in practice and if we were to scan strictly to a *tee*-**tum** tee-**tum** pattern we should have to stress syllables in ways that deform natural speech as in this line from Shakespeare's Sonnet 18:

Thou **art** more **love**ly **and** more **tem**perate.

The pattern, strictly applied requires a stress on that last syllable, -**ate**, but few nowadays would articulate. I shall discuss the properties and history of the *iambic pentameter*, and by extension other metrical lines in ways that will emphasize the importance of variation in more detail later in this chapter (see below 'Variation in Practice'). What the basic pattern does is act as a real but often intuited structure which the practising poet may vary but never violate.

There are however a number of other measures. Iambic lines might be longer and stress *six* of their twelve syllables making a **hexameter**, or, to take the name from the most standard French verse line, an **alexandrine**, like these translated from Pierre Corneille's *Le Cid*:

> No **day** of **joy** or **triumph** **comes** un**touched** by **care**,
> No **pure** content with**out** some **sha**dow **in** the **soul**.

Occasionally it can be even longer as in **Robert Southwell**'s (*c*.1561–1595) 'The Burning Babe':

> As **I** in **hoar**y **win**ter's **night** stood **shiv**ering **in** the **snow**,
> Sur**prised** I **was** with **sud**den **heat** that **made** my **heart** to **glow**;

Such a long line, the number of syllables make it a '**fourteener**', has generally been found hard to handle. A verse line needs a tension much as a washing-line does, and longer stretches can sag into incoherence. But the 'fourteener' has another life in which it is split into two segments in the pattern of four stress/three stress. This is also known as **ballad metre** or **common metre** that we met in Chapter 2 and is strongly associated with the **oral tradition**:

> The **King** sits **in** Dun**fer**ling **toune**
>   **Drink**ing the **blude**-reid **wine**:
> O **whar** will I **get** a **guid** sail**or**
>   To **sail** this **schip** of **mine**.

Used independently, the four-stress line and the three-stress line are known as **tetrameters** and **trimeters** respectively. Staying with iambic versions of these lines here is **Jane Cave** (1754–1813) speaking in the voice of her ladyship to 'Good Mistress Dishclout', an understandably sulky kitchen-maid:

> And **learn** to **know** your **fit**test **place**
> Is **with** the **dish**es **and** the **grease**;

and **Thomas Campion** (1567–1620) in 'Now Winter Nights Enlarge':

> Much **speech** hath **some** de**fence**,
> Though **beauty no** re**morse**.

Yet shorter lines, such as the two-beat ***dimeter***, or even a line with but one stress are uncommon, but here is the seventeenth century poet **Robert Herrick** (1591–1674) showing off his versatility to the senior poet **Ben Jonson** (1572–1637) by devising a stanza that includes lines of one stress up to pentameter:

> Ah, **Ben!**
> Say **how** or **when**
> Shall **we**, thy **guests**,
> **Meet** at those **lyric feasts**
> **Made** at the **Sun**,
> The **Dog**, the **Triple Tun**,
> Where **we** such **clusters had**
> As **made** us **nobly wild**, not **mad**;
> And **yet** each **verse** of **thine**
> Out**did** the **meat**, out**did** the **frolic wine**.

We can see that not all of these lines are iambic. For example, '**Meet** at those **lyric feasts** / **Made** at the **Sun**' are lines that both begin with a stressed syllable. In this pub-crawling poem, these inject some cheerful impetus by striking into the line without delay.

The metrical foot composed of a *stressed syllable* followed by an *unstressed syllable* – **tum**-ti – is called a ***trochee***, and thus the measure made of these feet is trochaic. The tale of Simple Simon's encounter is mostly trochaic:

> **Simple Simon met** a **pie**man
> **Go**ing **to** the **fair**
> Said **Simple Simon to** the **pie**man
> **Let** me **taste** your **ware**.

Trochaic metres, because of their incipient stress, are often used for poems with an urgent tone, sometimes to exhort someone, especially at the beginning. This is often true of hymns such as '**Praise** we the **Lord**', '**Bright**ly **did** the **light** di**vine**',

> **Christ** will **gather in** His **own**
> **To** the **place** where **He** has **gone**
> **Where** our **heart** and **treasure lie**,
> **Where** our **life** is **hid** on **high**.

This is a four-beat measure, making the lines *trochaic tetrameters*, but, as Herrick's lines have shown, trochaic feet can be used in other lengths of line.

Trochaic measures tend to draw attention to the verse's metricality, marking it off very clearly from ordinary speech. **Edgar Allan Poe** (1809–49) wanted poetry to have a mesmeric quality which carries the reader in a nearly musical reverie, blurring the meaning of the words. Thus he makes bold use of alliteration, rhyme, repetition and emphatic metres. In 'The Raven' he employs an eight stress trochaic line,

> **While** I **nod**ded, **near**ly **napp**ing, **sudden**ly there **came** a **tapp**ing,
> **As** of **some** one **gent**ly **rapp**ing, **rapp**ing **at** my **chamb**er **door** –

However we can see that these very long lines actually have a decided break in the middle:

> As of some one gently rapping, / rapping at my chamber door.

Such a break is called a *caesura* (from the Latin meaning 'cut') and is a feature we shall meet elsewhere. We might think the lines are really combined tetrameters, but elsewhere in the poem we can see that Poe wants the full continuous effect of the longer line:

> Ah, distinctly I remember it was in the bleak December;
> And each separate dying ember wrought its ghost upon the floor.

Besides the iambic and the trochaic feet there are two other, less common metres that employ not two but three syllables. These are the *dactyl* which goes / – – , *tum* tee tee, and the *anapest* which goes – – /, *tee tee* **tum**. This American spiritual's refrain uses the dactyl:

> **Steal** away, / **steal** away, / **steal** away / to Jesus

as does **Alfred Lord Tennyson** (1809–92) in 'The Charge of the Light Brigade':

> **Flash'd** all their **sab**res bare,
> **Flash'd** as they **turn'd** in air.

The *anapest* by contrast delays the stress, as in this anonymous tale of an 'Australian Courtship':

> But I **got** into **troub**le that **very** same **night**!
> Being **drunk** in the **street** I got **into** a **fight**;
> A **cons**table **seized** me – I **gave** him a **box** –
> And was **put** in the **watch**-house and **then** in the **stocks**.

In lines like these the effect is to strengthen the stress and so give the line a bouncing effect suitable to its knockabout subject-matter. In longer lines the anapest can evoke languor as here in 'Hymn to Proserpine' by **Algernon Charles Swinburne** (1837–1909) where the delayed stress falls on a series of long vowels:

> Thou art **more** than the **day** or the **morr**ow, the **seas**ons that **laugh** or that **weep**[.]

The beat can also be delayed for stirring purposes as in **Julia Ward Howe's** (1819–1910) 'Battle Hymn of the Republic' which begins many of its lines with anapests: 'He is **tramp**ling …', 'He hath **loosed** …', 'I have **read** …', 'In the **beau**ty …'. The famous first line is however iambic,

> Mine **eyes** have **seen** the **glory of** the **com**ing **of** the **Lord**.

though it is possible that scanning it this way is influenced by the marching beat of the tune which is now inseparable from these lines. Might Howe have meant to record a visionary moment, to exclaim in her eagerness? 'Mine eyes **have** seen …' could give us a more nearly anapestic line where the stresses are all on the most semantically important syllables:

> Mine eyes **have** seen the **glor**y of the **com**ing of the **Lord**.

This would make the line closer in measure to those that follow which after their opening anapests mostly put three unstressed syllables between each decided beat:

> He is **trampl**ing out the **vint**age where the **grapes** of wrath are **stored**;
> He hath **loosed** the fateful **light**ning of his **terr**ible swift **sword**;
>   His **truth** is **march**ing **on**.

Alternatively some might read these lines as a type of iambic where the two unstressed syllables as in *He has* constitute one rhythmic beat.

These possible variations take us back to a previous point and underscore that it is an unavoidable experience when we seek to scan lines: *regular measure is not absolute and fixed, and indeed is not wholly regular even in ostensibly regular poems.* Crucially, for instance, whilst we distinguish between stressed and unstressed syllables, that simple divide does not take account of the *different weights* of stress that we might hear. Returning to Howe's opening line we might easily hear a stronger beat on some of the stressed syllables:

> Mine **EYES** have **seen** the **GLOR**y of the **COM**ing **of** the **LORD**.

If this is how we hear the line, instead of the regular alternation of the first way that we scanned it, we could say we are giving greater stress to the beats in capitals than to those in bold. Alternatively, we might say that the line really only has those *four* beats, and that it bounds from one stress to the next across *three* unstressed syllables. This would mean that the line is less like the regular alternation of iambics and more similar to the strong stress line we looked at earlier.

All of this points to the obvious fact that the possible variation within a metrical scheme shows us how crude the simple *stress/*unstressed analysis of a line is. There are arguably many gradations of possible stress, several in even a single line. Some readers have tried to introduce a calibrated system which would give a value to each syllable ranging, say from 1 to 4 according to the strength of the beat. This might give us:

<pre>
2   3 1 3 1 4 2 1 3 1 2 1 4
Mine **eyes** have **seen** the **glo**ry **of** the **com**ing **of** the **Lord**.
</pre>

But *scansion* does not approach an exact science and very few of us I think would want to read poetry in this way. Even a regular line such as 'When I do count the clock that tells the time' whose metronomic alternation mimes the movement of a clock, is not in practice read so robotically. It does however draw attention to the *degrees* of stress that any reading aloud is going to make, and to the amount of variation in formal measures.

VARIATION IN PRACTICE

This brings us to a vital insight. I have referred above to variation of the underlying structure of the metrical line, including the *iambic pentameter*. The purpose of acquiring the technical expertise to scan metrical lines is *not* so that we dutifully anatomize every line we read, but to have the means to describe the general rhythmic pattern of a poem and – most importantly – the significant moments where that pattern *varies*. Almost always such shifts in the pattern are the most important moments. Even in metrical verse *rhythm* is always a more important concept than *metre*.

Shakespeare's Sonnet 94 is about nice, controlled people, but nonetheless is pregnant throughout with indignation. It begins with praise but praise that is guarded, and the guardedness is implied in the opening line's irregularity:

They that have **power** to **hurt** and **will** do **none**.

The stress on the first syllable, **They** – an inversion from the normal **v** \ of the iamb to the trochee, \ **v**, suggests a finger being pointed, and the further effect of this is to leave *that have* unstressed and so give the pivotal word **power** a very strong beat, one that is equalled by the next stress, **hurt**. *Power to hurt* is the poem's subject and the two words are the fulcrum on which the first line is balanced.

However, if we were to hear a beat on *do* at the end of the line, thus giving us three consecutive stresses, then the line does come weighted at that end. So far such an emphasis might be thought of either as a confirmation of the virtue of *they*, or as a gathering irony, that *they* might not be all they seem. This impression is strengthened at line 5 with another opening stress on *They* doubled by the immediate stress on the second syllable:

> **They right**ly are the **lords** and **own**ers of their **faces**.

The line has the regulation five stresses of the iambic pentameter, but is irregular in having thirteen syllables. This matters not at all since the important effect is to enlarge a sense of possible disgust should these **lords** *and* **own**ers turn out less virtuous than their **faces** show. The disgust ignites finally as the last line flares with sudden rage:

> For **sweet**est **things** turn **sour**est **by** their **deeds**;
> **Lil**ies that **fes**ter **smell** far **worse** than **weeds**.

The even tone of the regular 'For sweetest…' is transformed by the force of the **trochaic** inversion which makes the beat on the first syllable of *Lilies* so emphatic. Of course the **image** of rotting lilies is immensely powerful, but it is the variation of the measure which embodies the emotion in the poem.

Most often rhythmic effects work across several lines. Here is **Christopher Marlowe's** (1564–93) Doctor Faustus lamenting that he has the individual immortal soul that is about to be claimed by hellfire.

> Or **why** is **this** im**mor**tal **that** thou **hast**?
> **Ah**, Pythagoras' **met**empsy**cho**sis, were **that** true
> This **soul** should **fly** from **me** and be **changed**
> Un**to** some **brut**ish **beast**: all **beasts** are **hap**py
> For when **they** die
> Their **souls** are **soon** dis**solved** in **el**ements;

Now the basic measure of *Doctor Faustus* is **iambic pentameter**, but looking for regularity in these lines I am soon at sea. Line 1 is regular though **that** cannot carry the same pronounced weight as *im***mort**al; line 5 is nearly so but for the 'weak' ending on an unstressed syllable, **happ**y. The real interest lies elsewhere, in the effects created by the long second line, which seems to me impossible to scan conventionally but is a gift to an actor in its rolling out the syllables of that impressive-sounding phrase, *Py-thag-or-as' met-em-psy-cho-sis*. From there the lines run on in a sequence that, allowing for the mid-line pause at *brutish beast*, joins together (**enjambment**) five lines, including the simple change of key enabled by the very short *For when they die*. In the final line the drawn out sound of *dis***solved** means that the line does not need the normal fifth stress as it mimes Faustus' longing. Marlowe, like very many poets, is using a measure and playing changes upon it to create the particular rhythms he needs for his meaning.

Sometimes such variations will be yet more obvious as in the remarkable inventiveness of **John Donne's** *Songs and Sonets*. There he devises stanza forms which combine pentameter, tetrameter, trimeter and complete irregularity. Consider his love poem 'The Sun Rising':

> She's all states, and all princes, I,
> Nothing else is.
> Princes do but play us; compared to this,
> All honour's mimic; all wealth alchemy.

Any attempt to scan this metrically will very likely confuse us, but the lover's defiant exultation is marvellously carried in the rhythmic boldness of the staccato and surging effects. Later, eighteenth-century critics could not stomach Donne's free-handed way with formal metres, and it is significant that the revival of interest in his work and that of his Jacobean contemporaries, including the dramatists, did not take place until the early twentieth century and the beginnings of the *'free verse'* movement (see Chapter 5).

T.S. Eliot (1888–1965) was central to that movement, though he claimed emphatically that it did not exist. But what Eliot did insist is that 'the very life of verse' is the 'contrast between fixity and flux'. By this he meant that successful verse-lines do not continue to repeat an established pattern as exactly as possible, but operate in relation to it. In his essay 'Reflections on "Vers Libre"' (1917) he wrote:

> ... the most interesting verse that has yet been written in our language has been done either by taking a very simple form, like the iambic pentameter, and constantly withdrawing from it, or taking no form at all, and constantly approximating to a very simple one.
>
> (Eliot (1965) *To Criticise the Critic: And Other Writings.*
> London: Faber)

It is as though the 'simple form' radiates a force-field within which the poet works, sometimes closer to the exact pattern, sometimes further away. Attending to set measures therefore, for the reader as for the poet, is not a matter of slavish notation but of sensing variation, the tension between 'fixity and flux'. It was Eliot too who coined the phrase 'the auditory imagination' by which he meant 'the feeling for syllable and rhythm, penetrating far below conscious levels of thought and feeling, invigorating every word'. It is this 'auditory imagination' that we exercise and develop as we read poetry. Knowledge of the technicalities of **scansion** should increase our awareness as we read and give us the means to understand quite how a rhythmic effect is being produced. But if such knowledge is elevated into an exclusive mystery tasselled with Greek terminology it is serving neither the reader nor poetry. The knowledge should enrich, not replace reading, that is to say *hearing*. In the noises of words and the rhythms of their combinations we hear all the complex accumulations of meaning with which in all areas we try to make ourselves understood.

MEASURE: A HISTORICAL OVERVIEW

The history of measure in poetry in English is not only a matter of technical description. The changes in the style of the line are also a matter of culture and relate first to the history of the British Isles and later to the English-speaking world at large. In this part of the chapter I want to re-visit the measures outlined above but in a chronological way that connects them to linguistic and cultural change.

English mediaeval poetry moved through a varied series of metrical forms, especially in the latter part of the period. In Old English, the Anglo-Saxon verse line was heavily accented, usually, as in the eighth-century epic *Beowulf*, a pure stress line of four accents, but also alliterated and with a mid-line **caesura**. This pattern helped both reciter and audience as the poem was performed aloud (see Chapter 1). The lines tended also to be self-contained and sequential rather than carrying the sense fluidly through a long run of lines.

In the Middle English period, roughly the time between the Norman Conquest in 1066 and the rise of printing at the end of the fifteenth century, the language underwent considerable change: to look at a page of Old English is to see in effect a foreign language, whereas Chaucer, though unfamiliar, is at the least recognizable to the modern reader.

One important change was in syntax. Old English, like Latin and like German, is an *inflected* language, that is the forms of certain words change according to their exact role in the meaning of a sentence. Because a verb-ending for instance, includes the information of what its subject and tense are, the verb can be variously placed within a sentence and still make the necessary connections. In Old English verbs commonly come at the end of a clause or sentence, as in this line from the poem 'The Seafarer':

bitre breostceare ... gebiden hæbbe

The most literal translation of this might be:

bitter the cares in my breast [I] have abided

with the 'I' inserted because it had occurred in the original several lines earlier. Using modern English syntax we might have:

I have endured the most bitter anxiety.

Such a change in syntax clearly altered how a poet will order the space of the line. But the change has another significance for poetry. When a poet reverts to the *inversion* of subject and verb in the manner of Old English, this is especially noticeable and becomes foregrounded as a *gestural* feature in itself: *'When Suzi was a baby / A baby Suzi was'*. When **Ezra Pound** wrote his twentieth-century version of 'The Seafarer' he wanted to keep a sense of the original, and give a shock to what he felt had become stale modern usage. Therefore, using a version of Anglo-Saxon strong-stress metre, he compresses it and inverts:

Bitter breast-cares have I abided.

Both in this chapter and Chapter 5 on 'Free' Verse, we shall explore further this tendency to make something new through going back to the old.

A second new influence, felt particularly in vocabulary, was the absorption of the Romance languages, Latin, Italian and especially French following the Norman Conquest of 1066. Metrics in the later Middle Ages, roughly 1300–1500, became more various. The four-stressed Old English line continues in works like *Sir Gawayne and the Grene Knight* and, as we see here, in **William Langland**'s (?1331–?1400) *Piers Plowman*, although the caesura becomes less evident:

In a **som**er **seas**on whan **soft** was the **sonne**
I **shope** me in **shrouds** as I a **shepe** were.

But in the same period the ballad, or common metre, described above, flourished with its 4/3 stress pattern, a measure also employed in the *carol*, originally a dance song with a refrain:

As I **lay** upon a **night**
Alone in **my long**ing,
Me **thought** I **saw** a **wonder sight**,
A **maiden child rock**ing.

This example, from the fourteenth century, is also counting syllables to form an alternating pattern, as does this other verse from the same period where we can hear a virtually regular stress-syllable tetrameter:

Jesus **Christt** my **lem**mon **swete,**   beloved]
That **diyedst on** the **Rode Tree,**   [rood/cross]
With **all** my **might** I **thee** beseche,
For thy **woundes two** and **three.**

Chaucer was certainly writing ***patterned-stress tetrameter*** in his early 'Romance of the Rose':

Ful **gay** was **al** the **ground,** and **quaint,**
And **powdred, as** men **had** it **peint,**
With **many** a **fresh** and **sund**ry **flowr,**
That **casten up** ful **good** sa**vour.**

Savour, one of the many many French words that came into English at this time, will have been stressed as *sa***vour**. Chaucer was well acquainted with French poetry and introduced new forms like the ***rondeau*** into English (see Chapter 7), and it was probably with influence from this source that he came to lengthen his line to ten syllables (***decasyllabic***) and to stress five of them thus working it into ***iambic pentameter*** as in these lines from 'The Pardoner's Prologue' in his *The Canterbury Tales*:

For **I** wol **preche** and **begge** in **sond**ry **landes,**
I **wol** not **do** no **labour with** myne **handes.**

Chaucer's iambic pentameter did not however immediately dominate English metres. Between 1400 and the mid-sixteenth century poets were if anything yet more eclectic in their choice of line forms. But there were several influences at work that eventually consolidated English measures, and other aspects of poetic form, in the sixteenth century.

The first of these had to do with the development of the language and the attitude towards it among the literate classes. The fourteenth and fifteenth centuries saw an accelerated standardization of the language around the version of English that included the dominant city of London. Vocabulary, usage and spelling became much closer to what we can recognize as modern English, and the development of printing in the fifteenth and early sixteenth centuries carried this standardization more and more widely. At the same time, the official dominance and prestige of Latin and French, dating back to the Roman Empire and the Norman Conquest, began to decline among the English educated classes. Increasingly they became interested and committed to their own language as a valued medium of literate as opposed to 'common', or vernacular, communication. Yet, like Chaucer, this elite was multi-lingual and open to continental influence to a greater degree than at any time since. So, for instance, **Sir Thomas Wyatt** (1503–42) and **Henry Howard, Earl of Surrey** (1517–47) in the early and mid-sixteenth century imitated the forms, including the sonnet, they came to know mainly from the Italian poet **Petrarch** (1304–74), and fashioned the long Italian line into English decasyllables. They were educated in the Greek and Latin classics as they had been recovered during the *Renaissance*, and this classicism provided them with a self-conscious interest in *prosody* and metrics which could act as a theoretical framework for their experiments in poetry. One result of this was the development of scansion using the classical terminology I described earlier.

In some ways what was happening was that English poetry was being 'civilized' out of its earlier rough and rude habits by the exercise of sophisticated continental models that appealed to the courtier poets. **Thomas Campion** (1567–1620) for instance urged *quantitative* metrics on English poetry so that it might have the honour 'to be the first that after so many years of barbarism could second the perfection of the industrious Greekes and Romaines'. Practice, including Campion's own, was happily different, and despite the self-consciousness of poetic theory English verse in the Tudor 1500s continued to be pragmatically irregular, indeed all but 'barbarous', as the later, more determinedly classical, imitators and critics of the eighteenth century found it to be.

THE SPECIAL CASE: IAMBIC PENTAMETER

But we should pause at the *iambic pentameter* because it did become the single most salient and influential of English measures. It is the line of the Tudor sonnet tradition and, most significantly, of the Elizabethan and Jacobean verse drama of the late sixteenth and early seventeenth centuries. Later **Milton** employs it in *Paradise*

Lost, and, returning to a rhyming form, it is the basis of the heroic couplet of the eighteenth century. **Wordsworth** and other *romantic* poets used it extensively, and it has continued to figure in verse in English up to our own day.

The reasons why the iambic pentameter became and remained so dominant are far from simple to determine. For a long time it was claimed that it is the metre most 'natural' to English speech rhythms, and the instances of *iambs* in speech alluded to above give some credence to this. We might occasionally catch someone saying, 'he works at Mister Minit down the street', or 'you'll never see a team as good as Stoke', or even 'another losing season for the Jets', but this argument must be difficult to prove linguistically. It also begs the question of what was 'natural' to English speech rhythms when strong stress patterns were dominant in English verse. The argument would have to depend on establishing a distinct change in English speech patterns in the later Middle Ages as the Old English inheritance shifted into early modern English.

Alternative theories emphasize the artifice, rather than the naturalness of the verse line and relate the development of the iambic pentameter to social and cultural change. Thus its channelling through the work of a cosmopolitan, courtly elite might be seen as the process of 'smoothing' the crude stresses of the traditional English verse line into an equable alternation of tone more acceptable to an urbane ruling-class seeking to ease itself away culturally from the populace and their 'vulgar' *verses*. The role of poetry in the sophisticated play of the 'courtly love' tradition of *Renaissance* courts, and the emphasis given to this in literary history, certainly aids this impression. An instance of such socio-cultural division might be the scene at the end of Shakespeare's *A Midsummer Night's Dream* where the thumping versifying of the 'rude mechanicals" play (though most of it is in iambic pentameter) is mocked by the aristocratic audience.

But such a theory also needs to consider the Renaissance enthusiasm for the vernacular among a ruling group who, by their privileged access to Latin and French, had been able to set themselves culturally apart from the people for centuries. Moreover, if the literate elites were so keen to maintain their cultural superiority, they might have been expected to foster a more regular and classically-inspired metric than the iambic pentameter proved to be. In practice the iambic pentameter became an extremely flexible instrument, especially in the dramatic speech of the growingly popular Elizabethan stage. It could meet the demands of sounding plausibly like real people speaking – a demand that led to the abandonment of rhyme in favour of **blank verse** and of endless alliteration – whilst retaining the capacity for high-flown rhetoric. It can be fluent and continuous or set and reiterative as required. It possesses the capacity to move between 'fixity and flux' that Eliot noted. So, to better understand its success we need to look further into its technicalities. We might ask two questions: why is it *iambic* and why is it a *pentameter*?

In musical terms the sequence of unstressed syllable followed by stressed syllable, **v **, can be described as a rising rhythm. What are the implications of basing a measure on this impetus? The linguist Otto Jespersen in his 1933 essay 'Notes on Metre' made this suggestion:

> As a stressed syllable tends, other things being equal, to be pronounced with higher pitch than weak syllables, a purely 'iambic' line will tend towards a higher tone at the end, but according to general phonetic laws this is a sign that something more is to be expected. Consequently it is in iambic verses easy to knit line to line in natural continuation.
>
> (*Encyclopedia Britannica*, 'Prosody, Twentieth Century')

Following Jespersen's proposal, iambic metre aids verse which seeks to emphasize continuity. The argument of a **sonnet** with its frequently elaborate syntax, or the 'real speech' of characters in a drama, both need this kind of continuity. (A sense of closure, as Jespersen remarks, can be brought about by consecutive rhyming, as in the **couplet** that closes the sonnet or scenes in Elizabethan drama.) This kind of continuity where the reader's expectancy is carried along by a developing syntax that crosses the verse line is well exemplified in **Shakespeare**'s Sonnet 140:

> Be wise as thou art cruel; do not press
> My tongue-tied patience with too much disdain,
> Lest sorrow lend me words, and words express
> The manner of my pity-wanting pain.

The lines where the sense runs on without pause across the line-break (*enjambment*) –'do not press / My tongue-tied patience' – show in particular how the stress on the last syllable of each line, carries us forward to the next stage of the statement. We can also see, that while the first two lines can be readily measured out as conventional iambics, it is more likely that we will read them aloud – for the sense – with a very different sequence of stresses:

> Be **wise** as thou art **crue**l; do not **press**
> My **tongue-tied pati**ence with too **much** dis**dain**,

Again we see the basis of the regular measure acting as underlying pattern to enable particular variation.

The opening of Sonnet 91 presents a quite different effect:

> Some glory in their birth, some in their skill,
> Some in their wealth, some in their body's force,
> Some in their garments, though new-fangled ill,
> Some in their hawks and hounds, some in their horse;

The first words might be read conventionally, 'Some **glor**y ...', or, for greater attack, by stressing both opening syllables, '**Some glor**y ...' The following three certainly demand a stress on the opening syllable, '**Some** in their **wealth** ...' The movement here is not based on *syntactical* continuity in the manner of Sonnet 140, but on parallel repetitions. For the required emphasis the stress pattern is reversed from the iambic **v** \ to give a *trochaic foot* \ **v**. As we have seen with 'Simple Simon' above, a strong trochaic presence seems to fit the manner of emphatic repetition. An entirely trochaic metre tends towards the closure of every line and to require constant repetition to move the poem along. Longfellow's 'Hiawatha', written in trochaic tetrameter, is a famous example:

> **By** the **shores** of **Gitch**ee **Gum**ee,
> **By** the **shin**ing **Big-Sea-Wa**ter
> **Stood** the **wig**wam **of** No**kom**is,
> **Daugh**ter **of** the **Moon**, No**kom**is ...

The trochaic metre lays each line down in a fixed fashion, often inverting subject and verb – 'Stood the wigwam … Rose the firs …' – drawing attention to the verse's artifice. There is though a limited call for the manner and so a technical answer as to why verse since the sixteenth century has been mainly iambic may be because the rising rhythm assists the continuity of speech in dramatic poetry, and the fluency of thought and argument in much lyric poetry.

Now what of the ***pentameter*** half of the term, the line's length – why are *ten* syllables divided iambically? We have looked above at different lengths of line and of the difficulty of sustaining long lines without the tendency to fall into two. We can hear this happening in these 'fourteeners' from **Arthur Golding**'s sixteenth-century translation of the Roman poet Ovid:

> Then sprang up first the golden age, which of itself maintained
> The truth and right of everything, unforced and unconstrained

But a longish line does clearly assist fluency and continuity so how did the ten-syllable line achieve such popularity?

One theory points not to a decisive break between the longer line of medieval verse and the succeeding pentameter, but to the things they have in common. The older line tended to spring its stresses across ten and frequently more syllables. But as Middle English modulated into Early Modern English there was a great reduction of inflections and consequently many syllables ceased to be sounded, for example that terminal *e* as in the legendary '*ye olde Englishe tea shoppe*' now resurrected for tourists. Basil Cottle in his book *The Triumph of English 1350–1400* compares the sentence '*The goode laddes wenten faste to the blake hill*' which in Chaucer's day would have sounded each *e* and amounted to fifteen syllables, with its modern equivalent: '*The good lads went fast to the black hill*', a total of only nine syllables. Following this suggestion we might recognize a tendency for the medieval line of twelve or fourteen syllables to become a line nearer to ten as the spoken language changed.

Nonetheless there is a decisive difference between four and five-beat lines. As an even number four can readily be split

into two even parts. When allied with **rhyme** there is another
binary and overall we have a highly structured verse-form most
evident in the **quatrain**, as in the ballad 'The King sits in Dunferling
toune' we looked at earlier in this chapter. Even when the
syntax does not require even a slight mid-line pause (*caesura*)
we can perceive the see-saw rhythm. This is Puck, a figure from
the folk-world, speaking at the end of *A Midsummer Night's
Dream*:

> **If** we **shad**ows | **have** of**fend**ed
> **Think** but **this,** | and **all** is **mend**ed:
> **That** you **have** | but **slumb**ered **here**
> **While** these **vis**ions | **did** ap**pear.**
> **And** this **weak** | and **id**le **theme**
> **No** more **yield**ing | **but** a **dream,**
> **Gent**les **do** not | **rep**re**hend**
> **If** you **pard**on | **we** will **mend.**

Now for many purposes this degree of ostensible, nearly
symmetrical balance has attraction and virtue. But the five beat
line, which cannot be divided into rhythmically even portions,
offers the possibility of escaping the firmness of this structure
towards a greater fluency. It is not so long as to become unwieldy
in the mouth, but long enough to enable greater discursiveness.
Culturally, for the learned poets of the English sixteenth century,
it had the advantage of approximating the classical metres
of Greece and Rome and the model of Italian verse, as well as
sounding quite unlike the 'rude' popular tradition. (Especially
in his early comedies, the *Dream* and *Love's Labour's Lost*,
Shakespeare employs and parodies both these registers.) Thus did
poetry in Early Modern English shed the four-beat line along with
older devices such as alliteration and the regular caesura so as to
achieve a verse that could mime actual speech whilst still keeping
a measure elevated enough for rhetorical power. In evolving the
decasyllabic line it also extended the range of its stress base and
thus its flexibility.

Here is one final idea about the character of the ***iambic pentameter.***
In an intriguing essay called 'The Dimension of the Present

Moment' the Czech poet and scientist **Miroslav Holub** (1923–98) writes that while he can imagine eternity he finds great difficulty in figuring the present moment. In a series of swift, light-footed speculations he draws upon experimental psychology and musical data to propose that 'In our consciousness, the present moment lasts about three seconds, with small individual differences' (*The Dimension of the Present Moment*, 1990, p.1). This disarmingly simple notion he then allies with studies of the poetic line in a number of different languages with the broad conclusion that the outer edge of momentary attention at three to four seconds corresponds to the normal limit of a ten-syllable poetic line. We do not have to attach ourselves strongly to the science of these ideas to feel their possibilities. The neural effects of how we hear the rhythm and length of a line seems close to how we apprehend.

As we have seen, the analysis of measured verse can be quite complex. Much more difficult would be understanding how, within the processes of evolution, the first human speech for record and reiteration depended upon the recurrences of what we now call the poetic line. Nonetheless it is in the simple clap of the hand, the tap of the foot, that these metrical patterns have their foundation.

SUMMARY

In this chapter on formal verse we have examined:

- The poetic line and the importance of rhythm, beat and cadence.
- The distinction between rhythm and metre.
- The four main classifications of formal metres: syllabics, quantitative, accentual and patterned-stress.
- The terminology and method of scansion.
- The importance of variation, 'breaking the rules' of metre.
- The historical development of metre in English poetry with special reference to the iambic pentameter.

FURTHER READING

Attridge, Derek (1982) *The Rhythms of English Poetry*, Harlow: Longman.

—— (1995) *Poetic Rhythm: An Introduction*, Cambridge: Cambridge University Press.

Fussell, Paul (1979) *Poetic Metre and Poetic Form*, New York: Random House.

Holub, M. (1990) *The Dimension of the Present Moment*, Young, D., trans, London: Faber.

Leech, Geoffrey N. (1969) *A Linguistic Guide to English Poetry*, London: Longman, see Chapter 7.

Stallworthy, Jon (1996) 'Versification' in Ferguson, M., Salter, M.J. and Stallworthy, J. (eds) *The Norton Anthology of Poetry*, fourth edn, New York: Norton.

5

'FREE VERSE'

> When this Verse was first dictated to me, I consider'd a Monotonous
> Cadence, like that used by Milton & Shakespeare & all writers
> of English Blank Verse, derived from the modern bondage of
> Rhyming, to be a necessary and indispensable part of Verse. But
> I soon found that in the mouth of a true Orator such monotony
> was not only awkward, but as much a bondage as rhyme itself. I
> therefore have produced a variety in every line, both of cadences &
> number of syllables. Every word and every letter is studied and put
> into its fit place; the terrific numbers are reserved for the terrific
> parts, the mild & gentle for the mild & gentle parts, and the prosaic
> for inferior parts; all are necessary to each other. Poetry Fetter'd
> Fetters the Human Race.
>
> (William Blake, 'To the Public', Jerusalem)

So much of the theory, and the spirit, that gave rise to the notion
of *'free verse'* in the twentieth century can be seen in this address
by **William Blake** (1757–1827) writing at the outset of the
nineteenth. This chapter will explore the origins of what came to
be known in the twentieth century as 'free verse', and look at the
many directions this approach to the *poetic line* have taken.

As Blake acknowledges, poets have frequently chafed at the
formal demands they inherit, which is why Shakespeare in his
plays, and Milton in his epic poetry, 'derived' their verse from
rhyme and wrote *blank verse*. We have seen too in Chapter 4 how
measured verse regularized the numbers of *cadences* and *syllables*,
but that this regularity was not always strict in practice. But Blake
finds their measures 'monotonous'. He wants 'variety in every line'
and it is the *regulation* of *beat* that becomes the later liberators'
complaint against measured verse. When **Ezra Pound** (1885–1972)
joined the argument he urged poets 'to compose in the sequence of

the musical phrase, not in sequence of a metronome.' **Rhythm** then should not be timed by a pre-set mechanism, but suit the demands of the individual poem according to whether it is, as Blake writes, 'terrific' or 'mild & gentle'.

'FREE VERSE' AND LIBERATION

But the argument is not only technical but part of a wider claim to liberation. Blake's view of poetry is visionary, and for him its true voice is the original voice of humankind. He states that his verse is 'dictated' to him, not composed within the schemes of tradition. This pristine utterance of 'a true Orator' comes from divine inspiration and cannot be so confined. Indeed those schemes are but another part of the chains of culture that bind the natural freedom that is our original state: 'Poetry Fetter'd Fetters the Human Race.' Although two of its major influences in the twentieth century, Ezra Pound and **T. S. Eliot** (1888–1965), shared nothing of this romantic temperament, poetic allegiance or philosophy of Blake's, there is a powerful part of the *poetics* of 'free verse' which appeals to broader hopes of liberation. Let us therefore look at the modern evolution of 'free verse' as both a formal and a cultural development.

THE BIBLICAL LINE

In respect of 'numbers', the Biblical line might be described as 'free'. These lines are from Psalm 136:

> O give thanks unto the Lord; for he is good; for his mercy endureth forever.
> O give thanks unto the God of gods: for his mercy endureth forever.
> O give thanks to the Lord of lords: for his mercy endureth forever.
> To him who alone doeth great wonders: for his mercy endureth forever.
> To him that by wisdom made the heavens: for his mercy endureth forever.

The lines here are defined by what is to be said. Each has a variety of 'cadences & number of syllables' and is **end-stopped**, that is the end of the line coincides with the end of the sentence. But they do feature other gestures to make the lines memorable, notably the recurrence at their opening – 'O give thanks ...', 'To him who ...' – and their closing – 'endureth forever' – that rhetorical device of **anaphora**. The variations are built around these common elements. Blake's line in *Jerusalem* and elsewhere, is inspired by the Biblical model and sometimes employs similar recurrences:

> The land of darkness flamed, but no light and no repose:
> The land of snows of trembling & of iron hail incessant:
> The land of earthquakes, and the land of woven labyrinths:
> The land of snares & traps & wheels & pit-falls & dire mills:

Another, earlier poet, **Christopher Smart** (1722–71), in his *Jubilate Agno*, uses the style for his own distinctive devotional purposes:

> For I will consider my Cat Jeoffrey.
> For he is the servant of the Living God, duly and daily serving him.
> For at the first glance of the glory of God in the East he worships him in his way.
> For is this done by wreathing his body seven times round with elegant quickness.
> For then he leaps up to catch the musk, which is the blessing of God upon his prayer.

Smart is drawing upon the general manner of the verses in the Bible as set out in the **Authorized Version** of 1611, especially that of the *Psalms*, the *Song of Solomon* and the Magnificat of the Virgin Mary in Chapter I of St Luke's Gospel from which he takes the reiterative use of 'For ...'.

Both Blake and Smart were working in effect outside the mainstream of verse style. The model of the biblical verse gave them the amplitude their imaginations demanded but also a form closer to popular knowledge. After all, in the eighteenth century, the Bible was heard and read in churches, chapels and homes daily and weekly and would be far more widely familiar than the couplets of famous London poets of the period such as **Alexander Pope**. We can see a similar turn towards the biblical line in another poet seeking to mark a poetic space distinct from the tradition, the American **Walt Whitman** (1819–92).

'Not a whisper comes out of him of the old stock talk and rhyme of poetry … No breath of Europe'. This is Whitman in an (anonymous) review of his own first book in 1855. The main marker of what Whitman called his 'language experiment' is his shattering of measure. Again we can see the influence of the biblical line, augmented apparently by translations he knew of the Hindu sacred texts of the *Bhagavad Gita*. He makes great use of *anaphoric* structures, series and enumerations, exclamations and declamations ('Endless unfolding word of ages!'), but what he called his 'barbaric yawp' is also capable of the most delicate detailing of image and rhythm in moments of quietude such as this from Chant 6 of his huge poem 'Song of Myself':

> A child said *What is the grass?* fetching it to me with full hands;
> How could I answer the child? I do not know what it is any more than he.
> I guess it must be the flag of my disposition, out of hopeful green stuff woven.
> Or I guess it is the handkerchief of the Lord,
> A scented gift and remembrancer designedly dropt,
> Bearing the owner's name someway in the corners, that we may see and remark, and say *Whose?*

'Guessing' is characteristic of Whitman's style of intuition by which a flower on his window-sill 'satisfies me more than the metaphysics of books', so that the American colloquialism is a way of talking to the reader and suggesting a whole way of knowing. The use of the commonplace image of the dropped handkerchief in this mystical context is also part of Whitman's democratic voice. The placing of 'someway' too is a matchless touch as it particularizes the handkerchief that bit more and lengthens the line in a way that suggests the slightly longer time taken to look at it. For all his use of formulae and the round oratory of his public manner, Whitman does flex this style of free line to the most various and often subtle and intimate uses. This passage from one of his war poems, 'A Sight in the Daybreak Gray and Dim', begins, and nearly ends, with a tetrameter, but in between he stretches the lines with the utmost tact:

> Curious I halt and silent stand,
> Then with light fingers I from the face of the nearest the first just lift the blanket;
> Who are you elderly man so gaunt and grim, with well-gray'd hair, and flesh all sunken about the eyes?
> Who are you my dear comrade?

The inversion – 'silent stand' – in the first line establishes some formality, though he has admitted to simple curiosity. But then the tremulousness of his lifting the blanket is carried with those seemingly unnecessary, but in fact vital, extra syllables, 'the first', followed by the 'just' of 'just lift'. Generally Whitman makes his line coincide with the unit of sense and hardly ever uses run-on lines. Often the longer lines do have some kind of *caesura*, but here he manages to articulate the whole slow length in order to mime the action described.

The studied informality of Whitman's line is of a piece with his drawing his subject-matter from the familiar scene of ferries, streets and locomotives, and a *diction* happy to employ words like 'higgled', 'draggled', 'soggy' alongside the more high-toned 'esculent', 'obstetric', 'gneiss' and 'sextillions'. All of this comprises Whitman's radical – and deliberately American – revision of poetic norms, and anticipates not only the work of his most obvious imitators like **Allen Ginsberg** (1926–98) but all the significant changes to poetry in the twentieth century.

The line of **Gerard Manley Hopkins** (1844–89) is somewhat different but bears comparison with Whitman's. We noted in Chapter 4 how the *iambic pentameter*, with its equable alternation of unstressed and stressed syllables, can be seen as an imposition of educated sophistication. Hopkins wanted to return to the 'roughness' and energy of mediaeval strong-stress metres. Accordingly he developed a measure he called *sprung rhythm*, named for the way the line 'springs' across a varying number of unstressed syllables from one strong stress to the next. He also disturbs the alternating decorum of standard lines by jamming stresses together, jagging the lines with stutters of punctuation as his matter demands. This is from one of his religious sonnets, 'Carrion Comfort'.

> Not, I'll not, carrion comfort, Despair, not feast on thee;
> Not untwist – slack they may be – these last strands of man
> In me ór, most weary, cry *I can no more*. I can;
> Can something, hope, wish day come, not choose not to be.

Since the poem rhymes and uses the set form of the **sonnet**, it can hardly be called 'free verse', but the lines themselves entirely disrupt traditional measure with their staccato, gasping urgency which Hopkins makes yet more emphatic by his extra marking of stress. In his *Journals* Hopkins writes: 'You must not slovenly read it with your eyes but with your ears as if the paper were declaiming it at you ... Stress is the life of it.'

MODERNISM AND 'FREE VERSE'

Hopkins' poetry was not published until 1918 by which time the **modernist** movement towards 'free verse' was well under way. We have already glanced in Chapter 4 at **Ezra Pound**'s 1913 poem 'The Seafarer', a poem described as 'from the Anglo-Saxon'. Like Hopkins he has sought out earlier, less equable poetic manners to help him escape the inherited voice. Thus the poem is **syntactically** jagged, consonantal, often **alliterative** and set in irregular lines containing strong stresses.

> **Hung** with **hard ice-flakes**, where **hail scur flew**,
> **There** I heard **naught** save the **harsh sea**
> And **ice-cold wave**, at **whiles** the **swan cries**,
> **Did** for my **games** the **gann**et's **clam**or,
> **Sea**-fowls' **loud**ness was for **me laugh**ter,
> The **mews' sing**ing **all** my **mead-drink**.
>   (Pound (1968) *Collected Shorter Poems*. London: Faber)

'Some knowledge of the Anglo-Saxon fragments ... would prevent a man's sinking into contentment with a lot of wish-wash that passes for classic or "standard" poetry', wrote Pound in a typically pugnacious essay. The sentiment that verse must be dragged from 'contentment', a lolling posture wafted by the zephyrs of familiar rhythms, liquid consonants and mild assonance, pervades modernist *poetics* at this time. It goes along with disgust with the complacent, platform eloquence, 'the conventional oompa oompa', as one critic called it, of Edwardian public poetry in the years before the First World War.

Pound, who wrote bitterly about the waste and misery of the war, wanted to 'make it new', to avoid being gathered into the 'standard' voice of the time. So he sought models not only in Anglo-Saxon but in Provençal, Italian, Chinese and Japanese poetry. He put himself through a programme of defamiliarization aimed not just at making changes to his poetic line, but to subject-matter and, as we have seen in Chapter 3 describing the use of *persona*, to his tone of voice, 'casting off as it were complete masks of the self in each poem'.

T.S. Eliot was engaged in the same process at the same time and he found a decisive influence when, in 1906, he read the poems of **Jules Laforgue** (1860–87). The phrase 'free verse' translates the earlier French phrase *'vers libre'*, and French poetry, most obviously in the prose poems of **Charles Baudelaire** (1821–67) and **Arthur Rimbaud** (1854–91), had been seeking its own departures from formal verse, especially from the dominant *alexandrine*. **Stéphane Mallarmé** (1842–98) wrote in 1891:

> We are now witnessing a spectacle which is truly extraordinary, unique in the history of poetry: every poet is going off by himself with his own flute, and playing the songs he pleases. For the first time since the beginning of poetry, poets have stopped singing bass. Hitherto ... if they wished to be accompanied, they had to be content with the great organ of official metre.
>
> (*Selected Prose Poems, Essays and Letters*, 1956, p. 18)

In 1886 Laforgue described the direction his verse was taking in a letter:

> I forget to rhyme, I forget the number of syllables, I forget to set it in stanzas – the lines themselves begin in the margin just like prose. The old regular stanza only turns up when a popular quatrain is needed.

I'll have a book like this ready when I come to Paris. I'm working on nothing else. This place is a dump: eating, smoking, twenty minutes in the bath to digest – and the rest of the time: what else can you do but write poetry?

(D. Arkell, Looking for Laforgue, 1979, pp. 196–7)

I quote the circumstantial details here since they suggest something of the mood between exasperation and lassitude that Eliot evidently responded to in Laforgue and which colours the voices of decisive early poems such as 'Portrait of a Lady' and 'The Love Song of J. Alfred Prufrock'. In contrast to the anguish which wrings Hopkins' line, or the bracing stridency of 'The Seafarer', Laforgue cultivates the notion, though very knowingly, that he has fallen into *vers libre* as an idle accident. The speaker in Eliot's 'Portrait of a Lady' doodles with the line as with the emotions. Look here at the varying lengths and listen for where you think the stresses fall:

Doubtful, for a while
Not knowing what to feel or if I understand
Or whether wise or foolish, tardy or too soon ...
Would she not have the advantage, after all?
This music is successful with a 'dying fall'
Now that we talk of dying –
And should I have the right to smile?

(Eliot, T.S. (1917) 'Portrait of a Lady' in Eliot, T.S. (1974)
Collected Poems 1909–62. London: Faber)

In fact Laforgue did not forget to **rhyme**, though he did so irregularly, and Eliot follows suit. The whole final paragraph of 'Portrait of a Lady' from which the above lines come rhymes *a b c d e c a f f g e* (see Chapter 6 Rhyme). As we have already seen in Chapter 3, Eliot's idea of the line focuses on 'the contrast between fixity and flux'. The flux though is crucial for it embodies the casual and colloquial quality of voice that – as we saw in Chapter 3 on 'Tones of Voice' – shook early twentieth-century poetry. In 1917, in an essay 'Reflections on Contemporary Poetry', Eliot wrote:

> One of the ways by which contemporary verse has tried to escape
> the rhetorical, the abstract, the moralising, to recover (for that is its
> purpose) the accents of direct speech, is to concentrate its attention
> on trivial or accidental or commonplace objects.
>
> (Eliot, T. S. (1999) *Selected Essays*, London: Faber)

In Eliot's early work the line registers personalities too unsure of
themselves to be either certain or anguished. Idleness however has
always been the accusation of traditionalists decrying 'free verse'.
If this could be associated with the supposed debility of foreigners
so much the better.

THE MINIMAL LINE

The general movement of 'free verse' then is towards a democratic
informality that has a more flexible rhythm and a wider, more
colloquial, range of words. Once freed of measure the line has gone
in two main different directions. One has been towards minimalism,
reduction, and the other towards expansiveness, spread.

Poets who heard the full metrical line as 'oompa oompa' have
wanted to purge verse of elevation or pretension, to strip it down to
the barest elements, highlighting words with *semantic* content and
minimizing *syntactic* connection. The line in consequence tends to
be short. We have already seen in Chapter 3 how **William Carlos
Williams** finds a register for his 'nervous' sensibility – 'I didn't
go in for long lines' – and, 'very much an American kid', his own
cultural situation. The lines he uses in poems like 'An Early Martyr'
and 'Pastoral' are self-effacingly brief, and could be briefer, as in
this conversation with his barber:

Of death
the barber
the barber
talked to me
cutting my
life with
sleep to trim
my hair –

It's just
a moment
he said, we die
every night –

(Williams, 1988)

This poem eventually ends warmly, but this matter-of-fact opening is the more discomfiting for its terseness. This is not Williams at his most easy-going, as the opening inversion shows, 'Of death / the barber / the barber / talked to me', though the repetition is a recognizable exclamation of surprise. The line-breaks also quietly disrupt expectations not only of the metred line and the grammatical unit, but enable effects like the small shock of 'cutting my / life'. Overall what these broken lines do is make the ordinary chat of someone passing the time of day with his barber extraordinary. They wield shears, but hairdressers don't often draw our attention to death. Like many of Williams' poems its casual, jotted manner belies the penetration of his glance at the mundane.

In poems like these the visual element is important too. Isolated on a full page, the poem has a concentrated look, as though distilled on to the whiteness. Here is the strong visual dimension of the poem's 'deliberate space'. Williams has testified to the part played by the introduction of the typewriter into the compositional process. Its brisk mechanical motion and the even impress of the ink promotes a sense of simple fixity and of the poem as a physical object.

We sometimes speak of 'setting down' words. This has the sense of writing as something simple and fixed. In his long 'Autobiography' *Briggflatts* the English poet **Basil Bunting** (1900–85) finds his ideal in an analogy with stone-cutting:

The mason stirs:
Words!
Pens are too light.
Take a chisel to write.

Bunting's advice to an aspiring poet is to 'put away your poem till you forget it' and then 'cut out every word you dare', and then repeat this process again and again. In this way, Bunting believed, the poem, properly reduced to its impressive essentials, would become absolutely clear.

A very similar ideal of clarity can be seen in a poet who takes the Williams manner into a different scene, **Gary Snyder** (1930–). Like Bunting, their common aesthetic goal is to approximate the physical world as directly as possible on to the page, and to attend to sense and impression rather than thought. Snyder, a pastoral poet of the North American wilderness, likens the poem to a 'riprap', a mountain path laid in single stones: 'Lay down these words / Before your mind like rocks. / placed solid, by hands'. The lines have a set, bitten-off quality. This is the opening of Snyder's 'Mid-August at Soughdough Mountain Lookout':

> Down valley a smoke haze
> Three days heat, after five days rain
> Pitch glows on the fir-cones
> Across rocks and meadows
> Swarms of new flies.

> (Snyder, 1966)

Writing of Williams, Kenneth Burke wrote:

> The process is simply this: There is the eye, and there is the thing upon which that eye alights; while the relationship existing between the two is a poem.

This aesthetic normally finds its voice, or image, in the spare, minimalist short line. It is also an aesthetic which, in the modernist manner, aims for a depersonalized voice, one that allows only the minimum intervention of conscious thought or emotional response. Writing of Williams, another great American modern poet, **Wallace Stevens** (1879–1955) puts it like this:

> What Williams gives, on the whole, is not sentiment but the reaction from sentiment, or, rather, a little sentiment, very little, together with acute reaction.

Williams, says Stevens has 'a sentimental side', but continually reacts against it. This is of a piece with his 'passion for the anti-poetic', a passion shared by many of the poets who, like Snyder, embraced Williams' *poetics*, and especially the guarded austerity of the short, free line. It is a guardedness with respect to the 'I' as original poet, composer or artist, sole origin of the artwork, that found its extreme manifestation in 'found' or 'ready-made' works of art such as Marcel Duchamp's urinal (signed 'R. Mutt') offered for exhibition in New York in 1917 (and rejected).

However, such a line is not bound to such a relaxed tone, nor does it necessarily muffle its speaking voice. The Welsh poet **R.S. Thomas** (1913–2000) often uses a similar line, sometimes in an equally impersonal way, and with something of Snyder's stone-laying quality, if with a different, more imposing tone. But in 'Welsh', Thomas uses the same line for a very distinctly characterized voice:

Why must I write so?
I'm Welsh, see:
A real Cymro,
Peat in my veins.
I was born late:
She claimed me,
Brought me up nice,
No hardship;
Only the one loss,
I can't speak my own
Language –

(Thomas, 2000)

Of course this sounds much different from American colloquialism, but the spare line fits this grim, resentful shortness with words.

EXPANSIVENESS AND 'FIELD COMPOSITION'

The other stream of writing encouraged by the freeing of the line is expansive. Following Whitman the poem can be deliberately, often ostentatiously casual, keen to amble through the everyday bombardment of impressions without feeling any pressure to arrive at significance. The line is simply and suitably longer. Here is **Frank O'Hara** (1926–66) afoot with his own kind of vision in the beginnings of some almost randomly chosen poems:

- Ah nuts! It's boring reading French newspapers
  in New York as if I were a Colonial waiting for my gin
- The spent purpose of a perfectly marvellous
  life suddenly glimmers and leaps into flame
- I'm getting tired of not wearing underwear
  and then again I like it
  > strolling along
  feeling the wind blow softly on my genitals
- Totally abashed and smiling
  > I walk in
  > sit down and
  > face the frigidaire
- Light   clarity   avocado salad in the morning
  after all the terrible things I do how amazing it is
  to find forgiveness and love,

References to literature, art, music and the writing of poems abound in O'Hara's work, but the sub-text of these lines, like many of his openings, is 'this is not a poem'. He shares the modernist fear of the pretentiously 'poetic', but rather than trying to pare it away he seeks to bury it by being talkative and exuberant. Strong feeling, often in gusts, frequently lies at the heart of his poems, but it comes unsuspected, surrounded by the trivial, so that its true surprise is maintained. 'Light   clarity   avocado salad in the morning … the terrible things I do …', camouflage 'big' words like 'forgiveness' and 'love', and that abrupt line-turn, 'how amazing it is / to find', arrests us before we have seen them coming.

Because it denies itself a formal stance, the democratically colloquial register of modern 'free-verse' is always wrestling with the issue of how to phrase something really serious. It both wants to be part of the daily flow of everyday language and to be marked off from it. The poem above beginning 'Ah nuts!', 'Les Luths', is a love poem and, at heart, feels the traditional pains of love:

> everybody here is running around after dull pleasantries and
> wondering if *The Hotel Wentley Poems* is as great as I say it is
> and I am feeling particularly testy at being separated from
> the one I love by the most dreary of practical exigencies money
> when I want only to lean on my elbow and stare into space feeling
> the one warm beautiful thing in the world breathing upon my right rib.

The run-on lines here go to an extreme of cutting into the *syntax*, but in a way that does not disorient the reader as much as emphasize the speaker's impatience. The rhythm slows though over that hint at self-mockery in 'particularly testy' and 'the most dreary of practical exigencies'. Both are cleverly cumbersome prosy phrases between which, almost by-the-way, comes the crucial emotional phrase, itself a consciously recognized cliché: 'the one I love'. The lover's sweet pain is then drawn out in that last line with its series of firm stresses and a breath-catching *caesura*: 'the **one warm beau**tiful **thing** in the **world** / **breath**ing upon my **right rib**'. Free verse of course does not do away with *rhythm*. What it does do is bring in the opportunity for very particular, intuitive variation, Blake's 'variety in every line'.

For all the apparent self-effacement that goes with modernist free-verse, whether by clipping the voice, or by having it speak from within a spinning cloud of scenes, impressions and knowingness, idiosyncrasy is at the heart of it. The essential point of the unmeasured line is that it is *particular* to its occasion, bespoke not already patterned. **Charles Olson** (1910–70) in his influential essay 'PROJECTIVE VERSE' (1950), insists that when a poet departs from 'closed form' 'he [*sic*] puts himself in the open – he can go by no track other than the one the poem under hand declares for itself.' In effect Olson is developing the romantic tradition in which **Coleridge** formulated the idea of 'organic form'. This means, as Olson's countryman **Ralph Waldo Emerson** put it in the nineteenth century, that a poem is not an artefact, but 'like the spirit of a plant or an animal, it has an architecture of its own'. These ideas will be considered more fully in Chapter 8, 'Image, Imagination and Inspiration'.

Olson's aim is the entire abandonment of what he derided as the 'honey-head', 'the sweetness of meter and rime', in favour of a line based in the *breathing* rhythms of the poet. As for Williams, the typewriter becomes important since its precise calibrations enable the composing poet to 'score' the poem not only with conventional punctuation but by exact spacings, multiple margins and symbols such as the /. This 'field composition' can thus configure a poem across the full dimensions of the page. This is from Olson's poem 'The Distances':

> Death is a loving matter, then, a horror
>
>   we cannot bide, and avoid
>
> by greedy life
>
>   we think all living things are precious
>
>   – Pygmalions
>
>   a German inventor in Key West
>
> who had a Cuban girl, and kept her, after her death
>
> in his bed
>
>   after her family retrieved her
>
> he stole the body again from the vault
>
>   (Olson, 1993)

There is a concrete effect here in the use of the space of the page, but Olson's aim is more radical yet. He is trying to break, or at least stretch, the conventions of grammar and **syntax** in, as he puts it himself, 'the attack, I suppose, on the "completed thought," or, the Idea, yes?' Sentences may have deferred, or no full-stops. Parentheses may be opened but not necessarily closed in order to simulate the processes of uncompleted thought – perhaps the peculiar individuality of consciousness itself. In 'PROJECTIVE VERSE' Olson understandably shies away from 'an analysis of how far a new poet can stretch the very conventions on which communication by language rests'.

In the quest for liberation, 'free verse', as we have seen, has always sought connection with the 'naturalness' of speech. The entry on 'Free Verse' in *The Princeton Encyclopedia of Poetry and Poetics* describes it like this:

> All poetry restructures direct experience by means of devices of equivalence; all poetry has attributes of a naturalizing and an

> artificializing rhetoric. However, more explicitly than metrical poetry
> ... free verse claims and thematizes a proximity to lived experience.
> It does this by trying to replicate, project, or represent perceptual,
> cognitive, emotional, and imaginative processes. Lived experience
> and replicated process are unreachable goals, but nevertheless this
> ethos is what continues to draw writers and readers to free verse.

But 'Why imitate "speech"?' asked the American poet **Robert Grenier** (1941–) in 1971. 'I HATE SPEECH' he continues. He does so because he sees the injunction to follow the spoken word as but another constraint upon the poet. Moreover, since we have less awareness of the impositions of speech patterns, he argues that they form a constraint less obvious and so more confining than, say, an *iambic pentameter*. Grenier asks another, yet more radical question: 'where are the words most themselves?' I suspect it's impossible to answer. To ask it implies a utopian longing. Classical *rhetoric* and *poetics* asserted that words are 'most themselves' when fashioned to best effect. The *romantic* reaction, which remains dominant to our own day, privileges 'natural speech' as the pristine source for poetry. For Grenier – in a cadence reminiscent of Whitman – 'It isn't the spoken any more than the written': the words of the poem are 'words occurring' whether they hail from the written, the spoken, the dreamt, or wherever else.

Following Grenier we might well ask do we need more 'ordinary speech', or touched-up 'ordinary speech' as poetry can often be? Poetry that is, in **James Fenton's** (1949–) witty characterization, 'strictly free', can be as clichéd as a leaden sonnet. But, as a poet seeks rhythms that are truly surprising, she or he will sense when the sequence of words is falling into the easy arms of the reader's expectation, whether that be a dull metric or a worn colloquialism. But the background noise of rhythmical, as of all other linguistic cliché that surrounds the poet's ear is now more prolific than ever. It inhabits what we call 'information'. To be 'free' in verse is to be heard beyond that blurry, familiar noise – to be distinct. But 'the words most themselves' are not waiting somewhere else for us to find them, but are in the midst, part of the storm. The poetic line has to be tuned from the clamour. Here is **Geoffrey Hill** (1932–), forcing his way, head-down, through the blizzard of contemporary cliché in part 21 of his *Speech! Speech!*:

> SURREAL is natural ' só you can discount
> Ethics and suchlike. Try perpetuity
> *in vitro*, find out how far is HOW FAR.
> I'd call that self ' inflicted. Pitch it
> to the CHORUS like admonition. Stoics
> have answers, but nót one I go for.

(Hill, 2000)

SUMMARY

In this chapter on 'free verse' we have considered:
- The origins of 'free verse'.
- Its associations to ideas of liberation.
- The variations of the 'Biblical' verse line.
- Modernism and 'free verse'
- The use of 'free verse' as a feature of a democratic, informal style.
- Minimal and expansionist styles
- The opening of the page towards 'field composition'.
- Whether poetry should be close to speech.

FURTHER READING

Eliot, T.S. (1999) *Selected Essays*, London: Faber, see 'Reflections on "Vers Libre"'.

Hartman, Charles O. (1980) *Free Verse, An Essay on Prosody*, Princeton, NJ: Princeton University Press.

Kennedy, X.J. and Gioa, Dana (1998) *An Introduction to Poetry*, ninth edn, New York: Longman, see Chapter 11 'Open Form'.

Koch, K. (1998) *Making Your Own Days: The Pleasures of Reading and Writing Poetry*, New York: Simon & Schuster, see Chapter 2 'Music'.

Mayes, Frances (1987) *The Discovery of Poetry*, Orlando, FL: Harcourt, Brace, Jovanovich, see Chapter 7, 'Free Verse'.

Olson, Charles 'PROJECTIVE VERSE', in Allen, D. (ed.) (1960) *The New American Poetry 1945–1960*, New York: Grove Press; or in Herbert, W.N. and Hollis, M. (eds) (2000) *Strong Words: Modern Poets on Modern Poetry*, Tarset: Bloodaxe.

Preminger, A. and Brogan, T.V.F. (eds) (1993) *The New Princeton Encyclopedia of Poetry and Poetics*, Princeton, NJ: Princeton University Press, see 'Free Verse' entry.

Williams, W.C. 'On Measure – Statement for Cid Corman' (1954) in Herbert, W.N. and Hollis, M. (eds) (2000) *Strong Words: Modern Poets on Modern Poetry*, Tarset: Bloodaxe.

6

RHYME AND OTHER NOISES

> Mister Harris, plutocrat,
> Wants to give my cheek a pat,
> If a Harris pat means a Paris hat
> Bé bé!
> *Mais je suis toujours fidèle*, darlin', in my fashion
> *Oui, je suis toujours fidèle*, darlin', in my way!

I think these lines from a song by **Cole Porter** (1891–1964) include my favourite rhyme. The lines are blindingly simple but utterly ingenious in the way they manipulate *Harris, Plutocrat / pat* and then carry the sounds into the brilliant inversion of *'Harris pat'* and *'Paris hat'*. The song, 'Always true to you in my fashion' from Porter's musical *Kiss Me Kate* (1948) plays a series of such rhymes: 'vet/pet', 'Tex/checks/sex' – and it would not be impossible to believe that a less decorous version might have made the Harris word-play yet better by substituting 'ass' for 'cheek'.

Rhyme is a play with words and its first effect is pleasure. It comes from delighted surprise as words, remote from each other in meaning but which happen to sound alike, are made to coincide. One aspect of this delight can sport with meaning:

> Moses supposes
> His toe-ses
> Are roses
> But Moses supposes
> Erroneously.

Rhyme can make language disorderly because following its nose can entirely subvert normal sense, especially when words are corrupted to fit. But in other ways rhyme might be said to organize language into tidy shapes. There is a kind of 'click' as this happens like the neat fastening of a catch or two pieces of a jigsaw. With Porter's conjuring, this occurs with such bewildering speed that we are still figuring out what has happened as the song celebrates not only the character's but the composer's coup. Rhyme is often – as here – a matter of surface, and gains the kind of admiration we give to a magic or acrobatic trick.

But good rhymes can also embody meaning and we can see this here. The cheerfully and endearingly cynical character who sings Porter's song has a formula that works: the (euphemistic) 'Harris pat' = a 'Paris hat'. Algebra could not provide a neater equation.

AGAINST RHYMING

It must be said at the outset that many poets have done without the various qualities of rhyme. **Shakespeare** and the other Elizabethan dramatists employed predominantly *blank verse* as part of their simulation of natural speech on stage (though in his sonnets and other non-dramatic verse Shakespeare retained verse). When **Milton** came to write *Paradise Lost* he dismissed 'the troublesome and modern bondage of Rhyming' which had vexed many previous poets by its 'constraint to express many things otherwise, and for the most part worse than else they would have expressed them.' He described it in his preface to *Paradise Lost* as

> A thing of it self, to all judicious ears, trivial and of no true musical delight; which consists only in apt Numbers, fit quantity of Syllables, and the sense variously drawn out from one Verse into another.
>
> (Fowler (ed)., Milton, *Paradise Lost*, 1971, p. 39)

Milton's objections, that searching for 'the jingling sound of like endings' inhibits free expression, have been shared by many poets ever since, especially in the twentieth century. **Judith Wright** (1915–2000) writes in her manifesto poem 'Brevity':

> Rhyme, my old cymbal,
> I don't clash you as often,

or trust your old promises
of music and unison.

Nevertheless many people still like and expect poems to rhyme, and despite hundreds of years of blank verse, and a hundred years of *'free verse'*, rhyme is far from dead. Perhaps this is because its pleasures are felt in very different parts of the poetic spectrum. On the one hand rhyme is indispensable to all kinds of oral poetry from children's 'rhymes', folk songs and ballads to the rap and performance poetry of our own day because it is a strong *sound* effect and for the **mnemonic** qualities we've discussed above. Yet it can also offer the delight of surprise, of enjoying and admiring ingenuity as in the kind of cerebral, knowing sophistication shown by Cole Porter. In the ever-popular form of the **limerick** it can combine both these dimensions and please nearly everyone. When we consider rhyme in any poem however, we will always want to decide whether it is 'a thing of it self' or a deeply integrated part of the expression.

DEFINITIONS

In the rest of this chapter I want to describe and explore the definitions, and the different kinds, patterns and purposes of rhyme. This will include considering its aesthetic effects: how it works to provide closure to poems and parts of poems – and how sometimes it does not; how it helps to structure poems, and how rhyme confirms meanings and helps us to discover them. Whilst most attention will be given to **end-rhymes**, I shall also consider related sound effects such as **alliteration** and **assonance** and **consonance**.

According to *The New Princeton Encyclopedia of Poetry and Poetics* although every language contains the capacity for rhyme, there are some 4,000 poetries which make no use of it. In English however poems have often been known as 'rhymes', so closely has this feature been associated with the art. Rhyme is another characteristic that comes through the oral tradition and an additional **mnemonic** feature in early verse. It has always persisted in popular forms such as Cockney **rhyming slang** and is intrinsic to rapping and much contemporary **performance**, or **'slam'** poetry.

Again **recurrence** is at the heart of the pleasures of rhyme. Essentially it exploits an aspect of the coincidence of language. As I've already suggested in Chapter 1, language works not only along the axis of reference (meaning), but also among its own incidental associations. The *chance* that two words sound similar is one of these, and one with a great range of available subtlety. Thus a poem in rhyme is working along two axes: one travelling 'horizontally' along the line of its syntactically organized meaning, and another travelling 'vertically' down the line that connects the rhyming words. It is like an echo that still reverberates as the words move on. The relationship between these two axes is what determines how successful a poem in rhyme is. It should possess and connect reason and rhyme.

The *definition* of rhyme in English has to do with the arrangement of consonants and vowels. The family of rhyming effects can be described in the following seven types thus:

C = the **consonant; V** = the **vowel**. The recurring sound is highlighted.
1. **C** V C **C** V C e.g. **b**at **b**it = alliteration.
2. C **V** C C **V** C e.g. c**oo**l f**oo**d = assonance.
3. C V **C** C V**C** e.g. kna**ck** / so**ck** = consonance
   (could just be used as an end rhyme – see 5. below).
4. C **V** C C **V** C e.g. s**ock** / r**ock** = **full or strict rhyme**.
5. **C** V C **C** V C e.g. **cr**ick / **cr**ack = half, or slant, or pararhyme.
6. **C** V C C **V** C e.g. **kna**ck / **gna**t = reverse rhyme.
7. C **V** C **C** V C e.g. **wood** / **would** = identical rhyme or *rime riche*.

Purists would argue that the only 'proper' rhyming is *full rhyme* (4), where *the last two or more sounds are identical and the difference is in the preceding consonant*: sock/rock, bee/see, raft/daft, bill/fill, null/bull etcetera. Two polysyllables that illustrate this are d**emonstrate** and r**emonstrate.** The kinship of these two words is however disappointingly close to make a good rhyme. We would certainly prefer a greater difference, something like **Tony Harrison**'s (1937–) matching **haemorrhoid** and **unemployed** in his 'Divisions II'. Notice here that the success of the rhyme also depends on the rhythmic combination of syllables. The rhyming sound, coming at the end of the line, is obviously part of the final stressed syllable: – *rhoid* / *ployed* – but the cadence of the word has also to fit the rhythm of the line as a whole: *employed* would fill the rhyme but would not synchronize as **un***employed* does.

PATTERNS OF RHYME

Poets employ *end-rhymes* in a variety of patterns. The most apparent is the rhyming of successive lines into *couplets*, as here in **Mary Barber**'s (?1690–1757) 'The Conclusion of a Letter to the Rev. Mr C–':

> Her Husband has surely a terrible **Life**;
> There's nothing I dread, like a verse-writing **Wife**:
> Defend me, ye Powers, from that fatal **Curse**;
> Which must heighten the Plagues of 'for better for **worse**'!

In analysing verse we give each rhyming sound a letter, beginning with **a**, so these lines can be seen to rhyme **a a b b**. *Triplets*, as in 'To Sapho' by **Robert Herrick**, therefore go:

> Sapho, I will choose to go   **a**
> Where the northern winds do blow   **a**
> Endless ice, and endless snow: **a**
> Rather than I once would see,   **b**
> But a winter's face in thee,   **b**
> To benumb my hopes and me.   **b**

Or, in **Gjertrud Schnackenberg**'s (1953–), 'Supernatural Love':

> My father at the dictionary-stand   **a**
> Touches the page to fully understand   **a**
> The lamplit answer, tilting in his hand ...   **a**

(Schnackenberg, 1986)

Whereas couplets are commonly employed in extended *verse-paragraphs*, triplets usually form separate *stanzas*, although they may, like Schnackenberg's poem, run the syntax from one stanza to the next. Stanzas are often built around alternating rhyme schemes such as this **a b a b** scheme, also by Herrick:

> Gather ye rose-buds while ye may,
> Old Time is still a flying:
> And this same flower that smiles to day,
> To morrow will be dying.

Alternatively a *quatrain* might rhyme its outside lines and its inside lines in the pattern of **a b b a** as does **Ben Jonson** (1572–1637) in 'An Elegy':

> Though beauty be the mark of praise,
> And yours of whom I sing be such
> As not the world can praise too much,
> Yet is 't your virtue now I raise.

These basic patterns – **aa bb, abab, abba** – all highlight the obvious binary qualities of rhyme with all its implications of balance, symmetry, and the division and completeness of even number. The pairings of rhyme imply that nothing is odd, loose, or stands apart. It is an aesthetic of harmony and completion. As we shall see, longer stanza forms can use more elaborate rhyme schemes as part of the structure of the poem. As they do so the rhymes might appear much further apart, some seemingly abandoned until they are given their more remote echo. It is in the identification of such structures and echoes that the notation of rhyme is so helpful.

THE BEAUTIES OF RHYME

The aesthetic attraction – the beauties of rhyme – are very different. Sometimes we might gorge on a wonderful excess as in a poem like **Carol Ann Duffy**'s (1955–) 'Mrs Sisyphus' (1999) which plays exultantly on the words 'jerk', 'kirk', 'irk', 'berk', 'dirk', 'perk', 'shriek', 'cork', 'park', 'dork', 'gawk', 'quirk', 'lark', and 'mark'. There's plentitude too in these quatrains from 'Long After Heine' by **Gwen Harwood** (1920–95) which combine *internal rhyme* (rhyme *within* the line) with ingenious end-rhyme:

> The baby **screamed** with colic
>> the windows **streamed** with **rain**.
> She **dreamed** of a demon lover
>> like Richard **Chamberlain**.
>
> He **towered, austerely** perfect
>> in **samurai brocade**,
> and **hushed** the **howling** baby
>> with one **swish** of his **blade**.

(Harwood, 1991)

I've highlighted here not only the full end and internal rhymes but also the *assonance* of vowel sounds (towered / austerely / samurai), the *alliteration* of hushed / howling as well as the *half-rhyme* hushed / swished.

These are comic examples, but the religious poetry of **George Herbert** (1593–1633) also works with rhyme to shape his affirmations. This is the first stanza of 'Virtue':

> Sweet day, so cool, so calm, so bright,
>> The bridal of the earth and sky:
> The dew shall weep thy fall tonight;
>> For thou must die.

The next two of the four **ab ab** quatrains employ different rhymes for the key word 'die': 'eye' and 'lie'. None of these is exotic for simplicity is everything in this poem. In the last stanza 'die' is replaced by its opposite in meaning, 'lives':

> Only a sweet and virtuous soul,
>> Like seasoned timber, never gives;
> But though the whole world turn to coal,
>> Then chiefly lives.

The attraction of this poem is in its carefully judged composure. Its metre is simple and steady and the process of its imagery and ideas is paralleled in each of the first three stanzas with that recurrent crucial rhyme of the – **i.e.** sound. Then, as the rhyme changes so does the sense. The poem has the pleasures of calmness, compact shape and balance and the straightforward rhymes are an important part of this. They show us that whilst we may think of the effects of rhyme as something in themselves – especially when the juxtapositions have real surprise – rhyme is really set into the whole character and meaning of the poem.

RHYMING AND MEANING

Because of its binary character, rhyme is often used for *closure* of various kinds: the two parts come together like the shutting of a lid. A familiar example is the way that Shakespearean verse drama usually indicates the end of a scene by a rhyming **couplet**. The exhaustion of *King Lear* is tolled in a sequence of four rhyming couplets, including the last words of the faithful servant Kent:

> I have a journey, sir, shortly to go;
> My master calls me; I must not say no.

Couplets like this are called **closed** because they contain a whole sentiment or idea within their clearly defined boundaries. It is a **stichic** verse, which is to say that the poem proceeds mainly through distinctly punctuated lines as opposed to verse that flows through several lines. To eighteenth-century **neo-classical** poets who saw verse as primarily **rhetorical**, that is a way of clarifying and persuading an audience of long-established truths, the couplet is attractive because of its capacity for memorable summary. It is its associations with the effort of speech-making and grand persuasion that have gained this kind of couplet the title '**heroic**'.

For important summations or conclusions the couplet can have an **epigrammatic** quality, sometimes using humour and the surprise of the rhyme to achieve a deflating effect. This is well-shown in these lines by **John Gay** (1685–1732). The poem is called 'The Man and the Flea' and features a series of creatures, a hawk, a crab, a snail, and of course a man, discoursing upon how all Creation has been made for their particular benefit. Man boasts:

> 'I cannot raise my worth too high;
> Of what vast consequence am I?'

and gets an unexpected riposte:

> 'Not of th' importance you suppose',
> Replies a flea upon his nose.

The pride of Man is instantly deflated by this unlooked-for intervention which opens the pretensions of *high* / *I* to the ridicule of a flea, a flea educated enough moreover to employ words like *suppose*. Man cannot see what's on his nose never mind what's under it. Thus *suppose* / *nose* is a rhyme that is not merely incidental but essential to the meaning and tone of the poem.

In lines longer than Gay's four-beat **tetrameter**, this summative quality of the rhyming couplet can be complemented by related devices, as in these lines by the style's foremost exponent **Alexander Pope** (1688–1744). Here, in 'An Essay on Criticism', he wants to square the paradox that what we take to be natural, and thus think of as free and unconstrained, is in fact governed by laws of its own:

> Those RULES of old discovered, not devised,
> Are Nature still, but Nature methodised;
> Nature, like liberty, is but restrained
> By the same laws which first herself ordained.

In this instance the pairs of rhyming words, *devised* / *methodised* and *restrained* / *ordained* are associated in their meaning as well as in the coincidence of their sound. The second couplet moreover encapsulates a move in understanding. This goes from the notion of restraint alone, which we might think of as a troublesome leash, to the acknowledgement that the natural order is fixed. Pope is aiming to build an argument and so tries to carry us along the line of his thought in a series of clear, separate steps.

To this end the balanced, self-containment of the rhyme is often paralleled by a balancing effect within the ***iambic pentameter***. Usually this will involve a tiny break, or ***caesura***, half-way through the line. The lines above illustrate this, although, as so often in verse, the variation from it is equally important:

> Those RULES of old discovered, | not devised,
> Are Nature still, | but Nature methodized;
> Nature, like liberty, | is but restrained
> By the same laws which first herself ordained.

The caesura in the first line here is delayed so as to emphasize the assertion and push the opposite idea back before it. The alliteration, or **head-rhyme**, helps drive home the essential idea – 'discovered, not devised'. The second line is evenly balanced with Nature on both sides of the equation pivoting on 'but'. The third line allows an extra pause after 'Nature' to allow us to dwell on the relationship between Nature and liberty. But then the line runs on into the next, sweeping us along to its firm conclusion without any further break. That everything is *ordained*, with the strong implication of divine ordinance, is for Pope the last word. Although the closed couplet can be used for more intimate purposes, as here in Pope's 'Epistle to Dr. Arbuthnot':

> The Muse but served to ease some friend, not wife,
> To help me through this long disease, my life –

its primary mode is public and oratorical.

This is less true of **open couplets** where the sense can run on through lines with much less punctuation without necessarily matching components of meaning to the rhyming pairs. In these lines from **Christopher Marlowe**'s (1564–93) poem 'Hero and Leander', the narrator is striving to describe the beauties of the handsome youth Leander:

> Even as delicious meat is to the taste
> So was his neck in touching, and surpassed
> The white of Pelops' shoulder. I could tell ye
> How smooth his breast was, and how white his belly,
> And whose immortal fingers did imprint
> That heavenly path, with many a curious dint,

> That runs along his back; but my rude pen
> Can hardly blazon forth the loves of men,
> Much less of powerful gods;

These lines are rapturous rather than studied and the sensual excitement does not accept the measure of the couplet but flows enthusiastically across the endings. In running, or *strophic* lines like these the rhyme is much less important, serving the overall organization of the verse rather than its specific meanings. As Marlowe's own dramatic verse shows, when the pentameter is used like this, rhyme becomes redundant since the necessary pressure in the verse is felt in other ways.

But not all open couplets tend towards blank verse. In this poem, 'The Not-Returning', **Ivor Gurney** (1890–1937) imagines home from the trenches of the Western Front:

> Never more delight comes of the roof dark lit
> With under-candle-flicker nor rich gloom on it,
> The limned faces and moving hands shuffling the cards,
> The clear conscience, the free mind moving towards
> Poetry, friends, the old earthly rewards.
> No more they come. No more.
> Only the restless searching, the bitter labour,
> The going out to watch stars, stumbling blind through the difficult door.
>
> (Gurney, 1982)

As in this excerpt, Gurney's poem uses a mixture of couplets and triplets – although the poem's first line stays unrhymed. Unusually, too, for rhyming verse, the measure is irregular. So what purpose does the rhyme serve here? I think that in this case the customary tidying qualities of rhyme are an ironic counterpoint to the roughed-out quality of the verse. The last phrase, 'stumbling blind through the difficult door' is the poem's keynote. In its awkward word-order – 'Never more delight comes' – and its varying verse lines and punctuation, the poem embodies a sense of stumbling. It seems written under stress, almost improvised. The rhymes then represent some object to stumble towards, something to help keep coherence as the speaker feels everything dissolving. That the rhyme '*lit / on it*' is crude, and is succeeded by two **triplets** which include **half-rhymes**, shows how ironically distant these agonized, nearly broken lines are from the 'finish' we usually associate with rhyme. That it bothers with such artifice seems an irrelevance, but that it does so turns out to sound poignant and defiant.

BUILDING POEMS WITH RHYMES

I want to turn now to see how rhyme schemes work as part of the architecture of whole poems or the larger sections of poems. The couplet sequence of *aa bb cc* is **plain rhyme**, but as soon as rhyming words are separated further, even only to *ab ab* then the lines connecting the rhymes criss-cross and the rhyme becomes **interlaced**. **Terza rima** is a good basic example of this. It works in three line units, **aba bcb cdc**. This is the opening of **Thomas Kinsella**'s (1928–) 'Downstream':

Again in the mirrored dusk the paddles **sank**.	a
We thrust forward, swaying both as **one**.	b
The ripples widened to the ghostly **bank**	a
Where willows, with their shadows half un**done**,	b
Hung to the water, mowing like the **blind**.	c
The current seized our skiff. We let it **run**	b
Grazing the reeds, and let the land un**wind**	c
In stealth on either hand. Dark woods: a **door**	
Opened and shut. The clear sky fell be**hind**,	c

(Kinsella, 1996)

Terza rima was devised by the Italian poet **Dante** (1265–1321) for his huge three part poem *The Divine Comedy* and has found counterparts in the poetries of several European languages since. His choice of these **tercets** within his three part scheme was meant to allude to the Holy Trinity, but more generally the mode suggests forward movement and continuity. The closed couplet can be seen to be continually starting afresh, but with *terza rima* there is a sense of perpetual motion and of everything's being connected. The closure occurs with a single line, rhyming with the previous middle rhyme, as Kinsella does in his own very Dantean poem:

> The slow, downstreaming dead, it seemed, were blended
> One with those silver hordes, and briefly shared
> Their order, glittering. And then impended
>
> A barrier of rock that turned and bared
> A varied barrenness as toward its base
> We glided – blotting heaven as it towered –
>
> Searching the darkness for a landing place.

On the face of it, it seems strange that rhyme, which depends upon evenness, should work to bind three-line systems so strongly. The *villanelle*, originally a French form (see Chapter 7 'Stanza'), is a more compact example. This is a form comprising five three-line stanzas (*tercets*), each rhyming *aba*, and a closing *quatrain* rhyming *abaa*. The first and third lines of stanza 1 are also repeated alternately at the end of each succeeding stanza, culminating in the reappearance of both as the last two lines of the poem. Strictly, the rhymes should also be the same full sounds throughout. Here are the first two stanzas of **Dylan Thomas'** (1914–53) *elegy* for his father, 'Do Not Go Gentle into That Good Night':

> Do not go gentle into that good night,
> Old age should burn and rave at close of day;
> Rage, rage against the dying of the light.
>
> Though wise men at their end know dark is right,
> Because their words had forked no lightning they
> Do not go gentle into that good night.

(Thomas, 1952)

Thomas confines himself throughout to end words which rhyme with 'night' or 'day', two words of course which represent the poles within the poem's subject. To fashion such a feverishly emotional poem – 'Rage, rage against the dying of the light' – within this extreme discipline produces a special tension. The strict limitations on the poem's means, especially in the tight permissions of the rhyme scheme, construct a vessel to compress, and withstand, the pressure of the poem's feeling.

In 'Lycidas', in memory of his drowned friend Edward King, **Milton** shapes a highly individual version of the *elegy* which varies its line length, and, instead of stanzas, employs **strophic** verse-paragraphs of different duration. Rhyme is also used in unexpected ways that move between *plain* and *interlaced* patterns. In this fifth paragraph the poet is asking one the commonest angry questions of the grief-stricken: how could the divine powers allow this to happen? Associating King (Lycidas) with poetry, he concludes with the anguished recollection that in the ancient Greek myth the Muse could not intervene to save even her own son, the greatest of poets, Orpheus.

Where were ye nymphs, when the remorseless deep	a
Closed o'er the head of your loved Lycidas?	b
For neither were ye playing on the steep,	a
Where your old Bards, the famous Druids lie,	c
Nor on the shaggy top of Mona high,	c
Nor yet where Deva spreads her wizard stream:	d
Ay me! I fondly dream –	d
Had ye been there – for what could that have done?	e
What could the Muse herself that Orpheus bore,	f
The Muse herself for her enchanting son	e
Whom universal Nature did lament,	g
When by the rout that made the hideous roar,	f
His gory visage down the stream was sent,	g
Down the swift Hebrus to the Lesbian shore?	f

Earlier in this paragraph, the rhymes in the first seven lines have stayed plain, but then as the poet becomes more fraught the pace accelerates and the pattern changes. As we see the vision of Orpheus' severed head tumbling downriver to the sea, the rhymes rush over one another, a tumult caught in the only triple rhyme – *bore, roar, shore* – words we feel here as deep, harsh sounds. The first pairing is separated by two lines, the second by only one. These words beat heavily through the lines. We will see as well that the paragraph contains one, solitary unrhymed line, line 2: the abandoned *Lycidas*. When Milton brings his poem to its resolved conclusion 130 lines later, he gives his final paragraph the conventional harmony of **ottava rima** – a stanza form rhyming *abababcc*. The fifth paragraph has no such orderly convention, but the way the poet patterns both sections, irregular and regular, shows how important rhyme is to the structure of the poem.

All these instances of the different ways rhyme is used show the connection between rhyme and meaning. But rhyme does always depend upon coincidence, and its use might just be a celebration of the happy anarchy within the language that enables us to bring words together that would otherwise never keep company, like **Tony Harrison** rhyming *lah-di-dah / Panama*. We might exult for instance in discovering the rhyme in loan-words into English such as *crouton / futon*, and make the most of it by working up a poem about bed-crumbs. Some poems might be generated by pre-set rhymes, throwing their intentions entirely upon the mercy of rhyming accidents, or, as some have done, upon another's isolated rhymes which the poet then writes 'towards', as does **John Ashbery (1927–)** in 'The Plural of "Jack-In-The-Box"'.

SO, IS RHYME 'A THING IN ITSELF'?

Thinking about rhyme in this way takes us once more into the great poetic conundrum: does the poem find words to refine its intended meanings, the emotion or idea which is there, as the philosopher Collingwood says, 'before we express it', or are its meanings generated out of the energies of language? **Dylan Thomas'** rhymes in 'Do Not Go Gentle …' evidently belong in the first category for his choices, *night, light, bright, sight* belong predominantly in the same area of meaning, or **semantic field** as linguists call it, and others, *right flight height* and *day way pray* can all be said to 'belong' in the arena where we might think of death and dying. They form that *vertical* axis of association as the poem proceeds *horizontally* along and through its lines. (Since *they* in line 5 is a pronoun, and less substantive than any other of the rhyme words, it might be said to be out of key with the rest of the poem, though this would be a hard judgement.)

Another poem in which we can readily recognize the associations, if not the separate meanings, of the rhyme words is **Ben Jonson**'s (1573–1637) 'On My First Son'.

> Farewell, thou child of my right hand, and joy;
> My sin was too much hope of thee, loved boy:
> Seven years thou wert lent to me, and I thee pay,
> Exacted by thy fate, on the just day.
> O could I lose all father now! For why
> Will man lament the state he should envy,
> To have so soon 'scaped world's and flesh's rage,
> And, if no other misery, yet age?
> Rest in soft peace, and asked, say, "Here doth lie
> Ben Jonson his best piece of poetry."
> For whose sake henceforth all his vows be such
> As what he loves may never like too much.

The hard, self-reproachful thought here is that the poet invested too much in the joy of having a child, and prepared himself too little for what fate might bring. Still hard, and raging with exclamation, is the question of why we do not envy the release death brings, most of all from the trials of age. If there is one surprising rhyme it is *lie / poetry*. This is the idea most particular to the poet, and it might be objected that this drawing of attention to his craft has no necessary place in the lament. We might think that even as he is saying that all his poetry is as naught compared with his son, he is reminding us that he is a poet. The defence would be that this discounting of his art is part of throwing off delusion and vanity. We might even consider whether Jonson intends – or subconsciously produces – a pun on *lies* in the sense of deceit, thus associating, as writing of the period often did, poetry and untruth. The closing couplet, *such / much*, has a roughness to it befitting the baleful resolution to make this awful distinction between *loving* and *liking*. Throughout this poem there is a heavy-minded restraint in the way the rhyme words are fixed together.

This is very different from the rhyming of this next poem which, in subject and style, is a modern imitation of sixteenth- and seventeenth-century modes. This is the *abba abba* **octet** of 'Sonnet 23' by **John Berryman** (1914–72).

> They may suppose, because I would not cloy your ear –
> If ever these songs by other ears are heard –
> With 'love', suppose I loved you not, but blurred
> Lust with strange images, warm, not quite sincere,
> To switch a bedroom black. O mutineer
> With me against these empty captains! gird
> Your scorn again above all at *this* word
> Pompous and vague on the stump of his career.

(Berryman, 1990)

As a set, *heard, blurred, word* can be seen to have some affinity but it is not shared by *gird*, while *ear, sincere, mutineer, career* appear to have none at all. But, as the central exclamation exhorts, the poem is raising a mutiny against the conventions of the love sonnet with its familiar circuit of 'love', 'heart' and 'beauty'. 'I want a verse fresh as a bubble breaks', he writes in the sonnet's **sestet**, and this will involve unexpected rhymes more promiscuous than chaste in their associations. Berryman and Jonson have quite different approaches to rhyming. We might imagine Jonson looking down his classical nose at Berryman's extrovert style, and indeed think ourselves that he makes rhyme, as Milton says, 'a thing in itself', rather than something that serves the poem's sentiment and ideas. But whichever our preference, we can see how both poets employ rhyme as part of their total meaning, not just as a bolted-on device.

As we have seen there are several different kinds of correspondences in the company of rhyme from the **'head-rhymes'** of **alliteration**, the chimes of **assonance**, through **half-rhymes**, to the full, prominent **end-rhymes** of the **couplet**. Rhymes can also echo from the middle of lines, or diagonally from end to middle or back. **Emily Dickinson** (1830–1886) is one of the subtlest and most determined technicians of rhyme. One reason she is so, is that her poems seem at first so artless, even clumsy, and so conventional as to resemble nursery rhymes or the most mundane of hymns. But we soon see that here is an exceptional verbal intelligence which undermines the conventions she works with to produce through her wry styling the most astonishing sentiments and ideas. She makes much use of half-rhyme, both in endings and across the bodies of lines. A recluse herself it is perhaps not surprising to see how often the word *room* appears in her work and in only a handful of poems we can find it rhymed with *tomb, name, storm* and *firm*. This obliqueness is entirely characteristic and part of her philosophy, as when she writes,

> Tell all the Truth but tell it slant –
> Success in Circuit lies ...

This first stanza of a burial poem – # 216 in the standard edition, for she gave none of her poems titles – encapsulates the variety of her rhyming. I have highlighted all the rhyming effects.

> Safe in their Alabaster Chambers –
> Untouched by Morning –
> And untouched by Noon –
> Lie the meek members of the Resurrection –
> Rafter of Satin – and Roof of Stone!

> (Dickinson, 1951)

The criss-crossing here is very intricate. We can see for instance how *noon* and *stone* are half-rhymes, and how they slant to bring in the *s* and *t* sounds of *satin*. This echo in *satin* and *stone* is especially effective because of the opposite nature of the substances associated here in the material of the coffin and the tomb, both so far from the light of *noon*. Similarly the assonance of *rafter* and *satin* – the one word reminding us of hardness the other of softness – combine, as do the consonants of *rafter* and *roof*. Moreover we might see in *rafter* an **eye-rhyme** – that is a combination of letters that look as though they might rhyme although they do not – with the poem's first word *safe*. There are other delicate and eerie effects which help create the unnerving sense of this stanza such as the steady and then varying pace and beat of the rhythm. Then there is that astonishingly rich word *alabaster* whose *a* sounds are different from the others in that line and carries such **connotations** of deathly, clay-like whiteness. But the web of rhyming effects ensure complex associations between different words and lead to more and more implications. Dickinson's brilliance lies exactly in her understanding of that fascinating paradox of rhyme: its belonging in both 'simple' and 'sophisticated' modes. It is a brief, enigmatic poem but one that shows so much of what the poet has available in rhyme and other sounds.

SUMMARY

In this chapter on rhyme we have considered:

- Rhyme and word-play.
- The arguments against using rhyme; blank verse.
- Definitions of different kinds of rhyme.
- The character of different rhyme schemes.
- The aesthetic purposes of rhyme and how rhyme can enhance meaning.
- How rhyme schemes can shape a whole poem.
- A summary of the arguments for and against the use of rhyme.

FURTHER READING

Dickinson, Emily (1951) *The Complete Poems of Emily Dickinson*, Boston, MA; London: Little Brown and Co.

Thomas, Dylan (1952) *Collected Poems1934–52*, London: J.M. Dent.

Harrison, Tony (1984) *Selected Poems*, Harmondsworth: Penguin.

Hollander, J. (1989) *Rhyme's Reason: A Guide to English Verse*, new edn, London: Yale University Press.

Koch, Kenneth (1998) *Making Your Own Days: The Pleasures of Reading and Writing Poetry*, New York: Simon & Schuster, Chapter 2, 'Music'.

Wesling, Donald (1980) *The Chances of Rhyme, Device and Modernity*, Berkeley, CA: University of California Press.

STANZA

Let me hear a staff, a stanze, a verse.
(Shakespeare, *Love's Labour's Lost*, Act IV Sc. 2)

When the comic character Holofernes makes this demand he is either showing off by using three words where one will do, or he is uncertain which word to use. He wants Nathaniel to read him some poetry and in the 1590s the word *stanza*, to refer to a grouping of lines, was quite new in English. But, with the sixteenth century's attraction to Italian models, it was coming to displace the Old English word *staff*. The French word *verse*, then as now, could refer to a group of lines, a single line, or simply mean poetry in the generic sense.

After Nathaniel has read a dozen or so lines Holofernes interrupts him complaining 'You find not the apostrophus, and so miss the accent', in other words he is missing the correct places to pause. As we have seen, timing is essential to all aspects of the rhythm of poetry both for its sense and effects, so the 'apostrophus' – the pause – is vital.

DEFINITIONS

The original sense of *stanza* in Italian is 'stopping-place', a place to take a stand, and more particularly 'room'. These associated senses are exactly appropriate to the established sense of *stanza* in poetry. A poem in stanzas is one comprising a series of groups of lines shaped in the same way, and usually, although not always of the same length. As each group ends, the poem has a momentary stopping-place. The structure of each stanza itself provides a space for the words to work, for what, in his overblown way, Holofernes calls 'the elegancy, facility and golden cadence of poetry'.

For the American poet **Kenneth Koch** (1925–2002) a stanza is 'nothing more than organizing other forms of poetic music – rhythm and rhyme' (*Making Our Own Days*, 1998, p. 47). It is true that the organization of stanzas has traditionally been based on metrical patterns and on rhyme schemes. As we have looked at the variety of individual poetic lines and of their connections through rhyme, so in considering the stanza we are examining larger combinations.

But I think the purposes of the stanza go beyond the gathering of rhythm and rhyme. The stanza provides its own aesthetic experience for both the poet and reader. It also serves necessary functions for several different kinds of poems. In this chapter I want to explain some of those functions and suggest the nature of their aesthetic attraction. In doing so I shall widen the topic by including a description of free-standing forms, such as the *sonnet*. I consider those here because their shapes are basically stanzaic, and I shall present them in the context of the kinds of stanza they most resemble.

With the stanza, once again we can look for origins in the *mnemonics* of the *oral tradition*. The stanza of the oral tradition, as we saw in the discussion of *ballad* form in Chapter 2 'Deliberate Space', draws together the measures of the line, the repetitions of rhyme, and sometimes refrain, into comprehensible and memorable shapes. These normally coincide with sections of the ballad's narrative. The listener therefore is receiving the progress of the poem in distinct sections, like milestones along the way, and the performer has the same benefits of this segmentation, as well as the chance to recapitulate before going on. The stanza, even in the simple four-line ballad, is therefore eminently practical.

ALTERNATING VOICES

Such division need not only serve long *narrative* poems. Any poem that requires a balance or sequencing of voice or topic can use stanza-form. Here is an excerpt from a sardonic poem from the thirteenth century given the title 'How Death comes':

Wanne mine eyhnen misten   [eyes mist over]
And mine heren sissen,   [hearing hisses]
And my nose coldet,
And my tunge foldet
And my rude slaket,   [face goes slack]
And mine lippes blaken
...
Thanne I schel flutte   [shall pass]
From bedde to flore,
From flore to here,   [shroud]
From here to bere,   [bier]
From bere to putte,   [grave]
And te putt fordut.   [closed up]
Thanne lyd mine hus uppe mine nose   [lies my house upon my nose]
Of al this world ne give I it a pese!   [jot]

The poem has a very simple two-part structure: *Wanne* and *Thanne*.
The simple **anaphoric** structure – And / And / And // From / From /
From – devises instances of the two conditions, and the stanza-break
marks the movement from one to the other. Many early poems
use stanzas in this balancing way, or, in similar fashion, to itemize
various things on the way to their main argument. Thus another
mediaeval poem, 'The Five Joys of Mary', recounts each of those
joys in a centrepiece of five stanzas preceded by an introduction
and closed by a prayer. In more worldly mood, 'Bring us in good ale'
is repetitious in a way we know all too well as each boozy stanza
implores 'Bring us in no browne bread ... no beefe ... no mutton ...
no egges ... ' etc. etc., but 'Bring us in good ale.' Sequences which
mark time as they elaborate variations on the theme usually use
stanzas for each piece of their working.

The obvious artifice of stanza-form has meant that it finds little
place in verse-drama where a greater impression of naturalness
is needed. **Blank verse** generally is non-stanzaic, although this is
much less true in the twentieth century. However there are poems
which make use of dialogue, usually in the form of an argument,
and stanzas offer an obvious way of marking and balancing the
speakers. The debate in which students and schoolmen exercised
their powers of **rhetoric** was a staple of mediaeval and early-modern

education, and the argument between Body and Soul was a regular topic which also featured largely in **Renaissance** poetry. In poems like **Andrew Marvell**'s (1621–78) 'A Dialogue Between Soul and Body', the exchange is set out formally in ten line stanzas of rhyming couplets. The poem as we have it is thought to be incomplete but here are four lines of each of the complaints towards the other:

Soul
Oh, who shall from this dungeon raise
A soul enslaved so many ways?
With bolts of bones that fettered stands
In feet, and manacled in hands;

...

Body
But physic yet could never reach
The maladies thou me dost teach:
Whom first the cramp of hope does tear,
And then the palsy shakes of fear:

...

Another poem which uses this dialogue form, is **William Wordsworth**'s (1770–1850) encounter with the child in 'We Are Seven', a poem we have already encountered in Chapter 3, 'Tones of Voice'. The debate is between the worldly poet and 'the cottage girl', and though the poem uses the simple ballad stanza, the dialogue is not always divided between them. At the end for instance, the adult's exasperation and the child's insistence cut across each other:

'How many are you, then,' said I,
'If they two are in heaven?'
Quick was the little Maid's reply,
'O Master! we are seven.'
'But they are dead; those two are dead!
Their spirits are in heaven!'
'Twas throwing words away; for still
The little Maid would have her will,
And said, 'Nay we are seven!'

From these instances we can see how there are kinds of poems – narrative, sequenced and in dialogue – which virtually demand stanzaic form. But there are many stanzaic poems which do not fall even partly into these categories. I want now to consider a series of different types of shorter and then longer stanza forms and explore the effects they achieve in relation to their subject.

ONE-LINE FORMS

A one-line stanza must, on the definition given above, be a contradiction in terms. There are indeed few instances to be found, and some that might be considered are single-line sections of much longer poems. For example **Geoffrey Hill** (1932–) begins his sequence *The Triumph of Love* with the one-line poem,

Sun-blazed, over Romsley, a livid rain-scarp

and concludes it with the hundred-and-fiftieth poem,

Sun-blazed, over Romsley, the livid rain-scarp.

Between are poems of widely-varying lengths, but making a deliberate stopping-place after but one line, and then recalling it at the end of the volume with that one change from *a* to *the*, is bound to make us dwell on the image evoked. In what is frequently a turbulent poem employing several different **registers** and sudden alterations of subject and mood, this near-recurrence, again fore-grounded by its isolation has the effect of closure, perhaps even composure.

This gesture draws upon the spareness, the isolation of a few words taken out of the torrent of verse that so attracted **modernist** poets like **Ezra Pound** and **H.D. (Hilda Doolittle)** (1886–1961). Stanzas are meant to combine lines and then present them for attention in the space marked by the boundaries for the eye or ear. Isolating single lines makes this more intense. It is a technique **Jorie Graham** (1951–) employs extensively, as here, in 'Self-Portrait as Hurry and Delay [Penelope at her Loom]'. The poem is not comprised wholly of one-line stanzas but here is its conclusion:

17

the shapely and mournful delay she keeps alive for him the breathing

18

as the long body of the beach grows emptier awaiting him

19

gathering the holocaust in close to its heart growing more beautiful

20

under the meaning of the soft hands of its undoing

21

saying Goodnight goodnight for now going upstairs

22

under the kissing of the minutes under the wanting to go on living

23

beginning always beginning the ending as they go to sleep beneath her.

(Graham, 1987)

Actually section 16, which has four lines, ends 'it is', thus flowing straight into 17, 'the shapely and mournful delay...' But, as with each of the succeeding line-stanzas, 17 can be read as a beginning. Graham clearly wants this ambiguity of connection and separation besides creating a slow sensual effect by the pauses between her long lines.

TWO-LINE FORMS

We have seen in the chapter on **rhyme** (Chapter 6) how the **couplet** works not as a stanzaic form but within longer poems. But even without rhyme these small units have had an enduring attraction for poets right up to our own day. Proportion, symmetry, counterpart, felt as intuitively satisfying, seems basic to this. **Matthew Welton** (1969–) has a pair of poems, 'The Wonderment of Fundament' and the 'The Fundament of Wonderment'. Each has four sections comprised of two couplets. Usually the rhymes are full, but occasionally, as in this section, he uses **half-rhymes**:

> She makes her music, loosening her hands:
> the moment holds. But if the evening ends
>
> the coffee place will crowd, and trains will leave,
> and fields absorb what light the moon might give.

The gentle, seeming randomness of incident and imagery in these poems and their sportive **word-play** might seem at odds with the clarifying briskness of the eighteenth-century couplet, but each seems to me to act upon the other: the poem's wandering is given shape by the couplet while the normally firm outlines of the form are softened.

A few poets in English have experimented with a verse-form consisting of couplets adapted from Persian, Arabic and other poetries called the **ghazal**. Classically the form rhymed *aa ba ca da ea fa ...*, and in subject tends towards melancholy and a limited range of topic and imagery. **Judith Wright** (1915–2000) has adapted the form, not attempting the rhyme scheme but usually closing each pair of lines. In her sequence *The Shadow of Fire* she maintains a meditation upon the passing of time and age especially by evoking the seasons and the world of nature. This is one of the shorter poems, 'Dust', after the Japanese poet **Bashō**, (1644–94):

> In my sixty-eighth year drought stopped the song of the rivers,
> Sent ghosts of wheatfields blowing over the sky.
>
> In the swimming-hole the water's dropped so low
> I bruise my knees on rocks which are new acquaintances.
>
> The daybreak moon is blurred in a gauze of dust.
> Long ago my mother's face looked through a grey motor-veil.
>
> Fallen leaves on the current scarcely move.
> But the azure kingfisher flashes upriver still.
>
> Poems written in age confuse the years.
> We all live, said Bashō, in a phantom dwelling.

The form enables a strong sense of contemplation as the poem comes to rest at the end of each stanza before beginning again with a related but non-consecutive thought. In her poem 'Brevity' (see Chapter 6 'Rhyme') Wright speaks of her attraction to 'honed brevities' and 'inclusive silences', and the limitations imposed by her version of the *ghazal* ensure terseness and a stoical self-containment.

THREE-LINE FORMS

As stanzas stretch to three lines, so that emphasis on brevity can give way to greater expansiveness. In Chapter 6, 'Rhyme' we have seen how *terza rima* separates stanzas whilst spinning a thread to bind them together. There are two kinds of three-line stanzas, the *triplet* and the *tercet*. The *triplet* is the more traditional form in that it rhymes all three lines in a *monorhyme*, *aaa bbb ccc*, etc. Prolific rhyme usually tends to the comic and the triplet is the form **John Donne** (?1571–1631) uses in his verse letters where he wants a comparatively informal, jocular tone. This is one of those 'are you still alive, why haven't you written' openings, 'To Mr T.W.':

> Pregnant again with th' old twins hope and fear,
> Oft have I asked for thee, both how and where
> Thou wert, and what my hopes of letters were[.]

But before we think the triplet an essentially cheery form we should look at **Thomas Hardy**'s (1840–1928) adaptation of it in his 'The Convergence of the Twain (Lines on the loss of the *Titanic*)'. Here, in the third stanza, he evokes the sunken liner on the ocean floor:

> Over the mirrors meant
> To glass the opulent
> The sea-worm crawls – grotesque, slimed, dumb, indifferent.

There is no skip to these lines. There's symmetry in the *monorhyme* and in the double length of line 3, but there is a sombre awkwardness to the rhythm. That long third line especially just seems to stare at us unblinkingly.

Tercet is a more general term for the three-line stanza which might include other rhyme-patterns such as *terza rima*, but, particularly in the twentieth century, the grouping need not be rhymed. **Wallace Stevens** (1879–1955) came to use the form extensively. As this quotation shows however, his tercets are often not self-contained units. The passages, like this from 'Notes Toward a Supreme Fiction: It Must Give Pleasure, V', frequently stretch themselves across the stanza divisions:

> The elephant
> Breaches the darkness of Ceylon with blares,
>
> The glitter-goes on surfaces of tanks,
> Shattering velvetest far-away. The bear,
> The ponderous cinammon, snarls in his mountain
>
> At summer thunder and sleeps through winter snow.

(Stevens, 1955)

In such a case we might wonder what the point of the stanza is? As these lines show, Stevens is often exotic in his imagery, but he can also be quite prosy, especially when his ideas are to the fore. In both moods his sentences often enlarge themselves, stretching that bit further and creating their own rhythmic period. Stevens was always interested in ideas of order set against the flux of the world – what he called elsewhere, 'the meaningless plungings of water and the wind' – and the seemingly arbitrary tercet imposes an orderliness upon the ranging of his thought and imagination. He writes of a 'blessed rage for order' and he has an obvious rage for symmetry since his tercets are often formed into larger sub-sections and those into yet larger ones. This is true of 'Notes Toward a Supreme Fiction' where they are gathered into sevens, the sevens into tens, and the tens into three large sections. He varies this slightly at the very end of this long poem, but the intuitive desire for shapeliness is always apparent, even if it is contending against the varied character of his sentences.

William Carlos Williams (1883–1963), was a freer versifier than his near-contemporary Stevens, but also, especially in his late career, developed his own version of three-part form. He saw this as part of a new *prosody* too elaborate to detail here, but one obvious feature is its visual element as he steps this poem, 'Asphodel, That Greeny Flower', down and across the page:

> I cannot say
> > that I have gone to hell
> > > for your love
> but often
> > found myself there
> > > in your pursuit.

> > > > > > (Williams, 1988)

FOUR-LINE FORMS

Four-line forms are usually known as *quatrains* and reckoned to be the most common verse form in European poetry. Before the twentieth century quatrains would normally be rhymed either *abab, abba* – the second sometimes known as *'envelope' rhyme* – or *aabb*. As we have seen, it is the usual structure for the *ballad*, but also for far too many tones and styles to itemize here. As a whole poem, the compact and balanced quality of the quatrain lends itself to the witty compression of the *epigram*. **Tony Harrison**'s (1937–) mordant quip on secret police listening-devices, 'The Bedbug', is a good modern example:

> Comrade, with your finger on the playback switch,
> Listen carefully to each love-moan,
> And enter in the file which cry is real, and which
> A mere performance for your microphone.

> > > > > > (Harrison, 1984)

By contrast the shorter lines of **Alfred Lord Tennyson**'s (1809–92) long poem of grief, 'In Memoriam', use the form for an utterly different emotional state:

I sometimes hold it half a sin
  To put in words the grief I feel;
  For words, like Nature, half reveal
And half conceal the Soul within.

There is a very delicate modulation in the third and fourth lines here as that parenthesis, 'like Nature', and the extra, internal rhyme *half conceal*, cause a catch in the voice of the stanza's regular progress.

Having looked at three- and four-line stanzas this is a good point to consider a pattern which combines them to produce a form in itself.

Originally a simple Italian and French 'rustic' song, the *villanelle* has been formalized, especially in the use English language poets have made of it. The modern villanelle has a nineteen-line pattern that uses *five tercets* and a *final quatrain*. Strictly, these rhyme *aba* throughout, and the first and third lines recur at fixed points later in the poem. These reiterations and refrains seem to lend themselves to slow, mournful subjects, such as **Dylan Thomas's** 'Do not go gentle into that good night' that we looked at in Chapter 6. Certainly these first lines from two of the twentieth century's most notable villanelles suggest as much:

Time will say nothing but I told you so

(Auden, 'If I could tell you')

It is the pain, it is the pain, endures.

(William Empson, 'Villanelle')

I wake to sleep, and take my waking slow.

(Theodore Roethke, 'The Waking')

Here, to demonstrate the whole form, is Thomas's complete villanelle with its remarkably tight structure. I have marked the recurring lines.

Do not go gentle into that good night,
Old age should burn and rave at close of day;
Rage, rage against the dying of the light.

Though wise men at their end know dark is right,
Because their words had forked no lightning they
Do not go gentle into that good night.

Good men, the last wave by, crying how bright
Their frail deeds might have danced in a green bay,
Rage, rage against the dying of the light.

Wild men who caught and sang the sun in flight,
And learn, too late, they grieved it on its way,
Do not go gentle into that good night.

Grave men, near death, who see the blinding sight
Blind eyes could blaze like meteors and be gay,
Rage, rage against the dying of the light.

And you, my father, there on the sad height,
Curse, bless, me now with your fierce tears, I pray.
Do not go gentle into that good night.
Rage, rage against the dying of the light.

(Thomas, 1952)

FIVE-, SIX-, SEVEN-LINE STANZAS

Of course there is no reason why a stanza might not consist of any number of lines. Thus we can have **five-line quintets, six-line sestets** and **seven-line septets**, and in many respects their effects will be similar to the *quatrain*. The obvious variation is between odd and even numbers. In his 'Songs of Experience' **William Blake** (1757–1827) can use the quintet to disrupt the expectations of evenness, the comforts of balance that the quatrain gives. This is from 'A Little Girl Lost':

To her father white
Came the maiden bright:
But his loving look,
Like the holy book
All her tender limbs with terror shook.

We do not expect a father's 'loving look' to bring terror, especially as the couplets seem to have a child-like simplicity. The disruption we then experience is mimed in that fifth, clashing longer line.

The *sestet*, *sexain*, or *sextain* is again a stanza form that can offer closure, most often by developing the subject through the first four lines, perhaps by running them on, and then using a rhyming couplet to cap it. The version in *iambic pentameter* rhyming *ababcc* is known as the *Venus and Adonis stanza* after Shakespeare's use of it in his narrative poem 'Venus and Adonis'. Here nearly every stanza is complete in itself advancing the story of Venus's unrequited desire for the bashful (or teasing) Adonis in mini-episodes. At this point Venus has just pulled Adonis – but only from his horse:

> The studded bridle on a ragged bough
> Nimbly she fastens – O, how quick is love!
> The steed is stallèd up, and even now
> To tie the rider she begins to prove.
>> Backward she pushed him, as she would be thrust,
>> And governed him in strength, though not in lust.

Wordsworth's famous poem 'I wandered lonely as a cloud', uses the same rhyme scheme but in *iambic tetrameter* and uses the closing couplet as he registers the sudden sight of lakeside daffodils:

> For oft, when on my couch I lie
> In vacant or in pensive mood,
> They flash upon that inward eye
> Which is the bliss of solitude;
> And then my heart with pleasure fills,
> And dances with the daffodils.

Versions of the *sestet* have been used by many twentieth-century poets but few have revised it to a particular purpose with such an arresting result as **Keith Douglas** (1920–44) in his war poem 'How to Kill'. His four stanzas are self-enclosed, except for a bridge in the middle of the poem between stanzas two and three. Here, as a tank-commander in the North African battlefield, he gives the order to fire, and

Death, like a familiar, hears

and look, has made a man of dust
of a man of flesh. This sorcery
I do. Being damned I am amused
to see the centre of love diffused
and the waves of love travel into vacancy.
How easy it is to make a ghost.

(Douglas, 1966)

Douglas rhymes *abccba,* an *'envelope'* scheme which encloses
the speaker's chilling confession of amusement at the instant
evaporation of the human target at its centre. The outside half-
rhymes, *dust / ghost,* also associate to convey the dissolution into
death.

Six lines also form the basis for one of the most interesting of
poetic forms the **sestina**. This began with the Provençal **troubadour**
poets of the Middle Ages, notably **Arnaut Daniel** who was at
work in the late 1100s. The sestina consists of *six, six-line, stanzas,*
and concludes with *an **envoi** of three lines.* In its English versions
it usually uses a ten-syllable line. However, instead of a rhyme
scheme, the sestina repeats a series of six *end words* in each stanza,
but in a fixed pattern of variation in which the sixth moves up to
first in the next stanza and the others take up other corresponding
positions. The three-line envoi then contains all the six repeated
words. So, the words at the end of the lines of 'Paysage Moralisé' by
W.H. Auden (1907–73) are arranged in this pattern:

St 1:	*valleys mountains water islands cities sorrow*
St 2:	*sorrow valleys cities mountains islands water*
St 3:	*water sorrow islands valleys mountains cities*
St 4:	*cities water mountains sorrow valleys islands*
St 5:	*islands cities valleys water sorrow mountains*
St 6:	*mountains islands sorrow cities water valleys*
Envoi:	It is our sorrow. Shall it melt? Then water
	Would gush, flush, green these mountains and these valleys,
	And we rebuild our cities, not dream of islands.

Normally too the last word of the poem is the same as the last word of its first line, though not in 'Paysage Moralisé'. In this poem however, five of the six words belong easily in the same field of meaning, and the addition of the sixth, *sorrow*, adds a potential emotional charge that pulses through the poem.

There is a relentless, incantatory quality to the sestina, one that is obviously sustained in the longer version of the double sestina. In her book *The Discovery of Poetry* Frances Mayes points out that the **numerology** of sixes probably had specific significance to mediaeval writers. She also shows how each word of the six appears in adjacent lines to every other word twice. Thus, if we construct a hexagon with the points ABCDEF, and draw diagonal lines indicating these pairings, we have a graphically perfect hexagon with a symmetrical pattern of interior triangles. This net, or cat's- cradle structure presents the poet with a tensile form to hold subjects that reverse and reflect upon themselves without necessary resolution.

The **seven-line** stanza, or *septet*, can vary metre and rhyme scheme, or indeed have none. In English the form became established by **Geoffrey Chaucer** (*c.* 1343–1400) in his long poem on the Trojan war, 'Troilus and Criseyde'. He derived the stanza from French models in which the form was traditionally used for formal celebration and came to have the name of *rhyme royal*. As Chaucer uses it, it has a ten-syllable line and rhymes *ababbcc* and has the alternative name of *Troilus stanza*. The stanza is large and flexible enough to serve many purposes and was widely used in English poetry, including by Shakespeare in another narrative poem 'The Rape of Lucrece', until the early seventeenth century. Some practitioners introduced a longer seventh line, an *alexandrine* of six beats instead of the usual five. We might sense this to be a kind of pediment, the three/three evenness of the beat giving a base to the stanza. **John Donne** does this in 'The Good Morrow', which with typical eccentricity he rhymes *ababccc*. **Wordsworth**, in 'Resolution and Independence', also employs the longer last line but with Chaucer's rhyme scheme:

> All things that love the sun are out of doors;
> The sky rejoices in the morning's birth;
> The grass is bright with rain-drops; – on the moors

> The hare is running races in her mirth;
> And with her feet she from the plashy earth
> Raises a mist; that, glittering in the sun,
> Runs with her all the way, wherever she doth run.

Later in this poem the stanza carries far different moods, though none more sober than the tone of **W.H. Auden** in his great poem 'The Shield of Achilles' in which he uses both seven and eight-line stanzas:

> A ragged urchin, aimless and alone,
>   Loitered about that vacancy, a bird
> Flew up to safety from his well-aimed stone:
>   That girls are raped, that two boys knife a third,
>   Were axioms to him, who'd never heard
> Of any world where promises were kept,
> Or one could weep because another wept.

Each stanza in this poem is self-contained, and in this instance we can see the poet's very deliberate space containing a remarkable summarizing range. Each line contains its own clear *image* or idea, but the stanza is not only a sequence but a coordinated, sorrowing vision of dehumanization. The stanza's fulcrum lies in its *syntax*, specifically that colon at the end of line three. It is from that point that the observation of the particular child moves on to generalization. The purpose of the enclosure of the stanza's room could not be better illustrated.

EIGHT-LINE STANZAS

Eight-line stanzas are dominated by a particular form of Italian origin still known as *ottava rima,* or, more rarely, *ottava toscana*. *Ottava rima* uses a ten-syllable line which rhymes *abababcc*. It is a form to be found in several European poetries and came into English with the enthusiasm for Italian literature and culture of the sixteenth-century Tudor poets such as **Sir Thomas Wyatt** (1503–42). It was used subsequently by many poets including **Milton,** who chooses *ottava rima* as a stabilizing orthodox stanza after the turbulent series of different shapes he has used throughout 'Lycidas' (see Chapter 6 'Rhyme'). There the form is used with the greatest gravity, though the final couplet has a definite upbeat effect:

> At last he rose and twitched his mantle blue:
> Tomorrow to fresh woods and pastures new.

George Gordon, Lord Byron (1788–1824) however finds a quite different tone possible. He called the form 'the half-serious rhyme', and from this fragment, written on the back of the manuscript of his great serio-comic poem 'Don Juan', we can see what he means.

> I would to Heaven that I were so much clay,
>   As I am blood, bone, marrow, passion, feeling –
> Because at least the past were passed away,
>   And for the future – (but as I write this reeling,
> Having got drunk exceedingly to-day,
>   So that I seem to stand upon the ceiling)
> I say – the future is a serious matter –
>   And so – for God's sake – hock and soda-water!

With the parenthesis, the verse seems to be running out of control in the queasiness of the speaker's hang-over, but the metre and rhyme scheme hold it together and the variation of tone shows what can be encompassed in this space. The six-two pattern of the *ottava rima* enables the development of an idea, or mood, in the six lines, and then, in the couplet, the chance of a decisive conclusion. But it has great flexibility too in that the couplet can swivel at the very last to take the tone and subject in a different direction as Byron does above. Alternatively the divisions can be muted over a larger span of stanzas to produce more continuity. Among modern poets to use the form is **W.B. Yeats** (1865–1939) in such poems as 'The Circus Animals Desertion' and 'Among School Children'.

An eight-line pattern that comprises a form in itself is the *triolet*. A French form, but pronounced in English to rhyme with 'get' and 'debt' – as **W.E. Henley** (1849–1903) does in his 'Easy is the triolet' – the form uses just two rhymes and repeats some lines. The rhyme scheme is *ABaAabAB*, with the capital letters indicating the repeated lines. Edmund Gosse calls the form 'a tiny trill of epigrammatic melody' and it is given to the quick-footed lightness that repeated rhymes always bring. **Hardy** uses it for bird-talk. This is his 'Birds at Winter Nightfall':

> **Around the house the flakes fly faster,**
> *And all the berries now are gone*
> From holly and cotonea-aster
> *Around the house. The flakes fly! – faster*
> Shutting indoors that crumb-outcaster
> We used to see upon the lawn
> **Around the house. The flakes fly faster,**
> *And all the berries now are gone*!

Hardy's punctuation and syntactic play with 'Around the house the flakes fly faster' is so playful it amounts almost to a *parody* of the form.

THE SONNET

Having looked at how *couplets*, *quatrains*, *sextets* and *ottava rima* work, we can move now to one of the most prominent and important of forms, and one which combines some or all of these elements: the *sonnet*. The sonnet has been, and continues to be, successful not only in English but in a wide variety of European languages. Again its name comes from Italian, *sonetto* meaning a little sound or song, and its origins lie in mediaeval Italian poetry. **Dante** (1265–1321) and **Petrarca (Petrarch)** (1304–74) established the form and it was popularized in English during the sixteenth century. Normally the sonnet in English has **fourteen lines** of *iambic pentameter*. In Italian the line is *hendecasyllabic* (eleven syllables), and the French sonnet uses the *alexandrine* (twelve syllables).

From this we can see that the Petrarchan sonnet can require as few as four rhyme sounds, *abcd*, whereas the Spenserian requires five, *abcde*, and the Shakespearean seven, *abcdefg*. In part this reflects the greater difficulty of rhyming in English as opposed to Italian which has a great predominance of *-o* and *-a* word-endings.

But the more significant distinction is in the *thought structure* of the different styles. The **Petrarchan** is essentially a two-part structure: an idea or subject is expounded in the octave, and then, with the change of rhyme there is a *volta*, or 'turn', after which the sestet responds to or resolves the opening proposition. The

---

There are three principal forms of sonnet.

1. The **Italian**, or **Petrarchan** style: fourteen lines in divisions of eight and six, the *octave* and the *sestet*. The octave rhymes *abbaabba*, and the sestet either *cdecde*, *cdccdc*, or patterns that avoid closing the poem with a couplet such as *cdcdcd*.

2. The **Spenserian**: fourteen lines in three quatrains and a couplet and rhyming *abab bcbc cdcd ee*.

3. The **Shakespearean**, or **English**: also foregrounds the quatrain/couplet pattern and rhymes *abab cdcd efef gg*.

---

limitation to only two sounds makes the octave very compact as the rhymes overlap.

The **Spenserian** and **Shakespearean** by contrast might be said to be more volatile. Here, the changes in rhyme-sound from quatrain to quatrain encourage new turns of thought, and a step-by-step movement towards the definite closure provided by the couplet. As with so many poetic forms this strict division into 8/6 and 4/4/4/2 types is too simple to describe all sonnets written in the two modes. Shakespeare for instance makes the second quatrain of Sonnet 90 rhyme *cccc*. Also he often offers a distinct turn of thought after line 8 just as he sometimes waits, as in Sonnet 129, until the *couplet* before his idea develops and resolves. But since the main distinction is between the Petrarchan 8/6 pattern and the 4/4/4/2 of the Spenserian and Shakespearean styles, I shall concentrate on comparing just the two types.

The sonnet tradition, especially when closest to the Italian models, is associated with the sixteenth and seventeenth centuries and with a certain manner of usually anguished love poetry. For my example of the *Petrarchan* style however I have chosen a twentieth-

century sonnet, a love poem but with a different tone. This is by
Edna St.Vincent Millay (1892–1950):

I, being born a woman and distressed	a
By all the needs and notions of my kind,	b
Am urged by your propinquity to find	b
Your person fair, and feel a certain zest	a
To bear your body's weight upon my breast:	a
So subtly is the fume of life designed,	b
To clarify the pulse and cloud the mind,	b
And leave me once again undone, possessed.	a
Think not for this, however, the poor treason	c
Of my stout blood against my staggering brain,	d
I shall remember you with love, or season	c
My scorn with pity, – let me make it plain:	d
I find this frenzy insufficient reason	c
For conversation when we meet again.	d

(Millay, 1992)

Millay's sonnet demonstrates the function of the turn after line
eight to perfection. The *octave* bears witness to the erotic force
still exerted by the speaker's lover. Then in the sestet she musters
her 'staggering brain' to resist the conquering sexual attraction to
someone she evidently feels is bringing her nothing but distress.
This balance in the poem also represents the see-saw between heart
and head, body and mind, sexual urge and good sense, that suffuses
the whole poem. On the one hand she can choose very controlled,
distant words like 'propinquity' to refer to being physically close,
and then confess to being 'once again undone, possessed.' For the
conclusion, which, though it is not a couplet, is clinched in the
last two lines, she manages a put-down so haughty she might
be returning a visiting-card. However we always feel that the
control mimed by this carefully controlled sonnet is hard-won and
precarious. We feel that as soon as the last full-stop goes down she
might collapse.

The sonnet seems particularly suited to walking this fine line
between self-control and tumultuous emotion. We see it often in

Shakespeare's sonnets where we can frequently read a counter-implication beneath the ostensible argument. Here, employing of course the *quatrain* and *couplet* pattern of the **English** sonnet, is his Sonnet 138:

When my love swears that she is made of truth	*a*
I do believe her, though I know she lies,	*b*
That she might think me some untutored youth,	*a*
Unlearnèd in the world's false subtleties.	*b*
Thus vainly thinking that she thinks me young,	*c*
Although she knows my days are past the best,	*d*
Simply I credit her false-speaking tongue;	*c*
On both sides thus is simple truth suppressed.	*d*
But wherefore says she not she is unjust?	*e*
And wherefore say not I that I am old?	*f*
O, love's best habit is in seeming trust,	*e*
And age in love loves not to have years told.	*f*
Therefore I lie with her, and she with me,	*g*
And in our faults by lies we flattered be.	*g*

In this poem the lovers are exchanging duplicities. He, the speaker, is pretending to be younger than he is whilst she is pretending that she is faithful to him. But he knows she is unfaithful and she knows he is not so youthful. Moreover he knows that she knows this, just as she knows that he knows of her unfaithfulness, and this 'he knows that she knows that he knows …' goes on and on. The final couplet suggests that they get by with this tacit understanding, *lying* together in both senses of the term. The sonnet structure is good for argument and here its phases enable this mutual deceit to be revealed layer by layer. But is the speaker as worldly, even cynical, as he maintains? Do we also sense an emotional discomfort: anxiety about the fragility of the relationship, the pain of betrayal, the deep embarrassment of dishonesty?

Love has not been the sole subject in the sonnet tradition however. **Milton** and **Wordsworth** used the Petrarchan form to write polemical political sonnets. Like **Donne**, **Gerard Manley Hopkins** (1884–1899) found the argumentative capacity of the sonnet fit for his tussles with his conscience and God, and the intense emotion of his 'terrible sonnets' batter and strain the form to its utmost.

Another important feature of the sonnet in all its styles is the prevalence of *sequences*. Following Petrarch's example, Spenser, Sidney, Shakespeare and many other Elizabethan poets composed their sonnets into extensive sequences, usually exploring different aspects of one theme. This has been continued in such series as **Elizabeth Barrett Browning**'s (1806–61) 'Sonnets from the Portuguese', **George Meredith**'s (1828–1909) 'Modern Love', which varies the structure by adding two lines, and by many twentieth-century poets besides Millay including **Allen Tate** (1899–1979), **John Berryman** (1914–72), **Robert Lowell** (1917–77), **Geoffrey Hill** (1932–) and **Marilyn Hacker** (1942–). **Tony Harrison**'s sequence 'The School of Eloquence', ongoing over many years, uses a sixteen-line iambic pentameter pattern, strictly rhymed but stretching the form extensively in regard to vocabulary and line-endings, and covering a remarkable range of personal and social themes. **James K. Baxter** (1926–72) divides his thirty-nine 'Jerusalem Sonnets' into pairs of lines, sometimes rhyming, and other modern sonneteers such as **Ted Berrigan** (1934–83) ruffle the form yet more radically. 'The Sand Coast Sonnets' of **Les Murray** (1938–) include several styles, including one with fifteen lines, and indeed in his exuberant hymn to extravagance, 'The Quality of Sprawl', he cites as an example 'The fifteenth to twenty-first / lines in a sonnet, for example.'

But the attraction of the sequence persists, not merely because of tradition, but perhaps because of the opportunity to write extensively to related themes, even over many years, and to do so in a way that presents lots of new beginnings. It does not need the thread of **narrative**, even if each sonnet contains a little 'story' in its set progress. Rather the sequence enables fresh angles, different tones from the intimate and meditative to the comic and polemical. When written over time, for both writer and reader there is the nice juxtaposition of continuity of form against the other likely changes in subject, mood or style. This large-scale attraction of the sequence counterparts the enduring appeal of its component parts: the flux that can be contained – sometimes only just – within the single sonnet's walls.

NINE-LINE STANZAS

Returning to our numerical progress, nine lines would at first seem an arbitrary choice for a stanza. Just as we can see how the sonnet might plausibly be extended to sixteen lines but, *pace* Les Murray, not fifteen, so a nine-line stanza seems to lack the satisfying symmetry of even numbers. In fact the form devised by **Edmund Spenser** (?1552–99) for his long, fantastical narrative poem 'The Faerie Queene', proved successful not only for his poem but for many subsequent poets.

The **Spenserian stanza** comprises nine iambic lines: eight *iambic pentameters* and one, closing, **hexameter**. The rhyme scheme is *ababbcbcc*. In common with its nearest relative, *ottava rima*, the stanza is short enough to be pointed and precise, and ample enough for description and dilation. The ninth, longer, line has the effect of securing the footing of the stanza against its seeming imbalance. Here 'the gentle knight' confronts a monster:

> Therewith she spewd out of her filthie maw   [mouth]
> A floud of poison horrible and blacke,
> Full of great lumps of flesh and gobbets raw,
> Which stunck so vildly, that it forst him slacke   [vilely]
> His grasping hold, and from her turne him backe.
> Her vomit full of bookes and papers was,
> With loathly frogs and toades, which eyes did lacke,
> And creeping sought way in the weedy gras:
> Her filthie parbreake all the place defiled has.   [vomit]

Spenser's verse is notably sensuous in its descriptions and it was perhaps that association which drew some of the Romantic poets to imitate his stanza. **John Keats** (1795–1821) did so in 'The Eve of St. Agnes', and **Percy Bysshe Shelley** (1792–1822) chose the form for his elegy to Keats, 'Adonais':

> He will awake no more, oh, never more! –
> Within the twilight chamber spreads apace
> The shadow of white Death, and at the door
> Invisible Corruption waits to trace
> His extreme way to her dwelling-place;
> There eternal Hunger sits, but pity and awe
> Soothe her pale rage, nor dares she to deface
> So fair a prey, till darkness, and the law
> Of change, shall o'er his sleep the mortal curtain draw.

Both Spenser and Shelley use the length of the stanza to its utmost to unfurl long sentences whose controlled syntax is enhanced by the discipline of the few permitted rhymes.

Modern poets introduce more variation into stanzas clearly inspired by these examples. **Robert Lowell** (1917–77) employs only four rhymes in this poem, based on the hellfire sermons of the eighteenth century Massachussetts preacher Jonathan Edwards, 'Mr. Edwards and the Spider'. He places them mainly in the pattern of *ababcccdd*, and varies his line length whilst retaining Spenser's final hexameter:

> What are we in the hands of the angry God?
> It was in vain you set up thorn and briar
> In battle array against the fire
> And treason crackling in your blood:
> For the wild thorns grow tame
> And will do nothing to oppose the flame;
> Your lacerations tell the losing game
> You play against the sickness past your cure.
> How will the hands be strong? How will the heart endure?

Lowell also follows his predecessors in his grand tone, but just how different a register can be struck in this type of stanza can be heard in these lines from **Philip Larkin**'s (1922–85) 'Church Going'. Out on an excursion, the speaker has paused to venture into an empty church:

Yet stop I did: in fact I often do,
And always end much at a loss like this,
Wondering what to look for; wondering, too,
When churches fall completely out of use
What we shall turn them into, if we shall keep
A few cathedrals chronically on show,
Their parchment, plate and pyx in locked cases,
And let the rest rent-free to rain and sheep.
Shall we avoid them as unlucky places?

(Larkin, 1988; 2003)

Larkin uses the stanza in a deliberately understated way. Indeed it's easy to read the familiar manner of these lines with its commonplace phrases like 'in fact', 'at a loss' and 'out of use', without noticing how carefully it is crafted. For instance, at first sight – or hearing – the stanza appears to have an odd unrhymed sixth line, *show*. The rest of the poem reveals the same pattern until we notice that *show* can be heard as a half-rhyme with the *a* rhymes, *do* and *too*, and that this pattern obtains throughout the poem, mainly with half-rhymes like *on/stone/organ* and *font/don't/meant*. It is as though Larkin's structure is half-hidden from eye and ear.

Why? Maybe it is a game he is playing with himself and the reader in which he strikes a bluff, common-man pose, as unpretentious and unpoetical as can be, but quietly belies this by exercising such subtle but recognizable skill. Maybe too he needs the demands of the form as a discipline in composition. He is wedded to 'ordinary speech' in his choice of words and phrase, but in order to guard against an ease that might become just sloppy, he imposes these unobtrusive restraints upon himself to reach further levels of concentration. As with the demands of all set forms, Larkin's acceptance of these limits might be pushing him towards articulating more interesting things than he would otherwise say.

We could continue our progress through successive stanza lengths to examine **ten-line** stanzas such as those **A.D. Hope** (1907–2000) employs in his 'On an Engraving by Casserius'; the ingenious, **eleven-line** stanza of **John Donne's** 'The Relic'; and on to the enormous elaboration of Spenser's **eighteen-line** stanzas of his marriage hymn 'Epithalamium' with its variations of line-length and mixture of **plain** and **interlaced** rhyming. However the main features and resources of the longer stanza forms are by now established, so I will turn to some other line sequences which, like the sonnet, are forms in themselves.

RONDEAU AND RONDEL

The **rondeau** and the **rondel** are often associated with the **triolet** (see above) and also have their origin in mediaeval French poetry. Like much poetry their ancestry is in song, and especially the dance-songs of *rondes* or rounds.

Formalized into a literary convention, the **rondeau** became a fifteen-line form divided into a *quintet*, a *quatrain* and a *sestet*, and employing just two rhymes. A further distinguishing feature is that the first line is half-repeated at lines nine and fifteen. Experiment with these French forms was popular among English poets of the late nineteenth century, and again we can find **Hardy** using the form in 'The Roman Road':

> The Roman road runs straight and bare
> As the pale parting-line in hair
> Across the heath. And thoughtful men
> Contrast its days of Now and Then,
> And delve, and measure, and compare;
>
> Visioning on the vacant air
> Helmed legionaries, who proudly rear
> The Eagle, as they pace again
>   The Roman Road.
>
> But no tall brass-helmed legionnaire
> Haunts it for me. Uprises there
> A mother's form upon my ken,
> Guiding my infant steps, as when
> We walked that ancient thoroughfare,
>   The Roman Road.

A Roman road is a fine ancient subject weighted with significance. But in his typically contrary way Hardy upsets this expectation by saying that its meaning for him lies wholly in a childhood memory of his mother. The shift comes with that angular, almost awkward, 'Uprises there …' By the time 'The Roman Road' comes round for the third time its associations have become quite different.

The vestiges of these forms' beginnings in dance are surely visible in their continual return to where they begin. The first two of the *rondel*'s fourteen lines recur in the last two lines of the second quatrain, and in the last two of the third and last section which is a sestet. **Austin Dobson**'s (1840–1921) 'Too hard it is to sing' is an example. Confusingly, his near-contemporary **Algernon Charles Swinburne** (1837–1909), introduced a variant he called a *roundel* and wrote a 'century' of them, some lamenting the death of the composer Wagner. By this time though we are surely exhausting knowledge that might truly be called basic, though readers who want to see how a present-day poet employs the form might seek out **Sophie Hannah**'s (1971–) 'The End of Love' which works enjoyably round the refrain 'The end of love should be a big event. / It should involve the hiring of a hall.'

BORROWING FORMS

Scanning these different types of stanza and free-standing poetic forms, we can see how often their origins are in other languages and how much interchange there is between these different poetries. We have seen this kind of commerce over and over again in all aspects of poetic form: in poetry national and linguistic borders have always been highly permeable. Stanza form, because it relies much less upon the particular characteristics of a language (in contrast to the line, or rhyme for instance) passes back and forth very readily. Most transference involving the English language is with European models, but, as we have seen with the *haiku* (see above Chapter 2, 'Deliberate Space'), and the *ghazal* earlier in this chapter, other traditions have also been influential.

The *pantoum* is the Europeanization of the Malay form *pantun*. This is based in four-line form which rhymes *ab ab*, but it also includes internal rhymes and various kinds of correspondences between images and ideas. This translation is from Ruth Finnegan's excellent anthology *The Penguin Book of Oral Poetry*.

> Broken the pot, there's still the jar,
>> Where folk can come and wash their feet.
> And when the mynah's flown afar,
>> For comfort there's the parakeet.

In addition to the end rhymes, there is *jar/mynah*, and *come/comfort*, and these correspondences match the overall idea of compensation: the pot is broken, there is the jar; the mynah bird goes, there is still the parakeet.

In its European versions the **pantoum** consists of quatrains in which the second and fourth lines of each stanza become the first and third lines of the next, and so on. Eventually the very first line will reappear as the poem's last line and the third line of the poem as the third last. The form is too long to illustrate here but over its length it contrives a criss-crossing, mesmeric quality.

INVENTING STANZAS AND THE VERSE PARAGRAPH

The tension between containment and expansion is present in all these stanzas and their related forms. The history of poetry shows a nearly regular alternation between these competing demands. Here I want to compare a poem that uses most features of strict stanzaic shaping, but does so over a whole poem that has no given definition, with a passage that is not stanzaic at all but would be better called a *verse paragraph*.

The first is **Andrew Marvell**'s (1621–78) poem 'The Coronet'.

> When for the thorns with which I long, too long,
>> With many a piercing wound,
>> My saviour's head have crowned,
> I seek with garlands to redress that wrong:
>> Through every garden, every mead,   [field]
> I gather flowers (my fruits are only flowers),
>> Dismantling all the fragrant towers   [head-dresses]
> That once adorned my shepherdess's head.

And now when I have summed up all my store,
   Thinking (so I myself deceive)
   So rich a chaplet thence to weave   [coronet]
As never yet the king of glory wore:
   Alas, I find the serpent old
   That, twining in his speckled breast,
   About the flowers disguised does fold,
   With wreaths of fame and interest.
Ah, foolish man, that wouldst debase with them,
And mortal glory, heaven's diadem!
But thou who only couldst the serpent tame,
Either his slippery knots at once untie;
And disentangle all his winding snare;
Or shatter too with him my curious frame,
And let these wither, so that he may die,
Though set with skill and chosen out with care:
That they, while thou on both their spoils dost tread,
May crown thy feet, that could not crown thy head.

There is no point in pretending that this poem is easy. It is usually thought that poetry is betrayed by paraphrase, but this is the kind of arguing poem that benefits from our trying to put it into our own words.

The argument, I believe, goes like this. The poet, conscious that his sins have long served to add to the pain from the crown of thorns of his saviour Christ, resolves to make amends by turning from writing light love-verses addressed to his 'shepherdess' to poems glorifying Christ. Thus, in the system of *images* the poem employs, he will no longer make 'garlands' for her head, but a coronet of flowers to replace the crown of thorns. But, as he does so, he realizes that this new ambition is in truth driven by selfish 'fame and interest', that Satan, 'the serpent old' is subverting him. Finally he is reminded that only Christ can tame, 'disentangle', Satan's 'winding snare', and that in crushing Satan underfoot Christ will also tread on the poet's vain verses. Thus, paradoxically, the poem that was meant as a 'coronet' will crown Christ's feet rather than his head.

It is a testing, complex argument and this is engrossed in the structure of the verse and of the *syntax*. First the verse moves between *iambic pentameter* and the sharper, more emphatic three and four-beat lines. Secondly the rhyme scheme alters from the *envelope* pattern of *abba* to an *interlaced*, entangled pattern from where 'the serpent old' appears in line 13. This resolves briefly into plainness again with the exclamatory *couplet* 'Ah, foolish man, that wouldst debase with them, / And mortal glory heaven's diadem!', only to overlap again in the lines about Satan's 'slippery knots' and 'winding snare'. Finally, as the poem reaches its closing assertion, simplicity is restored with the couplet:

> That they, while thou on both their spoils dost tread,
> May crown thy feet, that could not crown thy head.

The poem's sentence structure is equally complex. The first sixteen lines consist of just two real sentences, each eight lines long. The first has the main verb 'I seek' and the second 'I find'. As he struggles to establish his task, and then to overcome the unsuspected pride that is undermining his good intentions, the poet wrestles through elaborate sentences beset with parentheses and subordinate clauses. Even the final sentence, the last eight lines, is not structurally straightforward but fights through more elaborate obstruction before arriving at the paradox that his flowers – that is his verses – must be withered and trodden underfoot to fulfil their proper function. Of course the whole poem can then be seen as a paradox since it cannot help but be the poem that the poet *says* he despises. Both the stanza and sentence structure of what the poet calls 'my curious frame', are tortuous, even tortured, as the work struggles to make sense of its contradictions. I'm tempted to say there was no ready-made stanza pattern that could accommodate Marvell's effort here, but that he needed this complex patterning to embody the difficulty of ideas and feeling. A 'freer' form would not do.

We can see such a 'freer' form however in the *verse paragraph* that displaces stanza form in much Romantic poetry. 'Frost at Midnight' is one of the poems **Samuel Taylor Coleridge** (1772–1834) called 'a conversation poem'. In some ways the relaxation into blank verse and the abandonment of stanza patterns by Wordsworth, Coleridge, and, before them, such poets as **James Thomson** (1700–48), is a return to the resources of Elizabethan blank verse, and even more so to the example of Milton. But whilst Wordsworth especially often sought Milton's grander notes, part of his and Coleridge's revolutionary poetic enterprise in *The Lyrical Ballads* of 1798 was, as we saw in Chapter 3 'Tones of Voice', to find an easier, more commonplace **register** for both description and meditation. Here is the last part of 'Frost at Midnight' in which the poet is speaking over his sleeping child:

> Therefore all seasons shall be sweet to thee,
> Whether the summer clothe the general earth
> With greenness, or the redbreast sit and sing
> Betwixt the tufts of snow on the bare branch
> Of mossy apple-tree, while the nigh thatch
> Smokes in the sun-thaw; whether the eave-drops fall
> Heard only in the trances of the blast,
> Or if the secret ministry of frost
> Shall hang them up in silent icicles,
> Quietly shining to the quiet moon.

This paragraph is the shortest of the four that comprise the poem's seventy-four lines. Clearly the poet has not been tempted into symmetry of organization. It is unrhymed and uses a **decasyllabic** line which is fundamentally **iambic** but with a high proportion **trochaic** inversions (the opening of lines 1, 2 and 6) and uncommon stress patterns in the second half of lines 4 and 5. Looking to the future of his child, the poet is in a reverie of hopefulness. The ten lines are but one sentence in which the assertion 'all seasons shall be sweet to thee' is the heart of the main clause. The seasons are then illustrated through the slow series of descriptive clauses in which details like the robin 'betwixt the tufts of snow', and the steam of 'the sun-thaw', seem to emerge as perfect **images** before his dreaming eye. But the slow stream of the sentence does not dribble away. The gentle action of the final image, 'the secret ministry of frost' hanging the icicles from the house-eaves, is strong enough to balance the sentence. The very last line,

Quietly **shin**ing to the **qui**et **Moon**

has just those four firm stresses, and, this, combined with the simple effect of repeating 'quiet', produces a wonderful sense of peace. The verse paragraph, by dispensing with so many of the staples of stanza-form, can risk becoming flatly 'prosy'. But in 'Frost at Midnight' we can see how the comparative looseness of the structure suits the movement of the poet's mind, his conversation with himself. Yet the line is still vital. That last line in particular shows us how the separate definition of the line gains an effect not available in prose.

The poet **Donald Davie** (1922–1995), also one of the most perceptive and rewarding readers of poetry, writes in his book *Purity of Diction in English Verse*, that Coleridge's 'conversation' poems signal 'one of the most momentous changes in the history of poetry'. It marks, he claims, the end of the '***Renaissance*** conviction about the poem as a made thing, thrown free of its maker … The poet hereafter is legislator, seer, scapegoat and reporter; he is no longer an artificer.' It is true that in the twentieth-century '*free verse*' largely jettisoned stanza-form as part of its liberation, and in the next chapter we shall be considering the nature and implications of this 'freedom' for poetry and the poet.

However it is striking how often in non-metrical and unrhymed verse line-groupings are routinely employed in poetry written in the 'modern' era. For my final instance of stanza-form I have chosen a twentieth century poem which patterns line, and rhyme into a highly individual shape, and one as subtle and demanding as any in the history of poetry. The poem is 'What Are Years?' by **Marianne Moore** (1887–1972).

> What is our innocence,
> what is our guilt? All are
>   naked, none is safe. And whence
> is courage: the unanswered question,
> the resolute doubt, –
> dumbly calling, deafly listening – that
> in misfortune, even death,
>   encourages others
>   and in its defeat, stirs
>
>   the soul to be strong? He
> sees deep, and is glad, who

accedes to mortality
and in his imprisonment rises
upon himself as
the sea in a chasm, struggling to be
free and unable to be,
    in its surrendering
    finds its continuing.

    So he who strongly feels,
behaves. The very bird,
    grown taller as he sings, steels
his form straight up. Though he is captive,
his mighty singing
says, satisfaction is a lowly
thing, how pure a thing is joy.
    This is mortality,
    this is eternity.

(Moore, 1984)

Because of the way these enigmatic sentences run across the strangely uneven lines, we might not much notice the rhymes, though some, *to be* / *to be* are **monorhymes** and others, *others* / *stirs* are **half rhymes**. We will quickly see that the poem comprises three nine-line stanzas, but until we look closely we might not see that these employ a *syllabic* pattern to define the lines, and that this is symmetrical. This is the architectonic pattern of the poem:

#	Stanza 1 No. sylls.	Rhyme	Stanza 2 No. sylls.	Rhyme	Stanza 3 No. sylls	Rhyme
1	6	a	6	a	6	a
2	6	b	6	b	6	b
3	7	a	7	a	7	a
4	9	c	9	c	9	c
5	5	d	5	d	5	d
6	9	d	9	a	9	e
7	7	e	7	a	7	f
8	6	f	6	e	6	e
9	6	f	6	e	6	e

If we look at the syllabic pattern we can see that each stanza is organized in exactly the same way. The first two and the last two lines of each stanza have the same number of syllables (6) as do the third and seventh (7) and the fourth and sixth (9). Only the fifth, middle, line stands alone with five syllables. Since the poem consists of three nine-line stanzas, and each stanza contains three different syllable groups – aside from the solitary fifth – it looks likely that the sense of the ratio 3:9 is important to the poem's building even without trying to attach any significance to these numbers themselves. Especially if it is turned through 90 degrees, this gives each stanza an arching shape centring on the solitary line:

In its latent visual shape what we have here is the ghost of an **emblem**, or even a **concrete** poem, but one that is still intensely centred on **semantics**. Those three centre lines are: *the resolute doubt // upon himself as // his mighty singing*, but lacking a verb we can't make syntactic sense of this. However, if we see the poem as an effortful, determined acceptance, and therefore defiance of death, realized in stanza three through the image of the captive bird rising and steeling himself to sing, then we can see that the *mighty singing* the bird takes *upon himself* constitutes the powerful paradox of *resolute doubt*. Looking at the last words of the unrhymed lines in each stanza we see: *are / question / death // who / rises / as // bird / captive / singing / joy*. Again we might read the heart of the poem's statement through this vertical axis. (If the third stanza had only three unrhymed lines like the first two, then the 3:9 ratio would have another dimension and the puzzling analyst's cup would run over. Perhaps it is significant that it is the word *joy* that surpasses symmetry.)

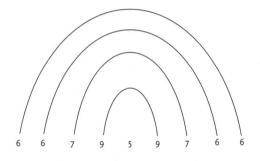

6 6 7 9 5 9 7 6 6

There is I believe a strong element of the puzzle in Moore's poem, including its concealed architecture. It has a problem-setting mischievous quality perhaps meant to belie the seriousness of its subject. This subject – mortality and how to face up to it – is difficult to approach without platitude and involves its own tensions. Under these pressures the poem is both awkward and elegant: awkward at first reading with those odd lines with their abrupt, anti-syntactical breaks, but eventually elegant as we come to see its underlying architecture. The poem shows there is no contradiction between the force of emotion and idea and the shaping of expression: 'So he who strongly feels, / behaves.'

CONCLUSION

Set forms can at first seem daunting to the beginning poet. Nonetheless *practice* within some of them can teach writers and readers important lessons about the possibilities of verbal pressure. Also they provide a different sort of liberation in that the page before us is not so intimidatingly blank. We have a shape to fill, lines of demarcation and an end in sight. To feel this it is not necessary to plunge into complex forms like the villanelle or sestina. Simply accepting a determinant such as a fixed number of words, perhaps on the model of another poem, can suffice to sense the concentration of poetic expression. Like all these poets before us we will then gain the experience of surprising ourselves with the words we find when we must think twice, or three, or more times before we can make the fit.

> **SUMMARY**
>
> In this chapter on the stanza we have looked at:
> - Definitions of the stanza as space and as pause, and its mnemonic qualities.
> - Its use in dialogue forms.
> - A series of stanzas ranging from one-line forms to longer, complex forms.
> - Several forms related to stanza-form but distinct in themselves, notably the sonnet.
> - Examples of forms borrowed from other poetries.
> - Invented stanza-forms and the use of the verse-paragraph.

FURTHER READING

Davie, Donald (1952; 1992) *Purity of Diction in English Verse*, Part II, I, Harmondsworth: Penguin Books.

Furniss, Tom and Bath, Michael (1996) *Reading Poetry, An Introduction*, Hemel Hempstead: Prentice Hall/Harvester Wheatsheaf, see Chapter 12 'The Sonnet'.

Hopkins, G.M. (1970) *The Poems of Gerard Manley Hopkins*, Gardner, W.H and Mackenzie, N.H. (eds), Oxford: Oxford University Press, see the religious 'terrible sonnets'.

Mayes, Frances (1987) *The Discovery of Poetry*, Orlando, FL: Harcourt, Brace, Jovanovich, see Chapter 8, 'Traditional and Open Forms'.

Millay, Edna St Vincent (1992) *Selected Poems*, Manchester: Carcanet Press.

Shakespeare, William (1986) *The Sonnets and A Lover's Complaint*, Kerrigan, J. (ed.), Harmondsworth: Penguin.

IMAGE – IMAGINATION
– INSPIRATION

What is man's body? It is a spark from the fire
It meets water and it is put out.
What is man's body? It is a bit of straw
It meets fire and is burnt.
What is man's body? It is a bubble of water
Broken by the wind.

(A Gond poem, from central India)

IMAGE AND METAPHOR

We might call someone *'daft as a brush'*; a mother feeling the child in her womb as specially vigorous might say it's *'like a frog in a sock'*; faced with an important decision we often say we are *'at the crossroads'*; on a good day *'things are looking up'*. All these phrases are making use of the figure of speech known as ***metaphor***. There are many different types of metaphor but they share the characteristic of *saying one thing in terms of another*. At the heart of metaphor, the *vehicle* which connects the subject of the utterance with the quality being evoked, is an ***image***: the brush, the lemon, the crossroads, the act of lifting the eyes. In the poem at the head of this chapter our body is first a spark, then a piece of straw then a bubble.

Metaphor is often seen to be the essence of the 'poetic', and prose that is coloured in such ways is often labelled 'poetic'. But poetry does not have a monopoly on metaphor, or upon the vivid evocations of descriptive imagery. The historian **Bede** (?672–735) likened human life to the flight of a bird that happens to swoop through a window and crosses a lighted hall before disappearing once more into the dark. Daily speech and prose of many kinds will often try to 'paint pictures' and to use metaphor, and not only to decorate a passage. Metaphor and its infinite variety of images is intrinsic to human language, and because consciousness of language is inseparable from poetry, we are bound to look at how it works, and at some of the interesting questions that follow.

At its simplest, in the *simile*, the metaphoric connection is explicitly made by using 'like' or 'as'. Here **Anne Askew** (1521–46) begins her poem 'The Ballad Which Anne Askew Made and Sang When She Was in Newgate' with a simile:

> Like as the armèd knight
> Appointed to the field,
> With this world will I fight
> And faith shall be my shield.

In other works the metaphorical intention will be more implicit and sometimes more sustained, as in this anonymous lyric, 'The Silver Swan', dated at 1612:

> The silver swan, who living had no note,
> When death approached, unlocked her silent throat;
> Leaning her breast against the reedy shore,
> Thus sung her first and last, and sung no more:
> 'Farewell, all joys; Oh death, come close mine eyes;
> More geese than swans now live, more fools than wise.'

Whatever sad event or melancholy mood inspired the poet, we will read this as a human lament. The swan is a *figure* through which the human voice complains not only of death, but of the condition of the world she leaves behind. The notion that the swan is mute until its last moments presents the neat poignancy, especially for a poet, of first words being last words and vice versa. Perhaps too the swan's muteness is a figure of restraint which makes her final condemnation of the world that much more powerful.

'The Silver Swan' works as an extended metaphor, or *conceit*, that is a figure of speech that is carried on beyond one moment's likening to develop a substantial idea.

'*Conceit*' is an interesting word in this context. The word has two other tendencies within its meanings. First it can mean an idea, or conception, but we are most likely to think of a second sense associated with self-regard and vanity. Our literary term has something of both implications for it carries an idea, but the working through of the metaphor is likely to display an ingenuity which some readers will find affected and self-admiring, as though the poet is keener to show off than to say something significant. Seventeenth-century poetry has often been disparaged for being 'lost in conceits', and the *Oxford English Dictionary* quotes one commentator who praises the classical Greek poets for ignoring such fancy elaboration: 'they did not call the waves "nodding hearse-plumes" … or laburnums "dropping wells of fire".'

WORDS AND 'THINGS AS THEY ARE'

This takes us deep into one of the most ancient controversies about poetry, and indeed language. The essence of human language is that it puts one 'thing' in place of another 'thing', that is that it makes unrelated sounds – and later their accompanying visual symbols – stand in for objects in the world and for what occurs in our minds. Metaphor – this further 'standing in place of' – extends this remove. Words are already images of the things they represent – 'signifiers' of what they signify – but metaphors are images of images. Writing on the theory of art in Book 10 of *The Republic*, the Greek philosopher **Plato** (327–247 BC), saw 'poetic' language as *refracting* reality. He likened this crucial difference between how a thing is and how words can represent it to the way refraction makes a stick look bent when it is put in water. This difference made Plato and other philosophers and other thinkers uneasy. They worry that the capacity of language to invent and elaborate, for its sounds and images to work upon the emotions, can carry us away from reality and truth.

The developing scientific culture of the seventeenth century also put a high premium on simple clarity in speaking and writing and set its face against 'the easie vanitie of fine speaking'. Sir Thomas Sprat in *The History of the Royal Society* (1667) complained of the 'many mists and uncertainties these specious Tropes and Figures have brought on our Knowledge'. Rather than 'pretty conceits' (it is interesting that the feminizing adjective 'pretty' is often applied here) we should aim, argued Sprat, for a plain, direct language which has 'as many words as there be things', and no more.

RHETORIC

Despite these anxieties, the Greeks, and every part of western culture since, has acknowledged and sought to deploy the power of words. So much of social life, and especially public life, involves persuasion. As soon as a parent encounters the question 'why?' at least some part of her response is going to involve persuasion. Teachers must find ways of engaging their pupils in their subject, lawyers seek to convince juries and of course politicians aim to sway us towards voting for them. All are using *rhetoric*: that is language shaped to persuade.

The full effect however has never been confined simply to the words themselves. The great Athenian orator, **Demosthenes** (383–22BC) is said to have had to overcome a stutter, and legend says he did so by practising his delivery with a pebble in his mouth and pitching his voice against the sound of the sea. Nowadays all manner of public figures take advice on how to present themselves on television and elsewhere. The *pitch* of the voice and the choice of a jacket are part of rhetorical effect, part indeed of another, newer sense of 'image'.

But our primary interest here is with the verbal dimension of rhetoric. We have already explored how different tones such as anger, pathos, humour, can be represented in poetic forms (Chapter 3 'Tones of Voice'). Within these registers orators deploy particular constructions of phrase for effect. They might for instance begin a series of sentences in exactly the same way. **Martin Luther King**'s (1929–68) celebrated civil rights speech which reiterates the phrase 'I have a dream that ... I have dream that ... I have a dream today' at the opening of each paragraph is an example of this. Such devices – or rhetorical figures – are quite deliberate, and many generations of students and orators, following the models of antiquity like Demosthenes and the Roman **Cicero** (106–43BC), practised them assiduously and knew all their specific names. One of them, *anaphora* – the figure used by King in his speech – we have encountered in a variety of contexts already.

We do not need to explore the particulars of classical rhetoric here. But it is important to recognize that there is a long tradition in which its deliberate strategies are also part of poetry. The Roman orator Cicero declared that 'the poet is very near kinsman of the orator' by which he meant that both aim to use all the resources of language, both intellectual and sensuous, to persuade the listener or reader.

Of course if we become too aware of the design the poet or orator has upon us then we might recoil, thinking that we are being got at, even conned. This is why we often use the word 'rhetoric' pejoratively, as in 'that's just rhetoric', meaning that the words sound good but lack substance. For a poet like **Alexander Pope**, who worked with the grain of this classical rhetorical tradition, devices must appear to arise in the argument simply to clarify what we can readily recognize as true. He puts it neatly in these lines from 'An Essay on Criticism':

> True wit is Nature to advantage dressed,
> What oft was thought, but ne'er so well expressed;
> Something whose truth convinced at sight we find,
> That gives us back the image of our mind.

But the eighteenth century *neo-classical* tradition Pope represents sees poetry as at heart rhetorical: that is that it consciously deploys the armoury of *metre, rhythm, syntax, metaphor, image, tone*, word choice and word sound in the interests of clarity and argument. Moreover this implies an actual or potential consensus of poet and audience. The audience will recognize in the poet's words what they in fact already knew to be true. Moreover it is the character of poetry, through its own techniques, to be especially impressive and memorable. At the end of his 'Anatomy of the World' **John Donne** evokes God speaking to the prophet Moses

> ...   He spake
> To Moses, to deliver unto all,
> That song: because he knew they would let fall

> The Law, the prophets, and the history,
> But keep the song still in their memory.

The 'song', the poem, will stay fixed in the people's mind after commandments or prophet's words are forgotten.

So we have a long-rumbling argument. Because it is a highly gestured, emphatic utterance, and often makes greater use of metaphoric and descriptive imagery, along with other verbal devices, poetry can have great rhetorical power. But these very qualities can also be seen to give it a dangerous potency. After all we can be persuaded towards bad as well as good. Thus poetry has often been seen as the distracting enemy of truth and right reason whether religious or scientific. The possibility that poetry might signify nothing has been a horror to many for centuries – as well as a source of joy to others.

IMAGE AND MEANING

The clash of substance and fantasy in poetry is brilliantly evoked in **John Ashbery**'s (1927–) poem about the process of writing a poem 'And *Ut Pictura Poesis* Is Her Name' (*ut pictura poesis* translates as 'as in painting, so in poetry'). After a few lines, says the poet, the poem needs 'a few important words … low-keyed, / Dull-sounding ones.' But as soon as these are provided by the comically mundane information that 'She approached me / About buying her desk', than the poem is in a street of 'bananas and the clangor of Japanese instruments'. The poet ponders this 'seesaw':

> Something
> Ought to be written about how this affects
> You when you write poetry:
> The extreme austerity of an almost empty mind
> Colliding with the lush, Rousseau-like foliage of its desire to
>   communicate
> Something between breaths, if only for the sake
> Of others and of their desire to understand you and desert you
> For other centers of communication, so that understanding
> May begin, and in doing so be undone.

(Ashbery, 1985)

Ashbery's idea is that disciplined, highly focussed verbal communication will be so 'austere' it could come only from 'an almost empty mind'. But 'the desire to communicate' is never so austere, but resembles – and inevitably a metaphor now appears – a luxuriant, multi-coloured forest full of monkeys and tigers of the kind painted by the French artist 'Douanier' Rousseau. For this poet, imagery seems to be the condition of thought.

IMAGINATION

Now, if we put together **image** and the related noun *imagination*, we bring to mind a powerful concept of the nature of poetry. Our 'rhetorical' poets formulating their careful arguments, or the 'makars' of the traditional ballad who did not seek for novelty and surprise in their metaphors, but just to tell a communal story, might be seen as constructors of poetry. There might even be said to be something *mechanical* about their method.

By contrast imagination suggests a quite different definition of poetry. Poetry is seen not as conscious process but as natural surprise, an utterance arising from the *non-rational* processes of the mind. Unbidden associations and illuminations spring into the poet's mind and thence to the page. 'Imagination' has often been regarded suspiciously. The words 'vain' and 'false' have often been attached to it. For **Samuel Johnson** (1709–84) 'imagination' was a negative state of mind he associated with depression: 'Imagination never takes such firm possession of the mind as when it is found empty and unoccupied.'

But for the **romantic** poets following hard upon Johnson at the end of the eighteenth century, the mental processes lying in the 'empty and unoccupied mind' could be welcomed as absorbing and in some profound sense truer than the processes of the conscious mind. In **William Wordsworth**'s (1770–1850) early poem 'Expostulation and Reply', the poet's 'good friend Matthew' accuses him of idleness. The poet replies:

'The eye it cannot choose but see;
We cannot bid the ear be still;
Our bodies feel, wher'er they be,

Against or with our will.
'Nor less I deem that there are Powers
Which of themselves our minds impress;
That we can feed this mind of ours
In a wise passiveness.'

In a companion poem, 'The Tables Turned', he exhorts his friend to
quit his books:

Enough of Science and of Art;
Close up those barren leaves;
Come forth, and bring with you a heart
That watches and receives.

Our minds can absorb knowledge passively, intuitively. What better
justification could you have for closing these particular 'barren
leaves' right now?

These poems of Wordsworth's are of course themselves rhetorical
in that they seek to persuade 'Matthew', and by extension us
as readers. But we see here a commitment to a different kind of
knowing, a different kind of mental action. It is imagination in the
sense of the mind's capacity to form concepts *beyond* those devised
from external objects. The articulation of such apprehensions
becomes one of the major tasks of Wordsworth's poetry, and again
and again he recalls moments, often from childhood, and usually
alone in the natural world, when such strange, profound sensations
overtake him.

Here in 'There Was a Boy' he is beside 'the glimmering lake'
at nightfall, imitating owls and listening to the echoes of his voice
come back over the water from the surrounding hills:

Then sometimes, in that silence, while he hung
Listening, a gentle shock of mild surprise
Has carried far into his heart the voice
Of mountain torrents; or the visible scene
Would enter unawares into his mind
With all its solemn imagery, its rocks,
Its woods, and that uncertain heaven received
Into the bosom of the steady lake.

What is 'carried far into his heart', enters 'unawares into his mind', is impossible to paraphrase. Wordsworth is not trying to convey a shared idea that his rhetorical skill will make us recognize, but to *express* something from his own deep experience that is at, or beyond the limits of words. It is not an idea that 'oft was thought', but an experience unique to him. Poetry is the means by which he can seek to recall and understand such 'mild surprise', and aim to put it before others. Poetry can do this because of its elasticity as a medium and because its sensuousness, especially the movements of its rhythms, can embody the charged excitement he remembers. Poetry now seems to be coming as though from elsewhere: the poet is *inspired*.

INSPIRATION

'Inspiration' is one of the great clichés associated with poetry. Until confronted by the cold realities of creative writing class, would-be poets loitered by guttering candles impatient for the moon-flash of the poem's arrival. As all my emphasis so far upon craft and artifice suggests, poetry is not always and only the product of such miraculous moments. Nonetheless, and however easy it is to satirize the poet's earnest expectancy, the experience of inspiration, and what it means for poetry, needs to be taken very seriously.

Inspiration in this sense is a metaphorical term. Its ground is the literal act of breathing, the taking in of air – respiration. **Walt Whitman** (1819–92), at the outset of 'Song of Myself', gathers his poetic forces in part through the act of breathing. Indeed his poetic being is intensely physical as it carries through to the voice:

> My respiration and inspiration, the beating of my heart,
>   the passing of blood and air through my lungs,
> The sniff of green leaves and dry leaves, and of the shore
>   and dark-color'd sea rocks, and the hay of the barn,
> The sound of the belch'd words of my voice loos'd to the
>   eddies of the wind[.]

For Whitman poetic inspiration is part of the untutored natural world. The lusty character of his poetic sensibility is marked here in the literalness of phrases like 'the passing of blood and air through my lungs', and the wonderful, arrestingly unpoetic 'belch'd words'. Inspiration for Whitman is no delicate zephyr.

This natural association has always been present in the metaphorical sense of inspiration. First it described religious experience where it is 'a breathing or infusion into the mind or soul' (*Oxford English Dictionary*): the great translator **William Tyndale** (?1494–1536) wrote of 'scripture geven by inspiracioun of god'. Later it acquired the more general meaning: 'the suggestion, awakening, or creation of some feeling or impulse especially of an exalted kind' (*OED*) – even if, occasionally, it might come courtesy of less exalted means. Thomas Hogg writes in his life of Shelley of 'the soft inspiration of strong sound ale'.

There is always something unbidden about the coming of such 'suggestion... awakening ... feeling ... impulse'. **Ralph Waldo Emerson** (1803–82) in his essay 'The Poet' (1844) writes that 'the poet knows that he speaks adequately ... only when he speaks somewhat wildly'. He describes the process like this:

> As the traveller who has lost his way, throws his reins on his horse's neck, and trusts to the animal to find his road, so must we do with the divine animal who carries us through the world. For if in any manner we can stimulate this instinct, new passages are opened for us into nature, the mind flows into and through things hardest and highest, and the metamorphosis is possible.
>
> (*Essays*, 1942, p. 218)

He goes on to say that the quest to 'stimulate this instinct' is 'why bards love wine, mead, narcotics, coffee, tea, opium, the fumes of sandal-wood and tobacco'. All these too have their place among the familiar accessories of poetic inspiration. Emerson however regards them as '*quasi*-mechanical': 'that which we owe to narcotics is not an inspiration, but some counterfeit excitement and fury.' Emerson's retreat from this implication of his ideas is hurried and anxious as he insists that 'sublime vision comes to the pure and simple soul in a clean and chaste body'. But he is grand and emphatic on the character of the mental state of true poetry. It is a condition, he writes, that helps the poet 'escape the custody of that body in which he is pent up, and of that jail-yard of individual relations in which he is enclosed.'

Emerson describes well the romantics' impulse towards transcendent freedom, a release from the dull drudgery of daily life. Images like these of imprisonment and release abound in his work, as they do in those of his contemporary **Henry David Thoreau** (1817–62). We meet them too in the images contrasting the earth-bound and free flight that recur in the poems of **John Keats** (1795–1821) envying his nightingale, and **Percy Bysshe Shelley** (1792–1822) saluting the skylark: 'Higher still and higher / From the earth thou springest / Like a cloud of fire'.

A poem that, as Emerson puts it, 'speaks somewhat wildly' is **Samuel Taylor Coleridge**'s (1772–1834) 'Kubla Khan'. It begins:

In Xanadu did Kubla Khan
A stately pleasure dome decree:
Where Alph, the sacred river, ran
Through caverns measureless to man
     Down to a sunless sea.

Nothing in the poem tells us who this Kubla Khan is and it has no narrative movement. But it is instantly effective with its exotic names and setting – Abyssinia, Mount Abora and Paradise come later – and the rhythmic excitement which tumbles the lines headlong towards that strongly stressed 'Down', and the sudden flat expanse of the 'sunless sea'. We are engaged but we probably don't know why.

As the poem continues other equally mysterious but fascinating images follow:

But oh! that deep romantic chasm which slanted
Down the green hill athwart a cedarn cover!
A savage place! as holy and enchanted
As e'er beneath a waning moon was haunted
By woman wailing for her demon-lover!

The 'woman wailing for her demon-lover' 'beneath a waning moon' is a tremendously compelling image, but is actually only there as part of a simile to describe the 'savage place'. In effect the image of comparison, does not serve to elaborate the 'deep romantic chasm'. Instead it disrupts the expectations of metaphor by taking over the interest of the lines. Then, as soon has it usurped the description and caught our fascination, it vanishes. We know no more of the woman or demon-lover. We do however return to the chasm in a series of images of pell-mell violence with the hectic eruption of the river from a 'mighty fountain' before, 'meandering with a mazy motion', it sinks 'in tumult to a lifeless ocean'. Strangely, ominously, at this moment Kubla can hear 'Ancestral voices prophesying war!'

So far the poem seems to be alternating between images of peace and repose in the picture of the 'stately pleasure-dome' set in its grounds with gardens, an 'incense-bearing tree', and walls and towers. This recurs immediately after the voices as 'the shadow of the dome' reappears 'floating midway on the waves'. Yet more strangely, it is now 'A sunny pleasure-dome with caves of ice!' All these images suggest a wondrous culture and civilization, but the alternating images are of the 'savage place', of the turbulent river out of whose roar can be heard those prophetic voices.

Now it changes once more with another memorable image:

> A damsel with a dulcimer
> In a vision once I saw:
> It was an Abyssinian maid,
> And on her dulcimer she play'd,
> Singing of Mount Abora.

With the *dulcet* **connotations** of the instrument the lines speak of a wondrous softness and ease. Now too we have another new presence: 'I'. Moved by this vision, the newly-revealed poet rises to a transport of creative enthusiasm:

> Could I revive within me
> Her symphony and song,
> To such a deep delight 'twould win me,
> That with music loud and long,
> I would build that dome in air,
> That sunny dome! those caves of ice!

And all who heard should see them there,
And all should cry, Beware! Beware!
His flashing eyes, his floating hair!
Weave a circle round him thrice,
And close your eyes with holy dread,
For he on honey-dew hath fed,
And drunk the milk of Paradise.

The exclamations which are such a feature of the poem become more numerous and intense in these lines and they pour breathlessly onward in one sustained rapture.

Yet what does it mean? The poet says 'could I *revive* within me ... I would build...' Perhaps he is writing of his anguished eagerness to recover his own creative strength, or, with less emphasis on 'revive', that he is inspired by this vision to emulate the wondrous creative labour of Kubla Khan and the Abyssinian maid. As his fever mounts the point of view changes yet again so that the poet is seen by 'all' as he desires to be seen, an exciting, even dangerously daemonic figure. The pace of the lines includes remarkable rhythmic changes:

And **all** should **cry**, Be**ware**! Be**ware**!
His **flash**ing eyes, his **float**ing hair!
Weave a **cir**cle **round** him **thrice**,
And **close** your **eyes** with **holy dread**[.]

The second line can be conventionally scanned as a regular *iambic tetrameter* like the first, but for me the growing urgency makes it vault across just two strong stresses to the third line which begins with the forceful stress on 'Weave', to the regular four beats of the fourth. This exhilarates the reader, catching us up into this strange thrill of the exotic and the possession of glamorous fantasy.

Famously, this is where the poem ends. It is subtitled 'a Vision in a Dream. A Fragment', for Coleridge said it was incomplete. Nor could he complete it, for he claimed that the poem was indeed the recollection of a dream, and that as he was 'instantly and eagerly' writing it down, he was 'unfortunately called out by a person on business from Porlock'. By the time he returned to his vision and the paper, he found that 'the rest had passed away like the images on the surface of a stream into which a stone has been cast, but alas! without the after restoration of the latter!' This is a great story of the excitement and the fragility of the imagination. It suggests the utter mystery of the process, as Emerson has it, 'the mind flowing into and through things hardest and highest'.

The apparent mystery however has not prevented scholars from trying to uncover its more material sources. Coleridge wrote the poem after lodging overnight at a farmhouse at Culbone near the Somerset-Devon coast in south-west England. His biographer Richard Holmes convincingly describes how the steep, enclosed combe leading down from Culbone to the sea might have encouraged Coleridge's imaginings of the 'sacred river'. More securely, Coleridge himself tells us that he was reading *Purchas' Pilgrimage*, a travel history which includes this passage:

> In Xanada did Cublai Can build a stately Pallace, encompassing sixteene miles of plaine ground with a wall, wherein are fertile Meddows, pleasant Springs, delightful Streames, and all sorts of beasts of chase and game, and in the midst thereof a sumptuous house of pleasure, which may be removed from place to place.
>
> (quoted in R. Holmes, 1989, *Coleridge: Early Visions*, p. 163)

Put this together with the note on the earliest known manuscript of the poem in which Coleridge describes it as 'a sort of Reverie brought on by two grains of opium taken to check a dysentery', and a picture emerges of a poem resulting from some observations of the surrounding countryside, a bit of near-copying from a book, and the hallucination caused by medicine he had taken for an attack of diahorrea. So much, we might think, for the inscrutable mysteries of the imagination.

But surely we should be wrong to think so. Even if we allow all these mundane contributions to the poem, the incomprehensible brilliance of the poem remains. And it is a brilliance that exceeds the subtlest interpretations, always finally elusive. The response of **William Hazlitt** in 1816 catches its quality when he writes: 'It is not a poem but a musical composition. We could repeat the opening lines to ourselves not the less often for not knowing the meaning of them.' (quoted in R. Holmes, *Coleridge: Darker Reflections*,

1998, p. 434). Other readers have worried about not knowing the meaning. Coleridge's friend, the essayist **Charles Lamb**, wrote to Wordsworth on 26 April 1816 about hearing Coleridge read 'Kubla Khan' aloud

> so enchantingly that it irradiates & brings heaven and Elysian bowers into my parlour while he sings or says it, but there is an observation Never tell thy dreams, and I am almost afraid that Kubla Khan is an owl that wont bear day light, I fear lest it should be discovered by the lantern & clear reducting [reducing] to letters, no better than nonsense or no sense.
>
> (quoted in Holmes, *Coleridge: Darker Reflections*, pp. 429–30)

Lamb seems undecided whether to place the greater weight in his mind upon the irradiation the poem brings him, or on his anxiety that the cold light of examination will show it to be meaningless. He has not been alone. The poem retains its great ambivalence. Whatever it is 'about', and whatever the true nature of its inspiration, the poem – and the legend that surrounds it – is a great model of one kind of poetic imagination. And a great poem.

POETRY AND LIBERATION

In Chapter 5 on 'Free Verse' we saw how **William Blake** saw formal verse as a symptom of imprisonment: 'Poetry Fetter'd Fetters the Human Race.' His fellow *romantics*, **Wordsworth**, **Coleridge**, **Keats**, **Shelley**, and in America **Emerson**, **Thoreau** and **Whitman**, and indeed the secluded **Emily Dickinson**, are all absorbed by the aspiration towards freedom. Their view of the range of the mind, conscious and unconscious, what they call imagination, is one part of this. For most, at least in their younger days, this striving for poetic freedom was part of a longing for political freedom, for the unfettering of the human race from poverty and oppressive government. The first generation of romantic poets – notably Blake, Wordsworth, Coleridge – spent their youth amid the ferment of change that brought about the American Revolution of 1776 and the French Revolution of 1789. The second generation of Byron, Shelley and Keats were also politically radical. In a very large degree Romantic poetry is a poetry of liberation. Sometimes, as in poems such as Shelley's 'England in 1819' or his 'The Mask of Anarchy', protest and the hope of freedom are *rhetorically* expressed. But for poetry the idea of liberation must amount to more than serving as propaganda.

The romantic account of poetry, which sees it as the inspired space of imagination, dramatically marks it off from other kinds of language. Poetry does not only look and sound different because of its peculiar formal characteristics, but its relation to language is quite other. 'Other', that is, to the way language normally works, which is to convey consecutive narratives or arguments in sentences governed by the efficient rules of *syntax*. Necessarily the speaker and hearer or writer and reader share the norms of communication and would prefer not to mystify one another. Nonetheless the romantic ideas and processes of imagination and inspiration present a radical challenge to poetry as *rhetoric*. As Charles Lamb's unease demonstrates, with a poem like 'Kubla Khan' the nature of the communication is different. It does not fall readily within the dominant circle of making sense. It may be , as Lamb fears, 'no sense'.

It is with these ideas in mind that I now want to move to consider poetry in the context and practice of one of the most profound liberation movements of our own day: the liberation of women.

FEMINIST POETICS

In the last forty or so years, the profile of poetry written by women, both past and present, has risen considerably, and as a result at least three topics have presented themselves. The first might be called historical and has to do with the revaluation of women poets of the past whose work has been passed over by literary history. Second there is the question of subject-matter: have women poets written about different topics by virtue of their interests and experience as women? Third there is a more complex and controversial discussion about the language and style of poetry by women: is it fundamentally distinct from that of men at the level of language and form? More controversially, *should* women poets strive to write in ways that are clearly female and owe less and less to the predominantly male poetic tradition? If poetry is itself 'other' with respect to conventional language use, is women's poetry 'other' in a yet further respect? These are the issues I want to discuss in this section.

In an essay called 'The Woman Poet: Her Dilemma', the contemporary Irish poet **Eavan Boland** (1944–) writes that the beginning woman poet very quickly becomes conscious of the 'silences' that have preceded her and which still surround her:

> Women are a minority within the expressive poetic tradition. Much of their experience lacks even the most rudimentary poetic precedent.

These 'silences' are those of all the women who might have written but for the assumptions of masculine dominance. They will become an indefinable part of her purpose as a poet. Boland's argument is that the overwhelming masculine presence in the poetic tradition inhibits and excludes the woman poet. 'Poetry' is the 'One' and she is the 'Other'. As **Elizabeth Barrett Browning** (1806–61) wrote, 'I look everywhere for grandmothers and see none.'

Many poets and scholars in recent years have sought to discover, or re-discover these 'grandmothers'. Aside from the anthologies of women's poetry, the newer historical anthologies of poetry in English published for the academic market now feature work entirely absent from their predecessors of even twenty years ago.

Two examples are Roger Lonsdale's *Eighteenth Century Women Poets* (1990) and *British Literature 1640–1789* (1996) edited by Robert DeMaria Jr. One of DeMaria's new inclusions is this poem by **Anna Laetitia Barbauld** (1743–1825). It is called 'Washing Day' and begins, in *neo-classical* manner, with the *Muses*:

> The Muses are turned gossips; they have lost
> Their buskined step, and clear high-sounding phrase,
> Language of gods. Come, then, domestic Muse,
> In slip-shod measure loosely prattling on
> Of farm and orchard, pleasant curds and cream,
> Or drowning flies, or shoe lost in the mire
> By little whimpering boy, with rueful face;
> Come, Muse, and sing the dreaded *Washing Day*.

Like many other poems in this collection, Barbauld's poem is not to be found in many previous anthologies of eighteenth-century poetry precisely because such a subject would not have been deemed fit for poetry, even when treated in the wry and ironic manner in which Barbauld approaches it. Here we arrive at the second topic concerning women's poetry: subject-matter. Where is the justifying precedent for writing about women's 'actual experience', subjects that have always been a central part of women's lives such as domestic tasks and childcare, what Boland calls the 'snips and threads of an ordinary day'? It might be argued that 'the dreaded Washing Day' is a slight matter, and that attending to it only reinforces women's domestic role. But that would not be a reason to exclude a poem like **Mary Jones'** (?–1778) 'After the Small Pox', which is a mordant criticism of the masculine perceptions that oblige women to rely on a pretty face. **Pope**'s 'The Rape of the Lock' (1714) is fascinated with female beauty and smallpox is a real if shadowy presence in his poem. But it was poets like Jones and **Lady Mary Wortley Montagu** (1689–1762) in her poem 'The Small-Pox', who can tell us of the woman's pain at hiding 'this lost inglorious face':

> How false and trifling is that art you boast;
> No art can give me back my beauty lost!
> In tears, surrounded by my friends I lay,
> Mask'ed o'er, and trembling at the light of day.

The work of recovery of barely noticed women poets is changing the perception of past poetry and helping fill the 'silences' that Boland laments.

This re-examination of what poetry might be written about has also drawn twentieth-century women poets to reconsider some of the celebrated Biblical and classical myths featuring women such as the stories of Eve, Medusa, Persephone and Eurydice that feature in the tradition. **H.D. (Hilda Doolittle)** (1886–1961) rewrote the story of Helen of Troy in her long poem 'Helen in Egypt', and more recently **Carol Ann Duffy** (1955–) has fashioned a satirical retelling of mythical stories from the woman's point of view in her volume *The World's Wife*. In her re-telling, the mythical Cretan aviator, whose pride in his artificial wings led him to fly too close to the sun, is about to take off from a hillock. Watching him, the long-suffering 'Mrs Icarus' ruefully concludes that her husband is yet another 'total, utter, absolute, Grade A pillock.'

So these are two of the issues regarding women and poetry: the historical matter concerning equality of attention to poetry by women, both past and present, and the revision and extension of subject-matter. Both bear upon the confidence and opportunity available to the beginning poet. But besides these, is that third topic: is poetry by women *marked* as such by its different use of language and form? How is it, or how might it be different?

One response to this question has come in the poetry and prose of the American poet **Adrienne Rich** (1929–). In an influential essay, 'When We Dead Awaken: Writing as Re-Vision' (1971), Rich makes her argument by describing the evolution of her own poetic career. She characterizes her early work as formal and distantly impersonal in that it uses metre, rhyme and stanza form and strives for an 'objective, observant tone'. She quotes her poem 'Aunt Jennifer's Tigers' (1951) in which a woman is embroidering a screen. This is the middle stanza:

Aunt Jennifer's fingers fluttering through her wool
Find even the ivory needle hard to pull.
The massive weight of Uncle's wedding band
Sits heavily upon Aunt Jennifer's hand.

(Rich, 1951)

The voice of these early poems was either third-person or cast in a male persona. Formal style, she writes, acted 'like asbestos gloves, it allowed me to handle materials I couldn't pick up bare-handed.'

But gradually the character of her work changed. Her new work

... was jotted in fragments during children's naps, brief hours in a library, or at 3:00am after rising with a wakeful child. I despaired of doing any continuous work at this time. Yet I began to feel that my fragments and scraps had a common consciousness and a common theme, one that I would have been very unwilling to put on paper at an earlier time because I had been taught that poetry should be "universal", which meant, of course, nonfemale. Until then I had tried very much not to identify myself as a female poet.

(*On Lies, Secrets and Silence*, 1980, p. 44)

These 'fragments and scraps' develop into a freer, less formal style, and she eventually finds the confidence to use the pronoun 'I'. She cites her poem 'Planetarium' as one where at last 'the woman in the poem and the woman writing the poem become the same person':

> I am a galactic cloud so deep   so invo-
> luted that a light wave could take 15
> years to travel through me   And has
> taken   I am an instrument in the shape
> of a woman trying to translate pulsations
> into images   for the relief of the body
>   and the reconstruction of the mind.

Unlike the voice of 'Aunt Jennifer's Tigers', the truly female poet will turn away from the inherited forms of the male-dominated tradition and be marked by a freer verse style in the manner of the 'field composition' we saw in Chapter 5 'Free Verse', and by confidently assuming the pronoun 'I'. For Rich, feminist poetics is liberationist and therefore romantic. It challenges previous forms, is iconoclastic towards the tradition – indeed rejects the viability and desirability of a single tradition – and it values subjective experience and its expression.

But none of this is uncontroversial. Eavan Boland, whilst admiring Rich, is sceptical towards what she senses as 'separatist thinking', and the identification of the poet, male or female, as a romantic outsider. She writes in her essay, 'In Search of a Language':

> The poet's vocation – or, more precisely, the historical construction put upon it – is one of the single, most problematic areas for any woman who comes to the craft. Not only has it been defined by a tradition which could never foresee her, but it is constructed by men about men, in ways which are poignant, compelling and exclusive.
>
> (Boland (1995) *Object Lessons*, p. 80)

She argues against that exclusion, that 'women have a birthright in poetry', and must have 'the fullest possible dialogue' with the poetry of the past, most of which is male. She warns too against what she calls 'the Romantic heresy'. The turn towards the subjective in poetry since Wordsworth has often declined, she believes, into 'self-consciousness and self-invention'. She is worried that women poets might replicate romantic ideas which have asserted the realm of imagination as *so* separate from, *so* different in kind, as to be incompatible with the process and experience of daily life. Her own poetry is not averse to the matter-of-fact either in setting or diction, as the opening to this poem 'Contingencies' suggests:

> Waiting in the kitchen for power cuts,
> on this wet night, sorting candles,
> feeling the tallow,
> brings back to me
> the way women spoke in my childhood –
>
> with a sweet mildness in front of company,
> or with a private hunger in whispered kisses,
> or with the crisis-bright words
> which meant
> you and you alone were their object –

(Boland, 1995)

Boland's style is one which aims to maintain connections with ideas and language as they are current outside the spaces of poetry. If for Rich the female poet must rise up from the kitchen table, for Boland it is a place to work. Her own subjectivity is part of her poetry as it is of her essays, but she is also a poet of argument not at all drawn towards 'no sense'.

Yet many writers do envision a female writing whose difference from male practice is deeply inscribed in how the language is used. In her essay 'The Laugh of the Medusa', the contemporary French writer **Hélène Cixous** (1937–) writes:

> Nearly the entire history of writing is confounded with the history of reason of which it is at once the effect, the support, and one of the privileged alibis.

(Cixous, 1976)

For Cixous then presumably real female writing will exist outside what I called earlier 'the dominant circle of making sense'. Thus it might seem possible to recognize an alliance of 'others'. Women stand outside these masculine norms, and so does poetic imagination which, from the point of view of reason, makes 'no sense'. In some poets – including men – she glimpses opposition to this dominance. In a rhetoric as strikingly urgent in its images of imprisonment and liberation as that of Emerson, she writes:

> There have been poets who would go to any lengths to slip something by at odds with the tradition – men capable of loving love and hence capable of loving others and of wanting them, of imagining the woman who would hold out against oppression and constitute herself as a superb, equal and hence "impossible" subject, untenable in a real social framework.

(Cixous, 1976)

But can this vision be seen in specific poems? Does 'Kubla Khan' 'slip something by at odds with the tradition'? Does the poetic 'other' have a further female dimension?

Some critics have seen the composure of 'masculine' techniques such as the *iambic pentameter*, and indeed grammar itself, as targets for subversion by female poets. Biographically it is easy to represent the reclusive **Emily Dickinson** (1830–86) as so at odds with her circumstances as to be 'an "impossible" subject' unable to be at ease in the 'real social framework' of a small New England town. But her deeper, transgressive difference at the level of language and style is often now seen in her rough broken surfaces and distorted hymn stanzas. Here are the last two stanzas of a poem which begins 'Why – Do They Shut Me Out of Heaven?' (#248):

> Wouldn't the Angels try me –
> Just – once – more –
> Just- see – if I troubled them –
> But don't – shut the door!
>
> Oh, if I – were the Gentleman
> In the "White Robe" –

And they – were the little Hand – that knocked –
Could – I – forbid?

(Dickinson, 1951)

Dickinson violates conventional syntax, ignores expectations to be more transparent, and is simply irregular even in her punctuation. Perhaps here we can see the kind of rejection of reasonable 'male writing' that Cixous and others seek.

Women's poetry, and ideas about it, is a rapidly changing and disparate field. To recur to my three topics, poets, scholars and readers – mainly women – continue to revalue the historical legacy. The resulting discoveries, and the writing of our contemporaries, is expanding ideas of what subjects poetry can take on. The third topic is more complex. All theories about poetry have prescriptions to claim that poems should be written this way and not that. Because in these times writing by women is urgently connected to social and political imperatives, the searches for definition and prescription are understandably forceful. To be free of the inherited forms of the male-dominated tradition was obviously going to be a desire of women writing. I think that its radical edge is bound up with the alternatives to the consecutive norms of rational process embodied in the notion of the imagination and the notion of inspiration.

But if we look at women poets since the seventeenth century, or, closer to our own time, at poets considered in this book like **Millay** and **Moore**, highly formal poets writing in the current of the tradition, can we say with confidence that in the styles and subjects they adopted they were wrong from the start? Is it true, as Cixous has claimed, that 'there has not yet been any writing that inscribes femininity', and how secure a definition of 'femininity' can there be? How *different* female use of language really is still needs, and is receiving, subtler analysis. A great deal of life in the writing and reading of contemporary poetry is energized by these questions, and out of it will come new poems to surprise us beyond our current imaginings.

SUMMARY

In this final chapter we have considered:

- The working of simple metaphor and image in speech and in poetry and some more complex instances.
- The historical debates around the relation of words, and metaphor in particular to the representation of reality.
- The purpose and character of rhetoric in relation to poetry.
- The concepts of imagination and inspiration and the impact they have had on poetry and ideas about poetry and the poet.
- How these concepts are allied to liberationist ideas.
- The ways in which poetry by women might be different from that of men and some different ideas about feminist poetic theory and practice.

FURTHER READING

Boland, Eavan (1995) *Object Lessons: The Life of the Woman and the Poet in Our Time*, Manchester: Carcanet Press.

Cixous, Hélène (1976) 'The Laugh of the Medusa', Cohen, Keith and Cohen, Paula, trans, in *New French Feminisms*, Marks, Elaine and Courtivon, Isabelle de (eds) Brighton: Harvester Press, 1981. Reprinted in. Walder, D. (ed.) (1990) *Literature in the Modern World: Critical Essays and Documents*, Oxford: The Open University/Oxford University Press.

Kermode, Frank (1957) *The Romantic Image*, London: Routledge.

Lawler, Justus George (1994) *Celestial Pantomime, Poetic Structures of Transcendence*, New York: Continuum.

Rich, Adrienne (1980) 'When We Dead Awaken: Writing as Re-Vision' (1971) *On Lies, Secrets, and Silence: Selected Prose 1966–1978*, London: Virago.

Stevens, Wallace (1960) 'Imagination as Value' in *The Necessary Angel* London: Faber.

Vickers, Brian (1988) *In Defence of Rhetoric*, Oxford: Clarendon Press.

Yeats, W.B (1900), 'The Symbolism of Poetry', in Jeffares, N. (ed.) (1964) *Selected Criticism*.

9

WRITING A POEM NOW

PHILOSOPHIES OF COMPOSITION

No one knows what contemporiness is. In other words they don't
know where they are going, but they are on their way.
(Gertrude Stein, quoted in interview with Rosemarie Waldrop)

THE MIGHTY DEAD

Some things never change for a poet of serious intent. There is
an empty space on the page, the screen, or in the ear and the poet
wants to fill it with something new, not to repeat the past. This
can be experienced as a nearly debilitating pressure as Coleridge,
writing of himself in the third person in his Notebook shows: 'he
rose, drew his writing-desk suddenly before him – sate down and
took the pen – & found that he knew not what to do' (quoted in
R. Holmes, *Coleridge: Early Visions*, 1989, p. 283). The painter
Benjamin Haydon, writing to John Keats at the time he was reading
Keats' *Endymion*, thinks over his own day's labours

on what I had done and with a burning glow on what I would do till
filled with fury I have seen the faces of the mighty dead crowd into my
room, and I have sunk down & prayed the great Spirit that I might be
worthy to accompany these immortal beings in their immortal glories,
and then I have seen each smile as it passed over me, and each shake
their hands in awful encouragement.

(*The Letters of John Keats*, Vol 1, 1958, H.E. Rollins (ed.), p. 124)

Artists of all kinds know Haydon's paradoxical experience: 'the mighty dead' (a phrase Keats had used in *Endymion*) intimidate because we feel we can never emulate their achievement, but at the same time their 'awful encouragement' offers a daunting yet tantalizing model of what we would like to reach in our way. At other times the artist might feel filled with hope and find, like Keats that

> The air that floated by me seem'd to say
> "Write! Thou wilt never have a better day."

This chapter will explore how practising poets in the present time seek to work through their good days and bad days. As Gertrude Stein suggests it is not always possible to gain a perspective to tell the writer if she or he is doing anything new, of her own time. The twentieth century, and now our own, have seen the development of new media and implements in sound and vision recording, typewriter and latterly word-processing and the internet. How do these affect poets who have grown up with them and write in this context?

HEARING VOICES

'If I knew where poems came from I'd go there' remarks **Michael Longley** (1939–). As we have seen in the section on 'Inspiration' in the previous chapter, the idea that poems have a mysterious source outside the purview of the mind's conscious processes is very powerful and it certainly persists into the present day. Many poets, for instance, cite periods of silence, the famous 'block', when, sometimes for years, she or he feels no impulse or possible beginning of a poem enter their mind. Equally they might experience an unaccountable torrent of creativity. **Geoffrey Hill** for instance published his first collection in 1959 and then only infrequently for almost forty years, until between 1996 and 2006 he doubled the corpus of his life's work.

These periods are as unpredictable as the sudden moments that can incite individual poems. **Fleur Adcock** (1934–) speaks eloquently of this experience.

What seems to happen is this: a phrase arrives in my head, usually when I am in a relaxed, dreamy state ... times when the barriers between the conscious and the unconscious mind are at their most permeable. This "given" phrase ... contains as it were the genetic fingerprint of what is to follow: the rhythm of the phrase indicates the rhythm and to some extent the tone, shape, texture and even the length of the finished poem; these qualities are all wrapped up in those few initial words as the embryo of a plant is wrapped up in a seed, and it is my job to nurture and encourage the seed until it expands into its final form.

(McCully (ed.), *The Poet's Voice and Craft*, 1994, p. 148)

With the addition of the metaphor from genetics, Adcock's account is cast in the romantic tradition of 'organic' composition as we saw described by Emerson, Coleridge and other romantic writers, that is that the beginnings of composition come unbidden and have a natural shape, likened here to the growth of a seed.

'Nice work if you can get it', might be the response to Adcock's description of a sceptic who always suspected poets of layabout tendencies. How can this reverie-born inception relate to the craft and graft of poetic form? For Adcock, who writes mainly within formal structures, 'the form finds itself' and then it is for her to work consciously and skilfully to complete it. But still the concept of the form finding itself, the process by which something historically shaped prior to and quite outside the mind of an individual poet can be sensed as intrinsic to the mind of that poet is hard to grasp, and certainly to explain.

In a 2009 interview with Anna Smaill for the *The Wolf* magazine, the American poet **Frank Bidart** (1939–) addresses this question from his own experience. In recent collections Bidart has moved to more formal structures in his poems, especially the use of stanzas. But in his own accounts of composition he has frequently described hearing his poems as almost dictated by what he calls a 'voice'. His interviewer wants to know if Bidart is 'still hearing the voice before it falls into the form?' Bidart replies:

Oh very much. On the other hand, things become possible for the voice if you have the right form; if you have the right, well, if you can

find the right stanza or the right shape for the voice on the page. But
I definitely still hear a voice. Sometimes I can't get the voice quite
right. I mean, sometimes I feel – "this passage in the poem has to be
a certain length"; and sometimes I don't know that right away. But as
I write and rewrite, it will become clear, say, "this has got to be nine
lines" or something like that. And I still can't get the movement right
within those lines, and I have to work very, very hard.

(*The Wolf*, issue 22, 2009, p. 39)

It seems that for Bidart his 'voice' is primary, but whilst in one
sense it seems to speak the poem, it does not do so in a way that the
poet can immediately catch what it says! Yet more paradoxically,
Bidart's later experience is that his use of a shape like the stanza
enables him eventually to 'hear' those exact words. Now Bidart
changes his terminology to refer to the 'pulse of the poem. I think a
good poem has a pulse of its own. It's not just a question of metre.
Finding the right stanzaic form helps one fix the pulse of the poem
on the page.'

'Pulse' is very like Fleur Adcock's explanation of how that
'phrase that arrives in my head' has a certain 'rhythm', and that
it was 'rhythm that first seduced me into liking poetry in the
beginning' in nursery rhymes, hymns, poetry her mother read to
her as a child and later poets. Now, she writes, 'I'm always conscious
of the rhythm without being in control of it', and like Bidart she has
the sense of dictation.

It is not necessary to become too metaphysical to understand
these poets' experience. What these and many other poets are
seeking to express is the importance of **rhythm** for verse. As we have
seen in previous chapters, particularly Chapter 4 'The Verse Line',
rhythm is the hardest quality to define whether it is embodied
in **measure** or in **free verse**. But the convergence of the words that
are **semantically** right with the more intuitive sense of the poem's
'pulse' or 'voice', like a body fusing with its shadow, is what the
working poet in most aspects of the genre seeks. (There are poets
who would dispute this formulation and we shall come on to other
ideas later.). As Duke Ellington said of jazz, 'it don't mean a thing if
it ain't got that swing'

UNDER PRESSURE

While we acknowledge the validity and importance of the intuitive element in composition, it is equally important to recognize and understand the role of conscious deliberation, the kind of effort that Fleur Adcock says feels 'comfortingly like work'. As we have seen, the greatest change to poetry in the twentieth century was the development of free verse, and the freedom from a canon of traditional forms continues to be enjoyed and to be radically extended in our own day. Nonetheless traditional forms, re-made for contemporary needs and speech, are still very widely used, and, as we shall see, new stipulations are invented.

The reasons for this are several. The unprecedented nature of free forms can induce a kind of anxiety in the artist. Fleur Adcock again expresses this cogently when she says that while she thinks free verse 'the purest type of verse, in that its rhythms are entirely innate and inherent … it has no rules by which to adjust them.' It is difficult to write 'because you can never be reassured by external considerations that you've got it right.' Exactly the same uncertainty is found in other kinds of artists. The painter **Matisse** (1869–1954) observed that 'to give yourself completely to what you're doing while simultaneously watching yourself do it – that's the hardest of all for those who do work by instinct.' **Brad Mehldau** (1970–) the jazz pianist has said in interview that improvisation offers 'incredible freedom' but also great responsibility because 'there is so much room for bullshit and nonsense. You really have to figure out what your identity is in all that lack of form.' In the absence of external norms to refer to composition must be accompanied by an improvising and ceaseless self-criticism. All of us who have presented a piece of writing we knew to be both lucid and peerless to other minds only to witness their utter incomprehension knows the penalties of myopic self-critique.

This last experience points towards another possible reason for the continuance of form in contemporary writing. Over the last generation across the English-speaking world 'Creative Writing' has become a part of the education curriculum, especially and most influentially in universities. Curricula require perceived rigour and a historical dimension, and in poetry the study and practice of traditional forms can supply demonstrable discipline. Technical skill and concentration is necessary to write verse and being set to write sonnets and sestinas is frequently seen as a way to inculcate these qualities in student – or apprentice – poets. The virtues of this in any respect whatsoever are of course disputed, and any influence impossible to measure, but the institutionalization of poetry composition is bound to have an effect on the art at large – I shall discuss some of the others later – and it is certainly possible that this is among them.

Nonetheless, over and above the arguments advanced above, the poet accepts prior stipulations, whether they be traditional forms or newly-invented ones, for one overwhelming reason. This is the one I quoted John Crowe Ransom sustaining at the end of Chapter 2: that the restriction forces the poet's mind below the surface of their readiest expression. It exerts a pressure towards new words and indeed new mental states. The antithesis of the dictum 'first thought, best thought', an imposed restriction frees the verbal mind to go beyond its most superficial expressions and consciousness. I shall now try to explore its operations in a few very different instances.

TAKING EXERCISE

In his description of the composition of his early poem 'The Thought-Fox' **Ted Hughes** (1930–98) tells how the idea came to him unexpectedly late 'one snowy night in dreary lodgings in London' after a year not writing, and how the poem was then written 'in a few minutes'. Hughes' account lends further credence to the part 'inspiration' plays in composition, notwithstanding that the poem itself deploys rhyme and **half-rhyme** and has a double subject in being about both the realization of a physical fox and the process composition: the image of the fox's footprints in the snow is also that of the print on the page. But equally Hughes has written very instructively about the process and virtues of set exercises to encourage and develop writing both in verse and prose. In his influential book *Poetry in the Making*, written mainly for school students and their teachers but readily transferable to older writers, he proposes a series of set tasks employing given themes or objects.

Crucially these begin with a strictly time-controlled session, often of no more than ten minutes.

> These artificial limits create a crisis, which rouses the brain's resources: the compulsion towards haste overthrows the ordinary precautions, flings everything into top gear, and many things that are usually hidden find themselves rushed into the open. Barriers break down, prisoners come out of their cells.
>
> (Ted Hughes, *Poetry in the Making*, 1967, p. 23)

The results may not always be so dramatically revelatory, but such exercises do exert a pressure that unceremoniously demystifies the candlelit preciousness of the poet at work. Such class-exercises have become a staple method in many creative writing classes with the aim of loosening inhibitions around the writing process and sometimes hopefully the imagination itself. These need not centre upon topics or themes but are often more technical, for instance imposing a small and very strict word-limit, say 49 words, not 48 or 50, or forbidding words containing a particular vowel. These repetitions have the salutary effect of forcing the writers to look at the particularities of words, how much essential work a word is doing, and what other words might be reachable. Again it is a means to escape the superficial and discard the cliché.

These exercises are of a piece with the long-standing tradition among poets of testing themselves by taking on the challenge of writing in different forms: ***couplets, sonnets, sestinas, limericks*** or whatever. Sometimes this might be quietly or noisily competitive. In the sixteenth century Scottish poets challenged one another to *flytings*, a competition in which each would improvise poetical abuse towards his opponent until one retired tongue-tied or listeners declared a winner. There are similar jousts in the sexual wars in Shakespeare's *The Taming of the Shrew* between Katharine and Petruchio and in *Much Ado About Nothing* between Beatrice and Benedick. In our own time, though hopefully without the abuse, poetry ***slams***, we have described in the section on performance poetry in Chapter 2 above. In such an arena the most prominent features of poetic form, strong ***metre***, often ***trochaic***, ***alliteration*** and full ***rhyme*** will most readily impress an audience and the manifest skill with which the poet can deploy them will be at a premium.

To explore this element of trying, and being tried by a form in contemporary composition I want to describe a recent poem, and its author's account of its writing. **Vona Groarke**'s (1964–) 'An American Jay' was published in her book *Spindrift* in 2009. The sixty-four-line poem follows an easy-paced autumnal day in the life of a poet teaching creative writing at an American college. Like 'the kids' she idles though some TV, goes to class, sets assignments, eventually arrives at supper and, back in front of the TV, falls asleep, all in an affectionately satiric and self-mocking fashion:

> My students smirk. I'm square. Fixed in the headlights
> Of form and tradition, I tell them, 'Next, it's an ode'.
> The news is welcomed like a bad dose of head lice.
>
> I remind Sally about the sonnet I'm still owed.
> She smiles, says she'll get to it after her midterm on *Hamlet*.
> I'm not sure if she thinks I'm quaint or just plain odd.
>
> I treat myself to Sancerre with my omelette.
> It's been a tough day and I still have a thesis on Nelly Sachs
> By a student who evidently hasn't heard of an umlaut
>
> To get through. Bill Clinton's on TV, playing sax.
> When I come to, a biopic of Tiger or Vijay
> Seems like the loneliest possible alternative to sex.

> (Groarke, 2009)

As you will see the poem is written in *terza rima*, three line *stanzas* rhymed *a b a* with the *b* rhyme carried on into the next stanza, *b c b* and so on, lacing the stanzas together as the subject proceeds.

In correspondence with me Vona Groarke tells how the poem began as a common project with a few other poets in which a bird's name and a poetic form was circulated for each to write a poem matching them up. The project did not develop but

I found that I really enjoyed writing Terza Rima. Being a poet teaching poetry involves both a chime and a chafe. It relies on and enjoys its predictabilities (as teachers must), but also introduces novelty and swerve. Like teaching, Terza Rima has its routines, and also, of course, its necessary surprises. And like terza rima, teaching is often a negotiation between inevitability and reinvention. To write about being a teacher and how that relates to the life from which poetry issues, I thought the form would provide opportunities and struts. I like how it requires end words to take cognisance of each other and also to provide the means of insinuating their own escape routes. I like how the rhyme pattern arcs between novelty and fulfilment: it seems to me a pattern for the pursuit of a dedicated and yet open vocation, if that's not stretching it too far. It's also great fun to write – it's like particularly intricate crochet with the casting off and picking up of variously coloured wools. I wrote this poem over a short enough stretch – maybe about three weeks, which for me is pretty immediate! But it was only last summer that the final brick got slotted in – the Sancerre of the last stanza (which up to then had been a Chablis). The newer version gave me a chime with 'sincere' earlier on in the poem, and that kind of cross-stitching seemed to me to be a vital part of what I want my poems to be: light-fingered, but also holding fast to the possibility of sincerity.

Here we can see a poet setting out by accepting an externally imposed pressure in initial subject (the bird) and poetic form. As the reader follows the poem he or she becomes more and more involved and curious about its virtuosity, continuing to ask how the poet is going to resolve each rhyming test and then marvelling at sequences like Hamlet / omelette / umlaut, and earlier the yet more remarkable equally / e-coli / ukelele, none of which would likely be achieved with the rhyming dictionaries she despises. Vona Groarke explains very well how she found not only pleasure in working with terza rima but how the style suits her subject, 'a pattern for the pursuit of a dedicated and yet open vocation'. She uses too a very tactile image to relay the experience and character of the verse form as 'intricate crochet with the casting off and picking up of variously coloured wools.' She is not so much in the 'headlights / Of form and tradition' as confidently behind them.

TRANSLATION

Translation has always been part of the western, and doubtless other poetic traditions. Contemporary poets are often stimulated by foreign language poets and poems whom they encounter either in the original or in translation. The custom of writing a poem 'after' or in 'imitation' of a preceding foreign work is commonplace. But for some poets today the model of a particular foreign language poet, or deep engagement with a second language, is crucial to the way they work and how their writing has developed.

Elaine Feinstein (1930–) is renowned as the foremost translator of the Russian poet **Marina Tsvetaeva** (1892–1941). Through this work, she says, Tsvetaeva became 'the most important single influence on my own work.' In a sense it seems she was 'ready' for this particular influence since as a young poet seeking her way in the 1950s she did not feel comfortable in any of the English poetic tendencies of her day, neither 'the Movement' poets associated with **Philip Larkin** (1922–85), nor 'the English intelligentsia poets' around **Jeremy Prynne** (1936–) whose poetics she admired but whose passion for geography and English local history felt alien. Whilst sensing a connection through her own family's East European roots, Feinstein acknowledges that her own life bears no comparison with Tsvetaeva's life of poverty and exile as a poet and mother in the desperate turbulence of revolutionary and post-revolutionary Russia culminating in her lonely suicide, yet she felt an affinity, albeit a 'dangerous' one. More precisely it was the effect of translating Tsvetaeva's verse that affected her own:

> Technically she taught me how intensity of passion creates a strong rhythm that will flow down a page even when held in stanzas. After working on my versions of her poems, I began to see poetry as a matter of the spoken voice pushing against the shape of the verses on the page. After that, I rarely used completely open forms.
>
> (E. Feinstein, *Strong Words*, eds. W.N. Herbert and
> M. Hollis, 2000, pp. 188–9)

Critics often write simplistically about poets finding their 'own voice' as though it is some latent, authentic gemstone deep in the writer's individual being. Elaine Feinstein's testimony shows how complex this quest can be and how subject to external influences, even one from an utterly different language.

The transactions between languages have been very much part of the formation of **Gwyneth Lewis** (1959–) as a poet. Brought up as a Welsh speaker she learned English as a necessary survival mechanism in the modern world. The pressures upon a minority language such as Welsh means, says Lewis, that 'to speak it is to know the sound of a long unbearable farewell.' To know Welsh however is to have access to another venerable literary tradition and to its forms. *Cynghanedd* is one of the complex poetic forms required in the verse competitions of the Welsh *eisteddfodau* or cultural festivals of Welsh-speaking Wales. As Lewis points out, *cynghanedd* was used in English by **Gerard Manley Hopkins** (1844–89) and influenced the style of **Dylan Thomas** (1914–53). **Wilfred Owen** (1893–1918) makes notable use of *half-rhyme* or *pararhyme* in his war poem 'Strange Meeting'– *escaped / scooped, groined / groaned, bestirred / stared* – and in doing so he drew upon the use of this technique in the mediaeval Welsh version of the style known as *proest*. For **Jon Silkin** (1930–97) in 'a world of disharmony and moral uncertainty the discord of pararhyme is a truer equivalent' to the cataclysmic experience of Owen and his contemporaries than full rhyme.

This kind of exchange between the languages continues to be an important part of Gwyneth Lewis' poetics, indeed she publishes poetry in both languages. Being bilingual she has a better claim than most poets who dabble in translation to recognize its nature and importance and she challenges some common assumptions about its practice.

> I'm one of those who believes that not only is translation possible, it's an essential element in every nation's culture. Poetry isn't only what's lost in translation – it's what's gained. In a culture the desire to translate is always a sign of strength. Only rich cultures are hungry for news of the outside world – paradoxically, voracity is a sign of plenitude ... Here I take it that the whole point of translation is to introduce a new element – of rhythm or thought – into a literary tradition. The point isn't to produce a version so culturally smooth that no one would ever

guess it was imported. There has to be something strange, novel and fascinating either about the style or cast of mind of the new piece.

(Gwyneth Lewis, *Strong Words*, W.N. Herbert & M. Hollis (eds), 2000, pp. 266–7)

Lewis' final point is especially important for English language poets. The hegemony of English as a world language makes the temptation for everything to sound 'English' in translation very powerful. But such a process of absorption can efface the distinct identity of a poem, or other literary work, as it is in its own language. It is truer to the original to retain words and phrasings that give a sense of it even at the cost of an initial roughness in English. The 'otherness' of the foreign language needs to be retained. At the present time the number of poets working in the Anglophone world whose first language is not English will be increasing as the metropolitan centres of the British Isles and the USA have more and more citizens from language backgrounds in, say, south Asia and Latin America. More and more writing poetry now will involve, as for a poet like Gwyneth Lewis, translation and writing across and between these language groups.

WHAT ARE WORDS?

At a poetry reading in Zurich on 14 July 1916 **Hugo Ball** (1886–1927) was carried to the stage (he was wearing a costume which meant he could not walk) and began to read from his work:

gadji beri bimba glandridi laula lonni cadori
gadjama gramma berida bimbala glandri galassassa laulitalomini
gadji beri bin blassa glassala laula lonni cadorsu ...

Before long the audience exploded, some with delight, some with outrage. This, the first of Ball's 'abstract phonetic poems', was not only a challenge to the nature of poetry as serious, significant speech – a 'criticism of life' as **Matthew Arnold** (1822–88) had grandly called it – but it jettisoned familiar language and with it any *semantic* intention, that is any attempt to 'make sense' in a poem.

Why did Ball do this? The DADA, 'anti-art' movement of which Ball was a founder in the early years of the world war of 1914–18, held the European society that had engendered such slaughter in contempt. For the Dadaists all its conventions, institutions and utterances were a pretentious and delusory sham. Against the 'sense' it propounded they posed nonsense, against 'order' anarchy. For Ball, who was a journalist, official discourse had been corrupted and so

> In these phonetic poems we want to abandon a language ravaged and laid barren by journalism. We must return to the deepest alchemy of the Word, and leave even that behind us, in order to keep safe for poetry its holiest sanctuary.
>
> (Hans Richter, *Dada, Art and Anti-Art*, 1965, p. 42)

So Ball's 'abstract phonetic' poems are intended to have a provocative social and indeed political effect. As we can tell from his terminology, for him the project had a religious dimension and not long after the exuberant evening in Zurich Ball turned away from Dada to live a religious life of poverty among the peasants of rural Switzerland. 'I have examined myself carefully,' he wrote, 'and I could never bid chaos welcome.'(p.43)

But the ideas and impulses of Ball and the other Dadaist poets can be seen as the wellspring of much radical poetic practice throughout the twentieth century and up to the present day. It gives rise to a progressive series of questions: what *is* poetry? what *are* words? what *is* language? is meaning possible? what *is* meaning? In my Preface to this book I wrote of the 'perpetual paradox' of poetry, of the attraction of two poles, one towards the desire 'to *say* something that is meaningful and memorable', and the other towards a desire to say *nothing*, but to rejoice in the peculiar nature of words themselves, their associations, their sounds, their visual shapes, or perhaps to invent new words. It is in considering poetry descended from Dada that we feel the pull of these two poles most powerfully.

HOW TO SAY NOTHING

The first way a poet might deny *semantic* expectations is to disrupt *syntax*. This is what **E. E. Cummings** (1894–1962) does here:

> anyone lived in a pretty how town
> (with up so floating many bells down)
> spring summer autumn winter
> he sang his didn't he danced his did.

(Cummings, 1994)

Here cummings (part of his refusal of linguistic convention was to eschew capital letters) begins by taking a conventional sentence – one that might be for instance 'John lived in a pretty New England town' – and by substituting 'wrong' parts of speech jolts us out of our easy expectations. cummings does this in this poem to a wider purpose, but some poets see their task, as Stefan Morawski puts it, 'to liberate the word from syntax' and to create texts where the 'principal coherence is sound, rather than syntax or semantics'. We have already looked at some practice of this kind towards the end of Chapter 2, 'Deliberate Space' and seen that this escape from semantics might focus on visual shapes as in *concrete poetry*.

But given that the whole of our education in language from infancy has been directed towards organizing sounds into words and words into syntactic chains that will enable us to share communication, if the chains are to be broken perhaps we cannot rely on the internal processes of our minds, determined as they might be by the formulae and conventions of everyday discourse, that is by *cliché*. It is to enable this that writers have sought to derive impetus and material from a plethora of existing texts, not necessarily literary ones.

The American poet **Charles Bernstein** (1950–) is one of the founders of $L=A=N=G=UA=G=E$ poetry mentioned in Chapter 2. We also encountered his colleague **Robert Grenier** towards the end of Chapter 5 on 'free verse' with his question 'where are the words most themselves?' and his description of poetry as 'words occurring'. Bernstein proposes ninety-seven exercises each of which will help words occur, and by minimizing the contribution of the conscious composing mind, perhaps allow them to be 'most themselves'. Here are a few suggestions from his list.

> Homophonic translation: Take a poem in a foreign language that you can pronounce but not necessarily understand and translate the sound of the poem into English (e.g. French "blanc" to blank or "toute" to toot).
>
> *
>
> Tzara's Hat: Everyone in a group writes down a word (alternative: phrase, line) and puts it in a hat. Poem is made according to the order in which it is randomly pulled from hat. (Solo: pick a series of words or lines from books, newspapers, magazines to put in the hat.)
>
> *
>
> General cut-ups: Write a poem composed entirely of phrases lifted from other sources. Use one source for a poem and then many; try different types of sources: literary, historical, magazines, advertisements, manuals, dictionaries, instructions, travelogues, etc.
>
> *
>
> Alphabet poems: make up a poem of 26 words so that each word begins with the next letter of the alphabet. Write another alphabet poem but scramble the letter order.
>
> *
>
> Collaborative Surrealist Language Event (I) (for two or more people): One person writes down a question without showing it to anyone else; simultaneously, another person writes down an answer; poem is formed by a series of these questions and answers. Alternate form: One question: multiple answers; vice versa. For example: "What is the pink elephant? The reason why it is so cold this week.// Is the door locked? / I have been faithful to thee, Cynara! in my fashion." (Cf: Robert Desnos's "Language Events")
>
> *
>
> Nonliterary forms: Write a poem in the form of an index, a table of contents, a resume, an advertisement for an imaginary or real product
>
> *
>
> the compositional method of Deer Head Nation: "You punch a keyword or keywords or phrase into Google and work directly with the result text that gets thrown up. I paste the text into Word and just start

stripping stuff away until what's left is interesting to me, then I start meticulously chipping away at and fussing with that."

*

Graphic design 101.1: Take a poem, first another's then your own, and set it ten different ways, using different fonts and different page sizes. Make a web version of the poem.

*

Proliferating styles. In 1947, Raymond Queneau, a founding member of OuLiPo (Ouvroir de Littérature Potentielle, or "Workshop of Potential Literature") published Excercises de Style, 99 variations on the "same" story. Each of this 99 approaches could take a place of honor in this list but best to turn to that work for the enumeration and explanation. For present purposes (if purposes doesn't strike an overly teleological chord), suffice it to say that an intial incident, mood, core proposition, description, idea, or indeed, story, might be run through the present list of experiments, though to what end only the Shadow knows, and maybe not even the Shadow.

*

Take a poem and erase all but one part of speech, leaving the visual layout intact, or read it backward or otherwise re-order it, or translate it (using any of the translation exercises listed here), Alternately, use these experiments as a way to rewrite or transform your own poems.

(http://www.writing.upenn.edu/library/
Bernstein-Charles_Poem-Profiler.html)

Bernstein's many references to such figures as **Tristan Tzara** (1896–1963), **Robert Desnos** (1900–45) and the Surrealists, and to **Raymond Queneau** (1903–76) and the French literary movement know as OuLiPo, underlines how Bernstein's poetics develops from Dada and subsequent models. All of these exercises subvert the notion of the single composing consciousness deploying, or 'mastering' language, and do so through the different means of randomization and chance, group composition, and 'found' materials, with the important new dimension offered by the internet. All seek, in Bernstein's phrase to 'de-lyricize poetry' and to maximize the 'objective', as opposed to the traditionally subjective orientation of poetry.

Many contemporary writers now employ some of these methods, either exclusively or as a part of their practice. As we have seen in Chapter 2 'Deliberate Space' and Chapter 7 'Stanza', **Matthew Welton** (1969–) is an innovator within this tradition. His second book, published in 2009, has a title 101 words long, presented in justified type, and includes the 'Six Poems by Themselves', mentioned in Chapter 2, where the twelve lines of each have different stanza formations but no words, giving them a ghost-like existence. Another sequence, 'South Korea and Japan', he constructs upon the World Cup finals fixture list. Another series entitled 'Four-letter words' consists of six poems labelled in turn *'eins zwei drei vier funf coda'* each made up entirely of words with four letters, none of them the expected ones, although *vier*, comprised only of invented words, plays teasingly close to the four-letter cliché. Like much other work in the book, this belongs in a collaborative music piece.

Perhaps the most sophisticated piece in the collection is 'I must say at first that it was difficult work'. The piece consists of six twelve-line stanzas in which each line is a sentence of twelve syllables. This is the first stanza:

A malaise that affects the demented at first

A masseuse with a thirst for delicious liqueurs

A monsieur who's inferring that discipline hurts
A moose in wet weather is disturbed as he walks
A mosquito, a butterfly, a tickler, a worm
A mouse with white fur was sick in the water

(Welton, 2009)

Welton acknowledges that he is adapting a procedure from the French writer **Raymond Roussel** (1877–1933), a member of the OuLiPo group, who began with one sentence, chose one word from it, and then derived the next sentence 'by finding a word loosely homophonic to that word, and then building a subsequent sentence that in some way incorporates the new word' and so on until a whole novel, *Impressions d'Afrique*, was written.

Welton refines this further. His first sentence, 'I must say that at first it was difficult work' (in fact a translation of Roussel's reported comment on writing his novel), generates a varied series of repetitions and alliterative and rhyming effects as follows. 'M' is the second letter of the title line and of the first stanza (and in fact of the first line of the subsequent stanza). Moreover *malaise masseuse monsieur moose mosquito mouse* are loose homophones and an internal rhyme associates *first thirst hurts disturbed worm fur*, indeed only two of the whole thirty-six lines do not employ the *ur* sound at least once through such instances as *termite burp version church alert desperate mezuzahs flirt Amherst impertinent absurd*. These do not exhaust the recurrences: the first fourteen lines began with the letter 'A' (seven 'A's and four 'Ands'), seven begin 'I'm', twelve with 'The' and the last two with 'Un-'. Matthew Welton writes:

> The point of course, is that in deriving one sentence from another ... the outcome might be less a distortion of the original than a text with an originality of its own. And maybe too it is significant that this method should feel more a game of chinese whispers than a traditionally poetic use of rhyme.
>
> (M. Welton, *We needed coffee but...*, 2009, p. 100)

Moreover the form in which it appears on the page in his book is not necessarily definitive. In readings he will copy each stanza on to a different card, shuffle them before the audience and read them in their new order – or in the one determined by audience members choosing a card.

How do poems such as these get written? Matthew Welton has described his approach to me in these terms.

> I was always impressed by the title of that collection of Williams interviews, I wanted to write a poem, for the way it suggests something done deliberately. And I suppose what I'm saying is that language itself is a found material, though one to which we become acclimatised. For me, it is in the poems that I make mathematically where I try hardest to make things sound 'natural' and avoid the angularity or disjointedness that can sometimes come in poems written through a very contrived process.

And as for the physical process itself:

> For a long time my writing process involved saying whichever poem I was working on over & over in my head & then, if I was happy with where I'd got it to in the course of my day, I'd write up a new draft when I got home. Pens & pencils & paper are all involved in the way I write &, as time has gone on, the paper I use has got bigger & bigger. I want to be able to see as many notes or drafts or versions as possible & these days that means working with A2 sketch pads or flip chart paper or long rolls of printer's paper that unscroll across the floor of my flat as the poem progresses.

Several points are particularly interesting here. First it may that the poems work from or with 'given' or 'found' materials, but that is only the spark to a clearly laborious compositional process. Second there is this need to keep as much material as possible in view during composition so that no possible avenue is forgotten or overlooked. Although Welton says that he also uses the computer for some aspects of poetic composition, the limits of the conventional rectangular screen with its rigid lines in which everything but a small portion of the work in progress is invisible at any given moment could not suit his method. A third point that emerges is the evident self-critical process. He is evidently monitoring the developing writing, 'to make things sound "natural" and avoid angularity and disjointedness', striving for effects he is 'happy' with. Even when working with the other 'imperatives' from visual artists or composers he writes that 'I've tried to put some poemness into what I've written, by which I think I mean I want them to stand alone without the images or the music.' In a work like 'I must say that at first it was difficult work' this 'poemness' is evident to me in the ancient verbal pleasure of *recurrence* but also in the variety of *rhythm* and *cadence* achieved within each reach of twelve syllables as well as the intriguing character of the images generated. These processes have their mechanical aspects but the poet still has to satisfy himself with any given result and this he does intuitively: this cadence, this form of phrase or rhythm, he feels 'happy' with. It just works.

THE MOVING TEXT AND DIGITAL POETICS

In 2010 it is obvious that the greatest single change in the realm of communications over the preceding ten years has been the extension of computer technology and the internet. If *speed* is the signature of this technology, and an hegemony over our attention the ambition of the corporations who wield most power within it, then poetry as both a 'slow art' which might be painstaking in its composition, cannot be skimmed with any profit and is domiciled in a small nook of our culture, might be thought to be alienated from it. But this is not proving to be the case in a number of respects.

The first advantage lies in availability of information. The activity of poetry has virtually no access to mass publicity in any of its media but simple internet facilities like email distribution lists enable people interested in poetry to be aware of one another and of publications, readings and other events and activities. Just one instance is indicative: in Manchester, England, the 'Dear List' poetry bulletin giving information about local readings other poetry events, founded as an email circular among friends in 2004, now has over 750 subscribers. Similarly through a plethora of websites and online archives a reader can access virtually any published poem together with biographical and background information and criticism, some of it ongoing as other readers contribute their more (or less) considered thoughts on a given poet. No longer confined to hunting out the poetry section in bookshops in order not to find a poet one is looking for, the internet can nearly always furnish a book even if it has been long out of print. Then of course specialist sites and facilities such as You Tube, Facebook and My Space provide every aspirant poet with a publishing platform, if not an audience.

None of this needs labouring, but is computing and the internet altering the way poems are written today and is this resulting in a distinctly different *kind* of poetry as opposed to a difference in distribution?

It is probably too early to tell but to begin an exploration of the topic I'll return to Matthew Welton's practice. Responding to my question about the use of computer technology Welton replied:

The poems of mine for which I first used the computer in the writing process were the ones where I set up a 'stencil' which repeats over & over with different words or phrases occupying the gaps each time. More recently I've been playing with the idea that any poem is only a version of the poem it might be, and I've been incorporating projections of rewritten versions of the poems into my readings. This takes place while I'm using effects pedals to generate new takes on the poem as I'm saying it, &, if it's working how I want it to, leads me into making up new stuff as I go along. For a lot of people working in music or the theatre or the visual arts this might not be such drastic stuff but I guess where poetry is concerned there is still a lot of unexplored territory. So far I'm having a lot of fun with it.

We see here the use of a computer tool, his 'stencil', to facilitate the kind of structuring we have already noticed in his work.

But more interesting I think is his idea that 'any poem is only a version of the poem that it might be'. Our default notion of a poem is of an artifact that is carefully worked and burnished through drafts until it is fixed in print and published. Poets whose work re-appears, might like **W.H. Auden** (1907–73) excise poems from later editions or present new versions, but always the aim of the set finished text remains. For many poets this is really the whole point: arriving *exactly* at what she or he wants to say with all the sensuous power that can be mustered, and the making of a book as a beautiful thing in itself, is a profound personal satisfaction. But in allying two variable media, the reading and the resources of the computer, Welton is saying that the poem need not aspire to this fixity, that it can exist in differing forms, a palimpsest that can be added to but just as importantly readily re-visit its earlier shapes.

This is a potentially significant move away from has been called 'codex practice', that is the writing of poetry (or anything else) conceived to find its medium in a bound book. Digital poetry moves away from this and in doing so is obviously novel, although at the same time we might discern the lineaments of two older media. The first is the written scroll which preceded the codex as a written object – it is no coincidence that we 'scroll' up and down the computer screen. Like the scroll the computer screen obscures all but one piece of text at a time but whereas the written scroll is less readily searchable than the codex, the computer's search keys mean that the digital scroll has no such disadvantage. How significant the hidden but *palpable* existence of the text of a printed book will prove to be psychologically important to reading only the development of e-reader devices will tell us.

The second medium which the digital scroll resembles, or potentially resembles, is of course the ***oral tradition***, which, as we have seen in Chapter 2 has always enabled fluidity, variation and improvisation. So the changes that may be offered by digital media are well summarized in this statement from Loss Pequeno Glazier of the Electronic Poetry Center at SUNY Buffalo:

> Writing is not a single monumental totality that can be measured. Rather, what can be charted is writing as an overlapping, hybrid, and extendable terrain of parts of writing, parts that fit together at times awkwardly and out of joint, to compose a textual continuum through which writing practices weave.
>
> (http.//epc.buffalo.edu/authors/glazier/dp/intro1.html)

These practices need not be individually authored. The technology readily enables participation, on the model of the blog, and so collaborative composition online becomes an easy and developing possibility. Put this together with the improvisational elements in ***performance poetry*** and a different, more freewheeling and flexible aesthetic emerges. Moreover the possibilities of multimedia begin to combine voice, word, image and music extend the character of poetry yet further.

CONCLUSION

As Gertrude Stein says, what is truly contemporary and will change the future can only be guessed at any given time. As this brief account indicates writing poetry now includes several different practices, some overlapping, some quite distinct. Poems are written for the page and book; they are written to be performed; they are written to be disseminated by the various means of the web; they are written in and for university classes and many other kinds of groups. These poems may continue to exploit the traditional modes of metre, rhyme and stanza – especially when composed for performance – or they may be exploring the freedoms in sound and visual space opened by the twentieth century's '*free verse*' revolution.

This range of possibility in contemporary poetry for both writers and readers is now more accessible than at any time in history. In comparison with cinema or popular music the reach of poetry remains, and is likely to remain, small. Nonetheless, the modern extension of literary education in schools and colleges has slowly enlarged that minority and two quite recent developments can further that growth.

First the capacity of information technology, as I have indicated above, makes the pursuit of an interest in poetry easier than ever before. The ability it gives to satisfy some nagging curiosity about **John Skelton** (*c.* 1460–1529), and then at another hour or day to read more of a present-day poet whose verse has caught our attention, means that as readers we can create our own fluid anthologies.

The second development is growth of creative writing in all parts of the English curriculum. Its best practice is always, I believe, in concert with reading, and its principal project is not the nurture of genius. Rather it works to add an expressive field to study, to enable students to discover the possibilities and the difficulties of working in language, and to understand the process and nature of literary texts by means other than the 'reverse engineering' of analysis and criticism. Moreover the staple presence of the 'workshop' in creative writing practice offers the experience and contribution of other minds as a measure for the writer's own interior sense.

Neither of these changes is of interest only to formal students of English. For some poetry might be a new discovery later in life, or one revived when the demands for qualifications are past. Whether pursued with intensity or sporadic interest, the endlessly extending library of poetry awaits, and the traditional tools of its practice, voice and pen, which have always been comparatively accessible, are now complemented by the two-way medium of the internet. If it is too much to say that the long-held ideal in art to break down the wall between producer and passive consumer has been achieved in the reading and writing of poetry now, then there is perhaps no other artistic practice where that wall is more permeable.

SUMMARY

In this chapter we have looked at:

- The traditional issues facing a practising poet.
- The experience of intuition in composition.
- The creative pressure of set forms.
- The role of set exercises in composition.
- Translation and its influence.
- The challenge to conventional expressive practice by the random and template generation of poetic texts.
- Digital poetics and the influence of the Internet.
- The place of creative writing in the contemporary sphere of poetry.

FURTHER READING

Adcock, Fleur (2000) *Poems 1960–2000*, Tarset: Bloodaxe.

Broom, Sarah (2006) *Contemporary British and Irish Poetry: An Introduction*, Basingstoke: Palgrave.

Herbert, W.N. and Hollis, Matthew (eds) (2000) *Strong Words: Modern Poets on Modern Poetry*, Tarset: Bloodaxe.

Lewis, Gwyneth (2005) *Chaotic Angels*, Tarset: Bloodaxe.

McCully, C.B. (ed.) (1994) *The Poet's Voice and Craft*, Manchester: Carcanet Press.

Richter, Hans (1965) *Dada: Art and Anti-Art*, London: Thames & Hudson.

Smith, Hazel (2005) *The Writing Experiment: Strategies for Innovative Creative Writing*, St Leonards, NSW: Allen and Unwin.

WEBSITES

www.poetryarchive.org. The British Library poetry archive including many sound recordings.

www.poetryfoundation.org. Wide-ranging contemporary poetry site associated with *Poetry* (Chicago).

http://epc.buffalo.edu/authors/bernstein.

10

CONCLUSION

I began Chapter 8 with a simple metaphor, 'daft as a brush'. This odd, yet ordinary phrase is a minute instance of the ceaseless creativity in human language, just one of its 'endless associations'. Such images are at the heart of our language-use. They enhance our rhetorical powers and suffuse that strangely occurring mental state we call the imagination, something made as much by the *unconscious* as the conscious mind.

Compared with what Ashbery calls 'other centers of communication', the poem is a free space for rhetoric and imagination. It might be tightly argumentative or loosely associative. It can combine so many aspects of experience, knowledge and ways of speaking. Some philosophy, a child's bedtime memories, geology and evolution, a bit of slang or verbal playfulness, can coexist here as in no other form. Because its sounds are so important – what we inaccurately but inevitably call the 'music' of its rhythms and metres – so much part of the power of this mix, is, as the critic Justus George Lawler says, 'nonconceptual'. Poetry works with ideas, but also within the subjective mystery of our consciousness, with the *qualia* of the mind when it is operating other than in its consecutive series. Its kinds are sometimes playful, and sometimes deal with the words that engage the most serious topics we know. In all its presences, the fascination, pleasure and impact of poetry inhere in the patterns of the language where form and content are truly indivisible:

'O body swayed to music, O brightening glance,
How can we know the dancer from the dance?'
(W.B. Yeats, 'Among Schoolchildren')

GLOSSARY

This glossary provides short definitions to all the specialist terms used in this book. These terms appear in the text in **bold**. The definitions here however are necessarily short. Most are discussed at some length in the appropriate chapters and these are indicated. Much fuller accounts, with many examples and histories, can be found in the exhaustive and excellent 1383 pages of the Princeton Encyclopedia:

Preminger, A. and Brogan, T.V.F. (eds) (1993) *The New Princeton Encyclopedia of Poetry and Poetics*, Princeton, NJ: Princeton University Press.

Accent In poetry, emphasis upon one particular syllable in speech, e.g. mass-ive. See also **stress**, the term most often used in this book for accent and **beat**.

Accentual-syllabic A measured line of verse which forms a pattern of accented and non-accented syllables. Also called **stress-syllable** lines. (See Chapter 4.) I have also referred to it as **patterned stress**.

Alexandrine A twelve-syllable line of verse, usually **accentual-syllabic**, with six **stresses** and a **caesura**. The standard metre in French poetry, sometimes adapted into English. (See Chapter 4.)

Allegory A literary work in which characters, settings and actions are all devised to represent, or **symbolize**, abstractions such as 'Good',

'Evil', Wisdom', etc. What is being represented does not emerge from the **image** or **symbol**, but is set in advance with the **images** chosen to fit.

Alliteration The repetition of *consonants* close enough together to be noticed by the ear. Usually appears on stressed syllables. **Alliterative** verse, mostly in Old and Middle English, normally forms the line by including three stressed syllables beginning with the same consonant. Occasionally alliteration is also referred to as **head-rhyme** when the repetition is on the first syllables of words.

Anadiplosis A **rhetorical figure** in which the last word of one phrase or sentence is repeated as the first word of the next. E.g. 'If you say he's mad, mad he is.'

Anapest A **metrical foot** of three **syllables** in which the first two are unstressed and the third stressed: **v v /**. The term comes from classical **prosody** where it referred to a foot of two short followed by one long syllable, (**See** Chapter 4).

Anaphora A **rhetorical figure** which repeats the same word or word at the beginning of a series of phrases, sentences or lines: e.g. 'Mad she thought him. Mad he seemed to be. Mad he surely was.'

Assonance The reiteration of the same *vowel* sounds close enough together to be noticed by the ear. It is more aural than alliteration because it not so visible on the page: e.g. 'the proud cow by the plough'.

Ballad A narrative poem in simple form that is derived from the **oral**, rather than literate tradition. The origins of the 'traditional', or 'popular', or 'folk' ballad are therefore usually unknown, and it will have been altered through its **transmission** as it has been sung or recited down the years. When more modern poets have wanted to recall simplicity they have re-invented the form, most famously Wordsworth and Coleridge in their *Lyrical Ballads* (1798). (See Chapter 2.)

Ballad metre The **metre** most commonly used for the ballad. Normally it alternates lines of four and three **stresses**. Also known sometimes as **common metre**.

Bard A traditional word for poet. It derives from the Celtic cultures of Wales and Ireland whose tribes had bards who recorded and recited verses, often in elaborate forms, both to entertain and to keep the history of their people. In modern use it is often at best mock-serious, as when Shakespeare is referred to simply as 'the Bard'.

Beat   The sound effects in all sorts of poetry in English, whether it has **measure** or is in **'free verse'**, rely upon the effective placing of **accent** or **stress**. A poem therefore will have **beats** (i.e. stresses, accents) which fall on particular syllables. But a poem is also said to have an overall **beat**, or **rhythm**. It is helpful to think of beat in poetry in a similar way as we do in music, though the relationship between poetry and music is eventually complex. (See also **metre** and Chapters 4 and 5.)

Beat poetry   Beat poets, Beat Generation: a group of American poets, first on the West Coast, who became prominent in the 1950s and whose work was in contrast to the formal, 'academic' poetry of the day. Its styles are free or open form (see **free verse**), sometimes improvisational, frequently recited or performed and its lineage is in **romanticism**.

Blank verse   Lines of poetry that do not use **rhyme**. In English it began in the sixteenth century and became the staple form for the dramatic verse of Shakespeare and his contemporaries because it enabled greater continuity, and sounded closer to natural speech than rhymed verse.

Burden   Occasionally referred to as *burthen*, it has several meanings. The most prominent is that of **refrain**, or repeated chorus, usually of a song, or song-like poem. It can also refer to the main theme or sentiment of a poem (or other utterance). Closer to music, a burden is the underlying aural effect, like the bass-line. More rarely, especially in biblical contexts, it can refer to a deliberate raising of the voice to recite.

Cadence   The word derives from Latin and Italian words for 'fall', hence we sometimes also speak of the **fall** of a poem. This especially refers to the **rhythm** as a poem, sentence or line reaches its close. More generally cadence refers to the overall rhythmic movement of one or more lines with regard to the placing of **stress** and other aural features.

Caesura   A term, derived from Greek and Latin **prosody**, denoting the break in a metrical verse line at a word boundary that is usually at half-way. It is in effect a pause, but a distinct one that falls at virtually the same point in the series of formal lines.

Carol Originally a mediaeval dance-song, usually for ring-dancing. Commonly it had 3/ 4-**stress** lines, all rhyming the same (i.e. **monorhyme**) and a shorter line that rhymed with its **burden**. As this dance tradition died out with the religious Reformation of the sixteenth century, the term became transferred to the modern sense of popular Christmas songs.

Classics, classical 'The Classics' is generally taken to refer to the literatures of Ancient Greece and Rome. For western poets, especially during and since the **Renaissance**, this literature has been held to set the standard of quality and permanence. Many also wrote in Latin and/or Greek and transposed classical forms into their own languages. When enthusiasm for classical models was most pronounced – for instance in English poetry of the late seventeenth and early eighteenth centuries – poets have been dubbed **neo-classical**. The terminology of versification (**prosody**) has been derived from classical examples even though they do not strictly apply to poetry in English. (See Chapter 4.)

Closed couplet A couplet which matches sentence structure, i.e. closes with a full-stop or other strong punctuation. (See **couplet**, **open couplet**, and Chapter 6.)

Common metre Four-line **stanzas** alternating 4 and 3 beat lines. Another name for **ballad metre**.

Conceit A particularly striking **metaphor**. Usually it is part of a larger pattern of **images**, sometimes continued through the whole poem – see **trope**. The more prominent and ingenious it is, the more marked and self-conscious its artificiality. Its English heyday was in the seventeenth century in the work of Donne and other poets.

Concrete poetry Visual poetry: strictly the words, or just letters, are offered as images which are as far as possible abstract, that is they are detached from their usual **semantic** function. Work of this kind, at the borders of poetry and visual art, was most prominent in the 1950s and 1960s. Less strictly, other poems such as the **emblem** poems of the seventeenth century might be said to have 'concrete' elements but their words are used semantically. All literate poetry, simply by its appearance in the space of the page, can be said to have a visual, if not 'concrete' dimension. (See also **sound poem** and Chapter 2.)

Connotative The secondary, or additional meaning of a word besides its primary meaning, i.e. its **connotation** as opposed to its **denotation**.

Consonance Broadly this can mean the overall harmony or concord of sounds. More specifically it includes the correspondence of certain sounds, as for instance in **assonance** or **alliteration**.

Couplet A successive pair of lines that rhyme, notated: *aa bb*, etc. In **closed** couplets the second rhyme coincides with a full-stop or other firm punctuation. In **open** couplets the sense is free to run on through to the next line and the sentence might end mid-line. **Heroic** couplets are closed couplets in **iambic pentameter** that employ a **caesura**. Adapted from **classical** models, it was seen as a **metre** suited to large, public subjects. In English it was used most prominently in the later seventeenth and eighteenth centuries.

Dactyl A metrical foot of three **syllables** in which the first syllable is **stressed** and the second two are unstressed: **/ v v**. The term comes from classical **prosody** where it was used to refer to long and short syllables. (See Chapter 4.)

Dada Sometimes called the 'anti-art' movement, Dada was an iconoclastic movement in the arts in the early part of the twentieth century. It sought to confound all of art's claims to profundity by, for example, replacing words with gibberish and entering 'ready-made' objects such as a typewriter cover or a urinal for art exhibitions.

Decasyllabic A line consisting of ten **syllables**.

Dialect Localized language use that has vocabulary, pronunciation and idiom particular to itself.

Diction The choice, or selection of words or phrases used. (See **lexis**.)

Dimeter A poetic line of *two* **feet**, usually containing two **stresses**.

Dramatic monologue A poem in which an identified character, or **persona**, is the sole speaker, that is the voice in the poem is 'playing' a role as in drama.

Dub poetry A form of **performance poetry** in which the words are spoken over the rhythms of reggae music. Its origins are in Jamaica and it was taken up in urban Britain in the 1970s.

Elegy A poem occasioned by the death of someone. It will normally expand to become a more general meditation on mortality. Usually quite formal in style and manner.

Emblem An 'emblem poem' is one that incorporates a visual image into the poem on the page. In English it was most practised in the seventeenth century.

End-rhyme A rhyme that occurs at the end of a line.

End-stopped   A line in which the end of the line and the punctuated end of the sentence or clause co-incide, as in the **closed couplet**. The opposite of **enjambment**.

Enjambment   A term from French meaning to step or stride across, it is the continuation, or **run-on**, of one line of poetry into the next; that is the **syntax** flows through the line-break. The opposite of **end-stopped**.

Envelope rhyme   A rhyme, usually a **couplet**, that is enclosed within another pair of rhyming lines: e.g. *a bb a*.

Envoi   Originally from French mediaeval poetry: a short poem, or section which acts as the conclusion, summary or 'send-off' of the whole work. It might repeat a **refrain** from earlier in the poem. (See also **sestina**.)

Epic   A long narrative poem, usually telling the tale of a single hero or group involved in a great historical event. The stories are likely to be legendary and involve divine as well as human characters. There is often a national or communal dimension to the epic in that it tells a story taken as vital to the collective history. Originally epics were **oral**, remembered and recounted over time. Epic was long held to be the ultimately significant poetic form. The major epics of western culture include Homer's *Iliad* and *Odyssey* (Greek), Virgil's *Aeneid* (Latin), Dante's *Divine Comedy* (Italian) and Milton's *Paradise Lost* (English). **Mock epic** is the imitation of epic features but with a comic dimension that pokes fun at the pretensions and pettiness of the characters involved.

Epigram   Not always in poetic form, it is a piece of writing that compresses an observation or saying into a very short space. It is often **satiric** and must be witty. In verse it will normally take the form of a **couplet** or **quatrain**.

Eye rhyme   Two words that look similar enough to rhyme but when voiced do not, e.g. *cough* and *rough*. It must be remembered that pronunciation changes over time and that what seems to modern ears to be only an 'eye-rhyme' might once have been an aural rhyme. It might also be used very deliberately as part of the visual aspect of poetry. (See also **half-rhyme**.)

Figure, figurative   In the context of poetry, the word is used in the same sense as in the phrase *'figure of speech'*, that is an expression used to lend colour or force to speech or writing. Most often this will be in the form of an **image** or **metaphor**. In **rhetoric** figures are of many particular, defined types such as **anaphora, anadiplosis** and hyperbole (deliberate over-statement or exaggeration for effect).

Flyting A live, oral poetic competition traditionally featuring the exchange of elaborate and ingenious insults. It is primarily associated with Scottish poetic tradition. See **slam**.

Foot A segment of a poetic line in **metre**. Normally this will be a combination of **stressed** and unstressed **syllables**. For example an **iambic** foot consists of two syllables, the first unstressed and the second stressed: *tee* **tum**. Thus, an **iambic pentameter** consists of *five* such feet. (See also **trochee, anapest, dactyl** and Chapter 4.)

Fourteener A poetic line containing *fourteen* **syllables**; less often used to describe a poem of fourteen lines. (See **sonnet**.)

Free verse / vers libre Most often taken to refer to poetry that has no recurring **metrical** pattern to its lines and does not use **rhyme**. More strictly it might avoid all kinds of **recurrence** such as **stanza** pattern and repetition of words or phrases as in any kind of **refrain**. The French phrase *'vers libre'* was often used in the early twentieth century because of the influence of French poets. (**See** Chapter 5.)

Full rhyme A rhyme in which the words involved have the last two or more sounds are identical and thus the only difference is the consonant earlier in the word, or line. The typical pattern is therefore **C**onsonant**V**owel**C**onsonant as in *knock / mock, insulate / regulate*. Sometimes known as strict rhyme. (See *rhyme,* half-*rhyme, head-rhyme, eye-rhyme* and Chapter 6.)

Genre, sub-genre In literature genre refers to the classification into 'types' or 'forms' or 'kinds', e.g. poetry, novel, drama. Within these, distinct genres, or 'sub-genres', might be defined, for example, lyric, dramatic and epic poetry, and within lyric such forms as the **sonnet**. Some controversy arises as to whether a genre is defined by form or subject, e.g. is the **elegy** defined by its subject – commemoration of the dead – or by traditional formal characteristics? How tightly or prescriptively genre can be defined has been a long-standing argument in literary studies as theorists propose new criteria and different classifications.

Ghazal A lyric poem in which a single rhyme predominates: *aa ba ca da ea*. Its origins are in Arabic, Persian and Turkish poetry. There has been considerable modern interest in imitating the form in English by poets including Adrienne Rich.

Haiku   A short form derived from Japanese poetry. Strictly it consists of just seventeen **syllables**, disposed across three lines in the pattern 5-7-5. Its subjects are normally resonant, momentary observations, often of the natural world. Translation into English that transposes its strict count is very difficult. However, imitation of the form in English, sometimes strict, sometimes less so, has been very popular since the early twentieth century. (See Chapter 2.)

Half-rhyme   A kind of **rhyme** in which the consonants of the two words sound the same but the vowels differ, e.g. *buck / back*. Sometimes known as **pararhyme**. (See also **rhyme, head-rhyme, eye-rhyme, proest** and Chapter 6.)

Head-rhyme (see alliteration)   The rhyming of the same consonants at the beginning of successive words, e.g. *big bucks*. As in **alliteration** except that it will only apply to two words not several.

Hendecasyllabic   A poetic line of *eleven* syllables. (See **decasyllabic**.)

Heroic couplet   Closed couplets in **iambic pentameter** that often employ a **caesura**. Adapted from **classical** models, it was seen as a **metre** suited to large, public subjects. In English it was used most prominently in the later seventeenth and eighteenth centuries.

Hexameter   A verse line of *twelve* **syllables** in *six* **feet**, normally with a **caesura**. The line is uncommon in English poetry but in **classical** Greek and Latin poetry it was the line for **epic** and other major poetry. Because of its prestige the **vernacular** languages of western Europe sought to find an equivalent. In Italian this was the **hendecasyllabic**, in French the standard **alexandrine**. In English the equivalent standard settled as the **iambic pentameter**. (See Chapter 4.)

Iambic   An iamb is term derived from classical **prosody**. In Latin it denoted a **metrical foot** consisting of a short **syllable** followed by a long. In English **accentual-syllabic** verse it became the most common foot in the form of an **unstressed** syllable followed by a **stressed** syllable, notated: / v, e.g. re**verse**, de**nounce**. The **iambic pentameter** is a line of *five* iambic feet, and is the most familiar metre in the history of poetry in English. It is for instance the basic metre of the verse of Shakespeare's plays. (See Chapter 4.)

Image, imagery   A general term, not confined to poetry. Essentially in **rhetoric** it is a **metaphorical** device whereby one thing is described in terms of another but with an emphasis upon a mental picture. In **romantic** poetry it becomes more expressive in itself, coming to stand in place of something not directly described. Thus, for example, when Wordsworth in 'Tintern Abbey' seeks to describe the 'presence', the 'sense sublime' he feels to be in Nature, he writes that 'its dwelling is the light of setting suns …' and this acts as an image to try to specify what he apprehends. In this sense an image is close to the more fixed notion of the **symbol**. (See also **allegory**.) Modernist poetry set great store by representing the concrete and sensuous, and thus by the importance of the image. Hence the brief flowering of **imagism**.

Imagism   A tendency in **modernist** poetry, and briefly a movement with an 'Imagist Manifesto', which urged the necessity of concrete, sensuous images as the basis of poetic practice. Its proponents included Ezra Pound and H.D. (Hilda Doolittle). For Pound the image should constitute 'direct treatment of the thing', but also broadened his definition to 'an image is that which presents an intellectual and emotional complex in an instant of time.'

Inspiration   Literally, from the Latin, 'breathing in'. This source points to the notion that poetic inspiration is natural and unconscious. It refers to the arrival in the poet's mind of ideas, words, images, figures that have no conscious source and result from no discernible craft or effort. In many poetries it has had divine associations – the breath of God, or the will of the **Muse** flows through the poet. It is very important to **romantic poetics**. It can also be associated with the processes of the unconscious mind as understood by modern psychology. (See Chapter 8.)

Interlaced rhyme   **Rhyme** where the correspondences are not adjacent as they are in the **couplet**, but two or more lines apart, therefore producing a criss-cross effect with other rhymes. In the sixteenth and seventeenth centuries there was a vogue for drawing lines, or brackets, to show the pattern of rhymes hence visualizing the interlacing effect. (See Chapter 6.)

Internal rhyme   A correspondence of word-sounds *within* the line rather than, as in conventional **rhyme**, at the end of lines. (See Chapter 6.)

Irony A **figure** in which what is *said* is the opposite of what is actually *meant*. The reader either realizes what is true from the beginning, or (hopefully) comes to understand it. *Dramatic irony* is when a speaking character thinks the opposite of what the audience, from its superior vantage point, knows to be true.

Lexis, lexical Vocabulary, but for linguists especially the words that carry substantive meaning, as opposed to those which serve grammatical functions like *the, at, to,* etc. Words can thus be divided into lexical items and grammatical items. (See **diction**, **semantic**, **syntax**.)

Limerick A highly popular form of comic verse that features in written and oral traditions. It is often nonsensical and frequently bawdy. Its form is very strict: *five* lines rhyming *aabba*; lines 1, 2 and 5 have *three* **stresses** and lines 3 and 4 *two*. (See Chapter 2.)

Lyric The type of poetry most readily associated with the chanted or sung origins of poetry, traditionally to the harp-like stringed instrument known as the *lyre*. We still refer to the words of songs of all kinds as lyrics, and poetry closest in style and span to songs, as opposed to poems that tell substantial stories or are the medium for drama, are defined as lyric. The form lends itself to expressions of personal feeling such as love. It is the most prominent of all the poetic genres.

Measure The term for the organization of the poetic line into a recurring set pattern, such as **metre**. Whether the line counts **syllables** or **stresses** it is regular. More broadly measure can be understood as the sense of order in other equivalences such as the length and form of **stanzas**. (See Chapter 4.)

Metaphor A broad and complex area. Most simply it can be described as a **figure** which expresses one thing in terms of another by suggesting a likeness between them. There are many different kinds of metaphor, some so embedded that it can be hard to remember that they are figures. For example, if someone is called 'bright as a button' their 'brightness' is being emphasized by the association with a shiny button. But 'bright', meaning clever, is itself a metaphor in which light is taken to stand for intelligence. Another type lies in a phrase like 'give me a hand'. Here 'help' is represented by the limb to represent what may or not be physical assistance. Metaphors are structured into **tenor**, *vehicle*, and *ground*. In the phrase '*happy as a clam*', the *tenor* is what is being said, i.e. 'X is happy'; the *vehicle* which carries this meaning is the 'clam'; the *ground* is what happiness and clams have in common, whatever that is. (See **allegory, conceit, image, symbol, trope**.)

Metre   A specific, recurring pattern of poetic **rhythm**. Typically in English a metred line will have a set number of **syllables**, or **stresses**, or a combination of stressed and unstressed syllables, i.e. **accentual/ stress-syllabic** metre. (See **foot** and Chapter 4.)

Mnemonic   That which aids the memory. Many features of poetry such as **metre, rhyme**, and repetition of words and phrases help memorization and are thus mnemonic. This is especially important in the **oral tradition**. (See also **Muse**.)

Modernism   In literature and the other arts, a loose, experimental movement in the twentieth century which sought to break with preceding styles. In poetry, modernism made formal challenges to such long-standing features as the verse-line, **rhyme** and **stanza**, initiating '**free verse**'. Also conventional **narrative** coherence was sometimes replaced by jump-cut juxtaposition of incidents without clear time-sequence or conclusion. Further, the assumed single speaking 'I' dissolves into a more elusive voice, or voices, sometimes seemingly speaking from the unconscious as well as conscious mind, or by a characterized voice or **persona**.

Monorhyme   An identical rhyme, though the words may mean different things, e.g. *caught / court.*

Monosyllable (see poly-)   A word comprised of just a single **syllable**. (A **polysyllable** is thus a word made up of two or more syllables.)

Muse   The idea of the Muse, or Muses, comes from Greek antiquity. Originally they were daughters of the principal god Zeus and Mnemosyne (goddess of memory; see **mnemonic**) and provided inspiration to artists in different **genres** and to different **sub-genres** within the arts, for instance *Calliope* was the Muse of **epic** poetry, *Erato* of love poetry and *Euterpe* of tragedy and **lyric** poetry. Poets since inspired by **classicism**, like Milton, used the convention of calling upon the Muses for inspiration. (See Chapter 3.) Much more loosely, and often comically, the Muse is invoked as a **metaphor** for poetic **inspiration**. (See Chapter 8.) Feminist poets and critics have questioned the mythology of male poets recognizing the feminine in only this way, and reconsidered what 'the Muse' might mean for women poets.

Narrative A narrative poem is most simply a poem that tells a story, that is a relation of events or facts placed in time so as to suggest causal connection and a pointed conclusion. (See **modernism** and Chapter 3.)

Naturalization A term sometimes used in the context of whether readers feel they 'know where they are' in a poem, that is with respect to who is 'speaking', what the setting is, what the process of the poem is. For example, naturalization might be more readily achieved in a **narrative** poem like Chaucer's *The Canterbury Tales* than in a **modernist** poem by John Ashbery. (See Chapter 3.)

Neo-classical Style that deliberately tries to emulate that of the **classics**, in English poetry most often used of work of he late seventeenth and early eighteenth centuries.

Octave In poetry, an *eight*-line **stanza**. (See **ottava rima**.) Also the first *eight* line section of a **Petrarchan sonnet**.

Ode A form of lyrical poetry, usually of considerable length, that treats significant subjects such as mortality, and often public events. Its tone is serious and the line and **stanza** forms often elaborate. It origins are in ancient Greek poetry where its name denoted chanting, or singing.

Onomatopoeia Traditionally this refers to the phenomenon of words sounding like what they mean, e.g. *swoosh, tick-tock*. Linguistically, this has been widely discredited, but onomatopoeic effects can be made once the context of the meaning has been established. *Princeton*: 'Sounds can never precede meaning: they can only operate on meanings already **lexically** created.'

Open couplets Couplets in which the sentence or clause does not close with the completion of the **rhyme** but runs on into the next line or lines. Thus, unlike in the **closed couplet**, the **syntax** and **couplet** do not coincide, indeed sentences might end mid-line. (See **couplet**, **end-stopped**, **rhyme** and Chapter 6.)

Oral, Oral tradition Poetry composed to be recited or chanted for a listening audience rather than the printed page. The roots of its tradition, as in the **ballad**, lie in pre-print, or even pre-literate cultures. Closer to our own day it continues to exist in such fields as children's rhymes and **performance poetry**. (See **ballad** and Chapter 2.)

Ottava rima (ottava Toscana) An *eight-line* **stanza** rhyming *abababcc*. As its name, and occasional alternative name suggest, it is Italian in origin. (See Chapter 7.)

OuLiPo A shortening of the French 'Ouvroir de Littérature Potentielle', a literary movement that developed compositional methods based on predetermined systems, for example texts in which each word must begin with the same letter, or a text that must exclude certain letters such as the important vowel *e*, or a poem whose lines might be read in any order. Mathematical schemes are also employed.

Pantoum The Europeanization of the Malay form *pantun*. This is based in four-line form which rhymes *ab ab*, but it also includes internal rhymes and various kinds of correspondences between images and ideas. (See Chapter 7.)

Parody An imitation of the style of a work, an author, or type of poem (or other writing) for mocking comic effect. (See **pastiche**.)

Pastiche Like **parody**, an imitation, but the result is meant to be a work in itself not merely a mockery of its model.

Pastoral Originally a type of poetry which pretends to imitate the simple songs of shepherds and extol the unaffected virtues of rural life as against metropolitan sophistication and corruption. It can therefore have a satirical or political edge. Under **classical** influence, it was seen as the most basic of forms, thus suited to a beginning poet before attempting the more demanding tasks of writing **lyric** and **epic**. More loosely it has come to refer to any poetry about rural life. (See Chapter 3.)

Patterned stress An alternative term I have used in Ch 4 to describe metres which have a recurring pattern of stresses as in an **iamb**, **trochee**, **anapest**, **dactyl**. See also **accentual-syllabic**, **stress-syllable**.

Performance poetry Generally any poetry presented to an audience in performance, as opposed to on the page, or indeed *from* the page. In recent years it has come to refer to poetry of large, entertaining verbal effect designed to impress a listening audience, the poets sometimes in competition with each other in what has become called a **slam**. (See **oral tradition**.)

Persona **Classical poetics** made a distinction between poetry in which the poet speaks in her or his own voice, and poems where it is understood that the poet has fashioned a character, or mask – i.e. a persona. For twentieth century poets like Yeats, Pound and Eliot, the use of a persona became a way of freeing themselves from **romantic** assumptions that identified the speaker in the poem and the poet. A strand of twentieth-century criticism regularly insists on seeing the 'I' in the poem as a persona rather than the writer him or herself. (See **dramatic monologue, modernism** and Chapter 3.)

Petrarchan   After the Italian poet Francesco Petrarca (English: Petrarch (1404–74). The adjective has two main references: (i) to the type of 8/6 **sonnet** form devised by Petrarch, and (ii) to a tradition of love poetry characterized by longing and a virtually religious devotion to the beloved. This last sense by no means represents the full character of Petrarch's work.

Phoneme   The most basic items in the sounds of a language. Phonemes are the sounds actually used by a particular language that will make a difference to the meaning of a word, e.g. if the phoneme that is the **k** sound in *cat* is replaced by the **m** phoneme we have the entirely different meaning of *mat*. (See **syllable** and Chapter 4.)

Pitch   In speech the contour of intonation, for example the rising movement in which questions are asked or denials delivered. In English poetry the patterning of **accent / stress** crucially affects the pitch and therefore sense of lines. (See also **tone**.)

Plain rhyme   Adjacent **rhyme** such as the **couplet**, or patterns as *abbacddc*, i.e. schemes that do not overlap, are not **interlaced**.

Poetics   A very broad term now frequently used to refer to many things other than literature. Regarding poetry, its simplest sense has to do with the theory of poetry, especially assuming that verse can be basically distinguished from prose. More locally it used to refer to the explicit theory, or practical principles, of some particular poet, or movement, or period in poetry.

Polysyllable   A word consisting of two or more **syllables** (*see* **monosyllable**).

Praise-song   A song or poem composed to express admiration, usually of a person or deity. Most often used in relation to traditional, **oral** poetries.

Proest   A Welsh poetic form which corresponds to **half-rhyme**.

Prosody   The study and analysis of verse form, mainly the sound-patterning of **rhyme** and **stanza**, and especially of lines in **metre**. (See **scansion**.)

Quantity / quantitative   English, and therefore poetry in English, is **stress** based. However other languages, including Greek and Latin measure the lengths, or quantities, of **syllables**, thus producing lines comprising patterns of these lengths. The terminology of this quantitative **prosody** has been carried over into English usage. (See Chapter 4.)

Quatrain   A **stanza** of *four* lines, normally rhymed. (See Chapter 7.)

Quintet   A term sometimes used to denote a **stanza** of *five* lines.

Rap poetry   The simplest definition given is 'talking in rhyme to the rhythm of a beat' but the beat is the one characterized by the style of rap music as it emerged from the African-Caribbean and African American communities in New York in the 1970s and 1980s. Also see **dub poetry**.

Recurrence   Quite simply that which recurs in the formal properties of a poem. Thus **metre**, **rhyme**, **stanza**, **alliteration** and all kinds of regular repetitions are instances of recurrence, as is the poetic line itself as it *recurs* to the left-hand margin. Arguably truly **'free verse'** would have no recurrent features.

Refrain   One or more lines repeated at intervals like a chorus. (See **burden**.)

Register   The choice of words and forms and tones appropriate to speaking to various audiences. (See also **pitch**, **tone**.)

Reiteration   Saying something over again – see **recurrence**.

Renaissance   Literally 're-birth' (from the French; in Italian *rinascimento*). It refers to the 'rebirth' of knowledge of, and emulation of the arts, architecture and culture of **classical** Greece and Rome, first in Italy and then more widely in Western Europe. The dates ought not to be stipulated too closely, but should stretch at least from Dante (1265–1321) to Shakespeare (1564–1616) and Milton (1608–74). Despite this admiration for the classics, the period sees the development of valued literature in Italian, French, German English and the other spoken vernacular languages of Europe

Rhetoric   The art of persuasion in language, first in speech-making but extending into writing. This was seen as a crucial public skill in Ancient Greece and Rome and through the **Renaissance**. **Classical** rhetoric employed formal **devices**, or **tropes** with which to enhance argument and hold an audience, and these practices were maintained by **Renaissance** and **neo-classical** poets. More broadly rhetoric can still be used to denote any deliberate strategies by which a poet forms the argument of his or her poem. In **romantic poetics** however, this idea of poetry as rhetoric – depending for its eloquence upon given forms – tends to be replaced by the notion of *expression*, personal in both content and form to the author. (See Chapters 3 and 8.)

Rhyme   The positioning of words of identical or similar sound for effect, normally at the ends of lines. There are many different varieties and patterns of rhyme. (See Chapter 6.)

Rhyme royal   A **stanza** of *seven* **decasyllabic** lines, rhyming *ababbcc*. Its first use in English was by Chaucer in his *Troilus and Criseyde* (?1482) and thus the scheme is sometimes called the Troilus stanza. (See Chapter 7.)

Rhyming slang   A Cockney (London dialect) feature in which things are referred to by a code phrase which bears no relation in meaning but does rhyme, e.g. *apples and pears* for *stairs*.

Rhythm   The Ancient Greek philosopher Plato called rhythm 'order in movement', and it is generally understood to be the 'flow' in the sounding of the line and the succession of lines. It will therefore include the effects of the sounds of individual words and **beat** or **stress**. There may be a recurring **measure** as in **metrical** verse, but **'free verse'** will also have rhythm.

Romantic   A various term with very many shades of meanings and applications which make brief generalization very insecure. Historically the romantic period in poetry is generally held to begin in English in the late eighteenth century, most notably in the poetry of Blake, Wordsworth and Coleridge, and remain the dominant influence throughout the nineteenth century. This has sometimes been called the 'romantic revival' on account of it being a rediscovery of the styles of Shakespeare and his contemporaries which had been occluded by the **neo-classical poetics** of the late seventeenth and eighteenth centuries. It is also seen to have re-discovered the forms and stories of the native, vernacular cultures of Europe, for example in the **ballad**, as against the dominant inheritance from Ancient Greece and Rome.

This points to the degree to which romanticism has been defined against **classicism**. Against the formality, respect for ancient models and **rhetorical** styles of neo-classicism, romanticism has been held to promote formal freedom, independence, and personal expressivity: nature as against culture, inspiration as against learning. (See Chapter 8.)

Rondeau Originally a French dance-song for *rondes* or rounds. Formalized into a literary convention, the **rondeau** became a fifteen-line form divided into a *quintet*, a *quatrain* and a *sestet*, and employing just two rhymes. (See Chapter 7.)

Rondel Another stanza form based on dance-song in the manner of the *rondeau*. It has fourteen lines shaped into two *quatrains* and a *sestet*. The first two lines of the poem recur in the last two lines of the second *quatrain* and in the last two lines of the sestet. There is also a little known variant known as a *roundel*. (See rondeau and Chapter 7.)

Satire Not confined to poetry, it is a mode which mocks some prevailing aspect of society or fashion. Its aim is always claimed to be didactic: that is to punish vice, corruption and pride through ridicule in order to improve conduct and society. (See Chapter 3.)

Scansion The practice of analysing, or *scanning*, lines of verse in order to determine their **rhythmical**, or more usually **metrical**, features. (See **prosody** and Chapter 4.)

Semantic Those aspects of language which pertain to meaning. (See **lexis**.) In poetry the semantic function of a word can be especially important as against, or in relation to the use of words for their sound, or sensuous qualities where meaning is secondary or even non-existent. A **semantic field** is the appearance of words in some proximity whose meanings can be associated.

Septet A *seven-line* **stanza**, rhyming or unrhymed. (See Chapter 6.)

Sestet Refers to a *six line* **stanza**, but more often to the second *six-line* section of the 8/6 **Petrachan sonnet**. (See Chapter 7.) Sometimes known as a **sixain**. See also **Venus and Adonis stanza**.

Sestina A form of *six, six-line, stanzas* concluding with *an* **envoi** *of three lines*. In its English versions it usually uses a ten-syllable line. However, instead of a rhyme scheme, the sestina repeats a series of six *end words* in each stanza, but in a fixed pattern of variation in which the sixth moves up to first in the next stanza and the others take up other corresponding positions. The three-line envoi then contains all the six repeated words. (See Chapter 7.)

Simile A basic form of **metaphor** in which the comparison is directly conjoined, usually with 'like' or 'as', e.g. 'black as coal'.

Slam A competition is which **performance poets** compete with the audience voting the winner.

Sonnet A major, long-lived lyrical form consisting of *fourteen* lines. Strictly, and most often, these are configured in one of several different rhyming patterns. The major ones in English are the **Petrarchan** model divided into sections of 8/6 lines and the Shakespearean in 4/4/4/2. The standard line is **iambic pentameter**. More recent sonnets, or 'sonnets', have dispensed with rhyme and pentameter, and sometimes with fourteen lines. (See Chapter 7.)

Sound poem A poem which makes no attempt to use words **semantically** but attends only to the sounds of the words, or, sometimes, does not use recognizable words at all. Its effects might be **onomatopoeic**. (See also **concrete poem** and Chapter 2.)

Spenserian stanza After Edmund Spenser (?1552–99), it comprises nine **iambic** lines, eight **iambic pentameters** and one, closing, **hexameter**. The rhyme scheme is *ababbcbcc*. (See Chapter 7.)

Sprung rhythm A term coined by Gerard Manley Hopkins (1844–89) to describe his variation on **strong-stress metre**. His long lines are built around a few strong **accents** with a varying number of unstressed **syllables** between them. The **rhythm** thus 'springs' across from one strong **beat** to the next. (See Chapter 4.)

Stanza A group of lines shaped in the same way, with the lines usually, although not always of the same length. Traditionally they would be rhymed, but by no means always, especially in the twentieth century. Stanzas can vary greatly in length and structure. They serve the function of segmenting the poem and providing pauses in its progression. (See Chapter 7.)

Stichic The name given to a series of lines in which the grammatical sentence and the line coincide, i.e. there is no run-on, or **enjambment**. (See **strophic**.) This produces an abrupt, staccato effect.

Stress (see accent, beat) The effect in all sorts of poetry in English, whether it has measure or is 'free', relies upon the effective placing of **accent** or **beat**, e.g. '**mass**-ive'. A poem therefore will have beats (ie stresses, accents) but also an overall beat, or rhythm

Stress-syllable Also **accentual-syllabic**, a metre in which **accented** and non-accented (stressed/unstressed) **syllables** alternate. They can be either *unstressed/stressed* (**iambic**), or *stressed/unstressed* (**trochaic**) or in other patterns. (See **anapest**, **dactyl**, Chapter 4.)

Strong-stress metre   A metre which depends upon a fixed series of strong **beats** without counting the number of unstressed **syllables** in between. (See **sprung rhythm** and Chapter 4.)

Strophic   The common, though with respect to **classical** models, loose meaning is of a series of lines in which the grammatical sentence flows on across the line-endings. (See **stichic**.) This is often a feature of the **verse paragraph**.

Syllabics   Measured lines which count **syllables**, not **stresses**.

Syllable   The segment of a word uttered with a single effort of articulation, e.g. *seg-ment*, (2 syllables), *ar-tic-u-la-tion* (5 syllables). It is syllables that bear **stress**. (See **phoneme, syllabics** and Chapter 4.)

Symbol   This is part of the same family as **allegory, figure, image** and **metaphor**: that is a symbol is something that stands in for, represents something else. Thus the colour red conventionally symbolizes 'Danger'. Symbols evolve, or are invented, because the 'something else' is usually a complex idea or emotion, an abstraction not easily expressible. The distinctions between symbol and **image, etc.** are not wholly clear, but the tendency is for symbols to have more fixed significations.

Syntax   The arrangement of words into sentences by the given rules of the language in order to create meaning. (See **lexis, semantics**).

Tenor   1 The tone, sometimes style of writing or speaking, often related to the level of formality. (See **pitch, register**, and Chapter 3.)

   2 In **metaphor**: *tenor* refers to *what* is being signified, *vehicle* to the **image** being used to signify, and *ground* to that which *tenor* and *vehicle* are seen to have in common. (See **metaphor**.)

Tercet   A *three-line* verse form, usually rhymed and usually employed as a separate **stanza**.

Terza rima   A verse form which links **tercets** together by **interlaced rhyme**: *aba bcb cdc ded*, etc. A form introduced by Dante for his *Divine Comedy*. (See Chapter 7.)

Tetrameter   An **accentual-syllabic** line of *four* **beats**, hence four **feet**. (See Chapter 4)

Tone   A much-used, if imprecise term to indicate the 'mood', 'colour', 'atmosphere' of a piece of writing as conveyed by its word-choice, rhythms, etc. An analogy can be made with the tones of a speaking voice, which is what is done in Chapter 3 of this book. (See also **pitch, tenor**.)

Transmission   The process by which poetry is conveyed to audiences through time. The term is most often used in the context of **oral** transmission of poetry and song, like the **ballad**, which is not written down.

Trimeter   An **accentual-syllabic** line of *three* **beats**, hence three **feet**. (See Chapter 4.)

Triolet   A fixed *stanza* form derived from French. It has eight lines of which the first is repeated three times, the second twice, and there are just two rhymes i.e. *AbaAabAB* (the capital letter denoting the repeated lines). (See Chapter 7.)

Triplet   A sequence, or **stanza** of *three* rhyming lines

Trochee, trochaic   A **metrical foot** consisting of *two* **syllables**, the first **stressed** the second unstressed, notated: / v. (In contrast see **iamb** and Chapter 4.)

Trope   A **figure** or **metaphorical** device, usually as part of deliberate **rhetoric**, where an **image** is standing for something else. The term is often used to refer to an *extended* **metaphor** where the scheme of likeness is carried on through several related images. (See also **allegory, symbol**.)

Troubadour   Poet-songwriters of eleventh- and twelfth-century southern France. Their **lyrics** were mostly on the themes of love, especially unrequited love for a superior or unattainable beloved. Although the men are best known, there were women troubadours. Their themes and styles had great influence on later **Renaissance** love poetry, and re-appeared in the interest of some modern poets, notably Ezra Pound. (See also **Petrarchan, Renaissance**.)

Venus and Adonis stanza   Named for the **stanza** form used by Shakespeare in his narrative poem *Venus and Adonis* though other poets used it before him. It is a six-line stanza rhyming *ababcc*.

Verse / poetry   (1) The terms 'verse' and 'poetry' are often used interchangeably, although this book is using 'poetry' almost exclusively. The use of verse often implies poetry that is formal, usually **metrical** and **rhymed**. It is sometimes seen as an old-fashioned term, or one to be used for simpler less serious poetry, as in 'children's verse' or 'comic verse'.

(2) A verse can also refer to a single line (the French *vers*), or a number lines (*verses*), or as another word for **stanza**, especially

if it is one that is short and comparatively straightforward like a **quatrain**.

Verse paragraph   A **stanza** form, but one that does not have a recurrent length or other set shape. It is thus a looser form, and although it does occur in longer **couplet** poems, it is mostly used in **blank verse**. (See **strophe** and Chapter 7.)

Villanelle   Originally a simple Italian and French 'rustic' song. The modern villanelle has a nineteen-line pattern that uses *five* **tercets** and a *final* **quatrain**. Strictly, these rhyme *aba* throughout, and the first and third lines recur at fixed points later in the poem. (See Chapter 7.)

Volta   The Italian word for *turn*, used for the moment when the 8/6 **Petrarchan sonnet** changes over from the **octet** to the **sestet**. It is a 'turn' in the rhyme scheme, almost always corresponding with a sentence pause, and a 'turn of thought'. (See Chapter 7.)

Word-play   A very general term to suggest the manipulation of words, especially when used for the sounds in themselves, or their various **connotations**. As 'play' suggests, there is often something sportive or *ludic* about this.

REFERENCES

ANTHOLOGIES

Several new anthologies of poetry in English have been published in recent years which have been re-edited from manuscripts, widened the range of their selection and provide excellent supporting information. Among these are:

DeMaria, R. (ed.) (1996) *British Literature 1640–1789: An Anthology*, Oxford: Blackwell.

Fairer, D. and Gerrard, C. (eds) (2003) *Eighteenth Century English Poetry: An Annotated Anthology*, second edition, Oxford: Blackwell.

Ferguson, M., Salter, M.J. and Stallworthy, J. (eds) (1996) *The Norton Anthology of Poetry*, New York: Norton. See essay 'Versification' by Jon Stallworthy.

Finnegan, R. (ed.) (1982) *The Penguin Book of Oral Poetry*, Harmondsworth: Penguin.

Heaney, S. and Hughes, T. (eds) (1982) *The Rattle Bag*, London: Faber.

Leonard, J. (ed.) (1998) *Australian Verse: An Oxford Anthology*, Melbourne: Oxford University Press.

Lonsdale, R. (ed.) (1990) *Eighteenth Century Women Poets*, Oxford: Oxford University Press.

Payne, M. and Hunter, J. (eds) (2003) *Renaissance Literature: An Anthology*, Oxford, Blackwell.

Pearsall, D. (ed.) (1998) *Chaucer to Spenser: An Anthology*, Oxford: Blackwell.

Schmidt, M. (ed.) (1999) *The Harvill Book of Twentieth Century Poetry in English*, London: Harvill Press.

Wu, D. (ed.) (1998) *Romanticism: An Anthology*, second edition, Oxford: Blackwell.

Wu, D. (ed.) (2001) *Romantic Women Poets: An Anthology*, Oxford: Blackwell.

* * *

The premier reference work in English for world poetry is:

Preminger, A. and Brogan, T.V.F (eds) (1993) *The New Princeton Encyclopedia of Poetry and Poetics*, Princeton, NJ: Princeton University Press.

* * *

Alexander, M. (ed.) (1995) *Beowulf*, Harmondsworth: Penguin Classics.

Allen, D. (ed.) (1960) *The New American Poetry 1945–1960*, New York: Grove Press.

Ashbery, J. (1985) *Selected Poems*, Manchester: Carcanet Press.

Arkell, D. (1979) *Looking for Laforgue*, Manchester: Carcanet Press

Attridge, D. (1982) *The Rhythms of English Poetry*, London and New York: Longman.

—— (1995) *Poetic Rhythm: An Introduction*, Cambridge: Cambridge University Press.

Auden, W.H. (1966) *Collected Shorter Poems 1927–57*, London: Faber.

Barrell, J. (1988) *Poetry, Language and Politics*, Manchester: Manchester University Press.

Bate, W.J. ((1971) *The Burden of the Past and the English Poet*, London: Chatto and Windus.

Bernstein, C. *see* Silliman (ed.) (1986).

Bloom V. (1983) *Touch Mi, Tell Mi*, London: Bogle-L'Ouverture.

Berryman, J. (1973) *The Freedom of the Poet*, New York: Farrar, Straus and Giroux.

—— (1990) *Collected Poems 1937–71*, London: Faber.

Bidart, F. (1997) *Desire*, New York: Farrar, Straus and Giroux.

—— (2008) *Watching the Spring Festival*, New York: Farrar, Straus and Giroux.

Blake, W. (1961) *Poetry and Prose of William Blake*, fourth edn, Keynes, G. (ed.), London: Nonesuch Press.

Blythe, R.H. (trans.) (1971) *Haiku*. Japan: The Hokuseido Press.

Boland, E. (1995) *Object Lessons: The Life of the Woman and the Poet in Our Time*, Manchester: Carcanet Press.

—— (1990) *Outside History*, Manchester: Carcanet Press.

Boland E. and Strand, M. (eds) (2001) *The Making of a Poem*, London & New York: Norton.

Brathwaite, E.K. (1973) *The Arrivants: A New World Trilogy*, Oxford: Oxford University Press.

—— (1995) *History of the Voice: The Development of Nation Language in Anglophone Caribbean Literature*, New York: New Beacon Books.

Brogan, T.V.F. (ed.) (1994) *The New Princeton Handbook of Poetic Terms*, Princeton, NJ: Princeton University Press.

Broom, Sarah (2006) *Contemporary British and Irish Poetry: An Introduction*, Basingstoke: Palgrave.

Browning, R. (1974) *Selected Poems*, Armstrong, I. (ed.), London: Bell.

Cave, N. (1997) *The Boatman's Call*, Mute Records.

Chaucer, G. (1957) *The Works of Geoffrey Chaucer*, Robinson, F.N. (ed.), London: Oxford University Press.

Child, F.J. (ed.) (1965) *The English and Scottish Popular Ballads.* 5 vols 1882–98. New York: Dover.

Cixous, Hélène (1976) 'The Laugh of the Medusa', trans. Keith Cohen and Paula Cohen. *Signs*, Summer 1976, I, 875–93.

Cottle, B. (1969) *The Triumph of English 1350–1400*, London: Blandford Press.

Cummings, E. E. (1994) *Complete Poems*, New York: W.W. Norton.

Davies, R.T. (1963) *Mediaeval English Lyrics: A Critical Anthology*, London: Faber.

Dennett, D.C. (1984) *Elbow Room: The Varieties of Free Will Worth Wanting*, Oxford: Clarendon Press.

Dickinson, E. (1951) *The Complete Poems of Emily Dickinson*, Boston, MA and London: Little Brown and Co.

Douglas, K. (1966) *Collected Poems*, London: Faber.

Duffy, C.A. (1999) *The World's Wife*, London: Picador.

Easthope, A. (1983) *Poetry as Discourse*, London: Methuen.

Eliot, T.S. (1917) 'Reflections on "Vers Libre"' in Eliot, T. S. (1965) *To Criticise the Critic: And Other Writings*. London: Faber.

—— (1917) 'Portrait of a Lady' in Eliot, T.S. (1974) *Collected Poems 1909–62*. London: Faber.

—— (1917) 'Reflections on Contemporary Poetry' in Eliot, T. S. (1999) *Selected Essays*, London: Faber

—— (1974) *Collected Poems 1909–62*, London: Faber.

—— (1999) *Selected Essays*, London: Faber.

Emerson, R.W. (1906; 1942) *Essays*, London, Dent; New York, Dutton.

Empson, W. (1961) *Seven Types of Ambiguity*, London: Penguin.

Ewart, G. (ed.) (1980) *The Penguin Book of Comic Verse*, Harmondsworth: Penguin.

Fenton, J. (1983) 'Letter to John Fuller', *The Memory of War and Children in Exile, Poems 1968–1983*, Harmondsworth: Penguin.

—— (2002) *An Introduction to English Poetry*, London: Viking.

Finley, M.I. (1979) *The World of Odysseus*, revised edn, Harmondsworth: Pelican Books.

Furniss, T. and Bath, M. (1996) *Reading Poetry, An Introduction*, Hemel Hempsted: Prentice Hall/Harvester Wheatsheaf.

Fussell, P. (1979) *Poetic Metre and Poetic Form*, New York: Random House.

Graham, J. (1987) *The End of Beauty*, New York: The Ecco Press.

Graham, W.S. (1979) *Collected Poems 1942–1977*, London: Faber.

Greenfield, S. (2000) *The Private Life of the Brain*, London: Allen Lane, The Penguin Press.

Grenier, R. *see* Silliman, R. (ed.) (1986)

Grigson, G. (1975) *The Penguin Book of Ballads*, Harmondsworth: Penguin.

Groarke, V. (2009) *Spindrift*, Oldcastle, Co. Meath: Gallery Press.

Gross, H. (1979) (ed.) *The Structure of Verse, Modern Essays on Prosody*, New York: The Ecco Press.

Gunn, T. (1961) *My Sad Captains*, London: Faber.

—— (1993) *Shelf Life: Essays, Memoirs and an Interview*, Ann Arbor, MI: University of Michigan Press.

Gurney, I. (1982) *Collected Poems of Ivor Gurney*, Kavanagh, P.J (ed.), Oxford: Oxford University Press.

Hall, D. (1991) *To Read a Poem*, Orlando, FL: Harcourt, Brace, Jovanovich.

Hannah, S. (1995) *The Hero and the Girl Next Door*, Manchester: Carcanet.

Hardy, T. (1976) *The Complete Poems of Thomas Hardy*, Gibson, James (ed.), London: Macmillan.

Harrison, T. (1984) *Selected Poems*, Harmondsworth: Penguin.

Hartman, C.O. (1980) *Free Verse, An Essay on Prosody*, Princeton, NJ: Princeton University Press.

Harwood, G. (1991) *Collected Poems*, Oxford: Oxford University Press.

Herbert, W.N. and Hollis, M (eds) (2000) *Strong Words: Modern Poets on Modern Poetry*, Tarset: Bloodaxe.

Hill, G. (1998) *The Triumph of Love*, Harmondsworth: Penguin.

—— (2000) *Speech! Speech!* Harmondsworth: Penguin.

Hollander, J. (1989) *Rhyme's Reason: A Guide to English Verse*, new edn, London: Yale University Press.

Holmes, R. (1989) *Coleridge: Early Visions*, London: Hodder & Stoughton.

Holub, M. (1990) *The Dimensions of the Present Moment*, Young, D. (trans), London: Faber.

Hope, A.D. (1986) *Selected Poems*, Manchester: Carcanet Press.

Hopkins, G.M. (1970) *The Poems of Gerard Manley Hopkins*, Gardner W.H. and. Mackenzie, N.H. (eds) Oxford: Oxford University Press.

—— (1980) *Selected Prose*, Roberts, G. (ed.) Oxford; Oxford University Press.

Hughes, T. (1967) *Poetry in the Making*, London: Faber.

Jakobson, R. (1987) *Language in Literature*, Pomorska, K. and Rudy, S. (eds), Cambridge, MA: Harvard University Press.

Jespersen, O. 'Notes on Metre', see Gross (ed.) (1979).

Keats, J. (1958) *The Letters of John Keats, Vols I and II*, Rollins, H.E. (ed.). Cambridge; Cambridge University Press.

—— (1975) *Letters of John Keats, A Selection*, Gittings, R. (ed.) Oxford: Oxford University Press.

Kennedy, X.J. and Gioa, D. (1998) *An Introduction to Poetry*, ninth edn, New York: Longman.

Kinsella, T. (1996) *Selected Poems*, Oxford: Oxford University Press.

Koch, K. (1998) *Making Your Own Days: The Pleasures of Reading and Writing Poetry*, New York: Simon & Schuster.

Kostelanetz, R. (ed.) (1980) *Text-Sound Texts*, New York: Morrow.

Laforgue, J. *see* Arkell, D. (1979) *Looking for Laforgue: An Informal Biography*, Manchester: Carcanet Press.

Larkin, Philip (1988; 2003) *Collected Poems*, London: Faber.

Lawrence, D.H. (1957) *The Complete Poems of D.H. Lawrence*, London: Heinemann.

Leech, G.N. (1969) *A Linguistic Guide to English Poetry*, Harlow: Longman.

Lennard, J. (1996) *The Poetry Handbook: A Guide to Reading Poetry for Pleasure and Practical Criticism*, Oxford: Oxford University Press.

Lowell, Robert (1950) *Poems 1938–1949*, London: Faber.

—— (1973) *The Dolphin*, London: Faber.

McCully, C.B. (ed.) (1994) *The Poet's Voice and Craft*, Manchester: Carcanet Press.

Mallarmé, S. (1956) *Selected Prose Poems, Essays and Letters*, Baltimore, MD: Johns Hopkins Press.

Mandelstam, N. (1975) *Hope Against Hope: A Memoir*, Harmondsworth: Penguin.

Mayes, F. (1987) *The Discovery of Poetry*, Orlando, FL: Harcourt, Brace, Jovanovich.

Millay, E. St. Vincent (1992) *Selected Poems*, Manchester: Carcanet Press.

Miller, J.H. (ed.) (1966) *William Carlos Williams: A Collection of Critical Essays*, Englewood Cliffs, NJ: Prentice-Hall.

Milton, J. (1971) *Paradise Lost*, Fowler A. (ed.), Harlow: Longman.

Montefiore, J. (1987) *Feminism and Poetry, Language, Experience, Identity in Women's Writing*, London and New York: Pandora.

Moore, M. (1984) *Complete Poems*, London: Faber.

Morgan, E. (1985) *Collected Poems*, Manchester: Carcanet Press.

Murphy, F. (ed.) (1969) *Walt Whitman, A Critical Anthology*, Harmondsworth: Penguin.

O'Hara, F. (1991) *Selected Poems*, Allen, D. (ed.), Manchester: Carcanet.

Olson, C. (1993) *Selected Poems*, Berkeley, CA: University of California Press. *See also* Allen, D. (ed.) (1960).

Opie, I. and Opie, P. (1959) *The Lore and Language of Schoolchildren*, Oxford: Oxford University Press.

Ostriker, A.S. (1986) *Stealing the Language: The Emergence of Women's Poetry in America*, London: The Women's Press.

Pinsky, R. (1988) *Poetry and the World*, New York: Ecco Press.

—— (2002) *Democracy, Culture and the Voice of Poetry*, Princeton, NJ: Princeton University Press.

Porter, Cole (1977) *The Best of Cole Porter*, London: Chappell & Co.

Pound, E. (1913) 'The Seafarer' in Pound, E. (1968) *Collected Shorter Poems*. London: Faber.

—— (1954) *Literary Essays*, London: Faber.

—— (1970) *The Translations of Ezra Pound*, London: Faber.

Raworth, T. (2003) *Collected Poems*, Manchester: Carcanet Press.

Rees-Jones, D. (2004) *Consorting with Angels: Modern Women Poets*, Tarset: Bloodaxe.

Rich, A. (1951) *The Fact of a Doorframe: Poems Selected and New*, New York: W.W. Norton.

—— (1980) *On Lies, Secrets, and Silence: Selected Prose 1966–1978*, London: Virago.

Richter, H. (1965) *Dada: Art and Anti-Art*, London: Thames & Hudson.

Ricks, C. (1984) *The Force of Poetry*, Oxford: Oxford University Press.

Roethke, Theodore (1965) *The Collected Verse of Theodore Roethke: Words for the Wind*, Bloomington, IN: Indiana University Press.

Rothenberg, J. (ed.) (1968) *Technicians of the Sacred: A Range of Poetics from Africa, America, Asia and Oceania*, New York: Vintage Books.

Rothenberg, J. and Quasha, G. (eds) (1974) *America A Prophecy, A New Reading of American Poetry from Pre-Columbian Times to the Present*, New York: Vintage Books.

Schmidt, M. (1998) *Lives of the Poets*, London: Weidenfeld & Nicolson.

Schnackenberg, G. (2001) *Supernatural Love, Poems 1976–2000*, Tarset: Bloodaxe.

Sexton, A. (1964) *Selected Poems*, London: Oxford University Press.

Shakespeare, W. (1986) *The Sonnets and A Lover's Complaint*, Kerrigan, J. (ed.) Harmondsworth: Penguin.

Silliman, R. (ed.) (1986) *In the American Tree*, Orono, ME: National Poetry Foundation.

Smart, C. (1980) *Jubilate Agno* (Fragment B,) Williamson K. (ed.) Oxford: Clarendon Press.

Smith, Hazel (2005) *The Writing Experiment: Strategies for Innovative Creative Writing*, St Leonards, NSW: Allen and Unwin.

Snyder, G. (1966) *Collected Poems*, London: Fulcrum Press.

Stead, C.K. (1967) *The New Poetic: Yeats to Eliot*, Harmondsworth: Pelican Books.

Stein, G. (1971) *Look at Me Now and Here I Am: Writings and Lectures 1909–45*, Harmondsworth: Penguin.

Stevens, W. 'Notes towards a Supreme Fiction' in Stevens, W. (1955) *Collected Poems*. London: Faber.

Tedlock, J. (1972) *Finding the Center: Narrative Poetry of the Zuni Indians*, New York: The Dial Press.

Thomas, D. (1952) *Collected Poems 1934–52*, London: J.M. Dent.

Thomas, R.S. (1963) *The Bread of Truth*, London: Hart Davis.

—— (2000) *Collected Poems 1945–90*, London: Phoenix.

Vickers, B. (1988) *In Defence of Rhetoric*, Oxford: The Clarendon Press.

Villa, J.G. (1980) 'Sonnet in Polka Dots' in Kostelanetz, R. (ed.) *Text-Sound Texts*. New York: Morrow.

Walder, D. (ed.) (1990) *Literature in the Modern World: Critical Essays and Documents*, Oxford: The Open University/Oxford University Press.

Waldrop, R. Interview. Available at www.conjunctions.com/webcon/cooperman.htm.

Welton, M. (2003) *The Book of Matthew*, Manchester: Carcanet Press.

—— (2009) *'We Needed Coffee But …'*, Manchester: Carcanet Press.

Wesling, D. (1980) *The Chances of Rhyme, Device and Modernity*, Berkeley, CA: University of California Press.

Whitman, W. (1969) *Walt Whitman: A Critical Anthology*, Murphy, F. (ed.), Harmondsworth: Penguin Books.

—— (1975) *The Complete Poems*, Murphy, F. (ed.), Harmondsworth: Penguin Books.

Williams, W.C. (1958) *I Wanted to Write a Poem*, Boston, MA: Beacon Press; (1969) London: Cape.

—— (1962) *Pictures from Breughel and Other Poems*, New York: New Directions.

—— (1966). *William Carlos Williams: A Collection of Critical Essays*, Miller, J.H. (ed.), Engelwood Cliffs, NJ: Prentice Hall.

—— (1972) *William Carlos Williams: Penguin Critical Anthology*, Tomlinson, C. (ed.), Harmondsworth: Penguin.

—— (1976) *William Carlos Williams Selected Poems*, Tomlinson, C. (ed.), Harmondsworth: Penguin.

—— (1988) *Collected Poems*, Manchester: Carcanet Press.

Woof, P. and Harley, M. (2002) *Wordsworth and The Daffodils*, Grasmere: The Wordsworth Trust.

Wordsworth, W. (1977) *Poems Volume I.*, Hayden J.O. (ed.) Harmondsworth: Penguin.

Wright, J. (1992) *Collected Poems*, Manchester: Carcanet Press.

Yeats, W.B. (1966) *Collected Poems*, London: Macmillan.

INDEX

Glossary entries are indicated by **bold** page numbers.

www.routledge.com/sociology

Research Methods: The Basics

Research Methods: The Basics

Nicholas Walliman, Oxford Brookes University, UK

Research Methods: The Basics is an accessible, user-friendly introduction to the different aspects of research theory, methods and practice. Structured in two parts, the first covering the nature of knowledge and the reasons for research, and the second the specific methods used to carry out effective research, this book covers:

- Structuring and planning a research project
- The ethical issues involved in research
- Different types of data and how they are measured
- Collecting and analysing data in order to draw sound conclusions
- Devising a research proposal and writing up the research

Complete with a glossary of key terms and guides to further reading, this book is an essential text for anyone coming to research for the first time, and is widely relevant across the social sciences and humanities.

Pb: 978-0-415-48994-2
Hb: 978-0-415-48991-1

For more information and to order a copy visit
www.routledge.com/9780415489942

Available from all good bookshops

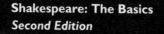

Shakespeare: The Basics
Second Edition

Shakespeare: The Basics

Sean McEvoy, University of London, UK

The second edition of this best-selling guide demystifies Shakespeare's plays and brings critical ideas within a beginner's grasp. The text provides a thorough general introduction to the plays, based on the exciting new approaches shaping the field of Shakespeare studies.

Demonstrating how interpretations of Shakespeare are linked to cultural and political contexts, and providing readings of the most frequently studied plays in the light of contemporary critical thought, *Shakespeare: The Basics* explores:

- Shakespeare's language
- the plays as performance texts
- the cultural and political contexts of the plays
- early modern theatre practice
- new understandings of the major genres.

Fully updated to include discussion of criticism and performance in the last five years, a new chapter on Shakespeare on film, and a broader critical approach, this book is the essential resource for all students of Shakespeare.

Pb: 978-0-415-36246-7
Hb: 978-0-415-36245-0

For more information and to order a copy visit
www.routledge.com/9780415362467

Available from all good bookshops